TROUT
FROM A BOAT

To my late wife, Cathy
and to our three sons
Benjamin, Jonathan and Duncan

TROUT
FROM A BOAT

Tips, Techniques and Experiences

Dennis Moss

First published in Great Britain by Merlin Unwin Books Ltd, 2007

ISBN 978 1 873674 97 0

Published by:
Merlin Unwin Books Ltd
Palmers House
7 Corve Street, Ludlow
Shropshire SY8 1DB, U.K.

The author asserts his moral right to be identified as the author of this work.

British Library Cataloguing-in-Publication Data:
A catalogue record for this book is available from the British Library.

Designed and typeset in Caslon by Merlin Unwin Books Ltd.
Printed by 1010 Printing International Ltd.

Contents

Foreword by Sandy Leventon   vii

Introduction   1

PART ONE: THE PRACTICALITIES OF BOATFISHING   4
  1. Boat Fishing Basics   5
  2. Of Lines and Leaders   21
  3. A Word about Hooks   31
  4. Choosing the Right Flies   39

PART TWO: RESERVOIR TROUT FISHING   54
  5. Reservoir Trout Fishing   55

PART THREE: WILD FISHING   82
  6. Salmon and Seatrout from a Boat   83
  7. Brown Trout Boat Fishing   107
  8. Irish Lough Fishing   115
  9. Wild Trout Boat Techniques   121

PART FOUR: OUTSTANDING DAYS BOAT FISHING   143
  10. A Spring to Remember   145
  11. Mayfly on the Corrib   152
  12. A Night to Remember on Sheelin   158
  13. Corrib Caenis at Dawn   161
  14. Sheelin Bloodworm   172
  15. A Very Late Night on Lough Arrow   178
  16. The Back End   184
  17. The Longest Day   193

Acknowledgements

Without the encouragement and support of my late wife Cathy, this book would never have been written. And our sons Benjamin, Jonathan and Duncan have always been a great help to me, particularly in matters concerning new technology!

I would also like to pay tribute to a very close friend, Vaughan Lewis, for not only being a great fishing companion, but also for sowing the seed of this book in my mind. He never let the matter drop until I actually put pen to paper. My thanks to Sandy Leventon for writing the foreword to this book and also for accepting and publishing my first magazine article, when he was editor of *Trout and Salmon*. Roy Westwood, who worked for IPC Magazines Ltd, published my articles in *Stillwater Trout Angler* and kindly supplied some of the photographs which appear in this book. I'd like to thank the tackle company, Leeda, for supplying the material for the Para Drogue; and Peter Gathercole, the photographer, for supplying the wonderful photos of the flies in this book. The author Alex Schwab, who knows Lough Currane well, has also been generous in supplying some of his photos.

Finally, heartfelt thanks to all my Irish friends, particularly Lawrence McCarthy, Denis O'Keefe and John Donlon who have made me so welcome in their country.

Foreword

by Sandy Leventon

The first article Dennis Moss submitted to me as editor of *Trout and Salmon* was, I think, in the '80s. Immediately I knew that here was no run-of-the mill pot boiler. It was obviously written by someone who had thought long and hard about his subject, and whose ideas and recommendations had been the subject of intense personal scrutiny before he felt justified in committing them to paper.

Dennis's honesty and integrity – no fly-by-night untested theories for him – shone from his typewriter and led me to ask him for more contributions, which I am delighted to say he duly delivered.

One can be certain, therefore, that whatever Dennis writes about – tactics, locations or fly patterns – has been exhaustively tested and examined. After cutting his fly-fishing teeth on our big reservoirs (and, for instance, enjoying astonishing success with big over-wintered Rutland rainbows), Dennis co-launched Wychwood Tackle, manufacturer of, among many other fly-fishing innovations, the collapsible drogue that was to earn him the gratitude of thousands of boat-fishers. After several highly successful years, Dennis sold the company and moved to the west of Ireland, where he now pursues his passion for wild fish in wild places.

With the publication of this book, Dennis's vast experience and inquiring mind have been put to good use, and I defy any boat-fisher not to profit from it.

Sandy Leventon
Editorial Consultant
Trout and Salmon magazine

Introduction

Why choose to write a book exclusively about boat fishing? I could have written this book about lake fishing from the bank, or river fishing, but I feel that I would not have written to my strength. Boat fishing is my greatest interest. It is the many variables of boat fishing with which we have to come to terms if we want to be successful that so intrigue me.

There are those who believe that boat fishing is 90% luck. I would suggest that they have clearly never come to terms with a discipline that is rather more complex than it might appear. And yet to be successful requires little more than getting the basics right. These anglers fail because, quite simply, they do not apply themselves correctly.

Many of the methods we now employ on still-water fisheries lend themselves to both bank and boat, indeed some of the tactics would have been devised for bank fishing – especially the imitative methods. For boat work these methods have simply been modified! Clearly, the angler must adjust his technique for fishing from a moving platform. But technique and tactics are not the only things we need to adjust. When pursuing wild fish we have to make allowances for the weather, its effect on both fish and fly hatches, stock densities and the fish's behaviour patterns, particularly wild brown trout whose reactions are quite different to those of stocked fish – especially rainbow trout.

I firmly believe that lakes are more difficult to read, and therefore far more difficult to come to terms with, than rivers. Any angler with a good sense of watercraft will, given time, come to terms with both faculties, but an angler who has truly come to terms with lake fishing, especially on the bigger fisheries, will find the adjustment to river fishing much easier than someone doing the reverse.

I love river fishing and like nothing better than to fish a long beat on a good river working from pool to pool. To hunt fish on a river to the accompanying sound of flowing water, particularly broken water on a quiet summer's evening, is so evocative – it is like a good piece of music, you want to hear it and experience it over and over again.

Atmosphere, emotion and the need to hunt are all part of my fishing. I can enjoy a day fishing a moorland stream for small under-nourished brownies just as much as I do fishing for the brown trout on the vast spaces of a large limestone lough. Both settings give me that feeling of wildness, remoteness, that are so important to me. But these emotions have nothing to do with reading the water and applying fishing tactics that might work. These skills we must learn if we are to be successful.

The tactics we use on rivers are much more circumscribed, so too is the reading of the water – the grey area between right and wrong is not so vast. If you are river fishing for trout you are hoping to time your visit to coincide with a hatch of fly and if you are after migratory fish you will look at the water levels. You will then cover a pool, working through the lies using a method that suits the conditions. You know instinctively where the fish are likely to be, which way they are facing, and how best to approach them in order to present your fly without being seen.

This is not so obvious on stillwater. Even if you time your visit to coincide with a hatch of fly, you are still faced with problems such as location, weather, method and the direction in which the fish are swimming. It seems to me there are always a lot of 'ifs' in fishing, but in stillwater fishing on wild waters the number of 'ifs' seem greater. That is why I feel some river anglers never fully come to terms with stillwater fishing for they cannot think problems through as rationally as

they can on the river. What might appear obvious on a river doesn't seem to be so clear-cut on a stillwater; it is as if, without a water current as a guide, the river angler cannot apply the same logic. So they assume there is a lot of luck involved. Well, when it comes to fishing, luck will always play its part, but in any type of fishing – river, sea or stillwater – you also need to do some things right and to do them right consistently.

The methods described here may not be cutting edge, so those wishing to learn the very latest techniques may be disappointed. But with wild fish or mature, grown-on stock fish, presentation comes second to location, and is I feel more important even than fly pattern.

You cannot catch fish without first finding them. You then present an artificial to them without alarming the fish. Once you have achieved this you then work on the fly pattern, and here again keep things *simple*. I have caught the majority of my fish on a mere handful of fly patterns; presentation is far more important than the fly. That is why dry fly is such a good method for taking educated fish. It is the easiest method to achieve a good presentation. With wet fly, where movement and colour are the triggers, it is far harder to achieve

a presentation that will fool an educated fish. That is why I place the wet fly third in my range of methods for fishing for the bigger trout and is now a tactic that I use more at the back-end with larger flies when the fish become more aggressive. Big trout are not necessarily the most cunning or wiliest of fish, but they will have seen many artificial flies. To catch such fish requires nothing more than a good understanding of the basic principles which I shall discuss – applying the correct method, in the right place, at the right time. It isn't cutting edge, it is just common sense.

It is June 2005, the evening and early-morning fishing had begun. On the 15th a good friend persuaded me to go out for an evening of buzzer fishing on Lough Corrib. I caught two fish, both over 3lbs. Again, on the 17th, fishing from 9.30 to 12.30, in ideal conditions, I caught another brace: one weighing 5lbs 4oz and the other 7lbs 2oz. An exceptional brace of wild browns, but it didn't end there. Buoyed by my run of luck and an infectious madness to go fishing, that only a keen angler will know, my friend persuaded me to go out the following morning to fish the caenis rise. With very

little sleep between us we were out on the lough at 5am the next morning, June 18th, and I caught a further 3 trout from the caenis rise, the best fish weighing 4lbs. It was a window of quality fishing that, by the end of July, fishing either early morning or late evenings, ended with 42 fish. I have never been a numbers man, and I wasn't after numbers, I was fishing for quality wild brown trout.

Fishing short sessions at the key times whenever the opportunity arose, I picked up one or two fish, my best bag from a single session was eight. And the average weight of those wild trout was such that I do not think I will ever better it. They will live with me for the rest of my life. Of the 42 fish, 20 weighed between 4lbs and 7lbs. The method was dry fly, a simple technique, with no frills attached, and we used our knowledge about the movements of fish. We sought trout trout moving in areas known to us, we fished particular times (the late evening for the buzzer, or early morning for the caenis). It was an unforgettable period of fishing.

Such a result is well within the scope of any angler and I hope that this book will inspire and help you to achieve this.

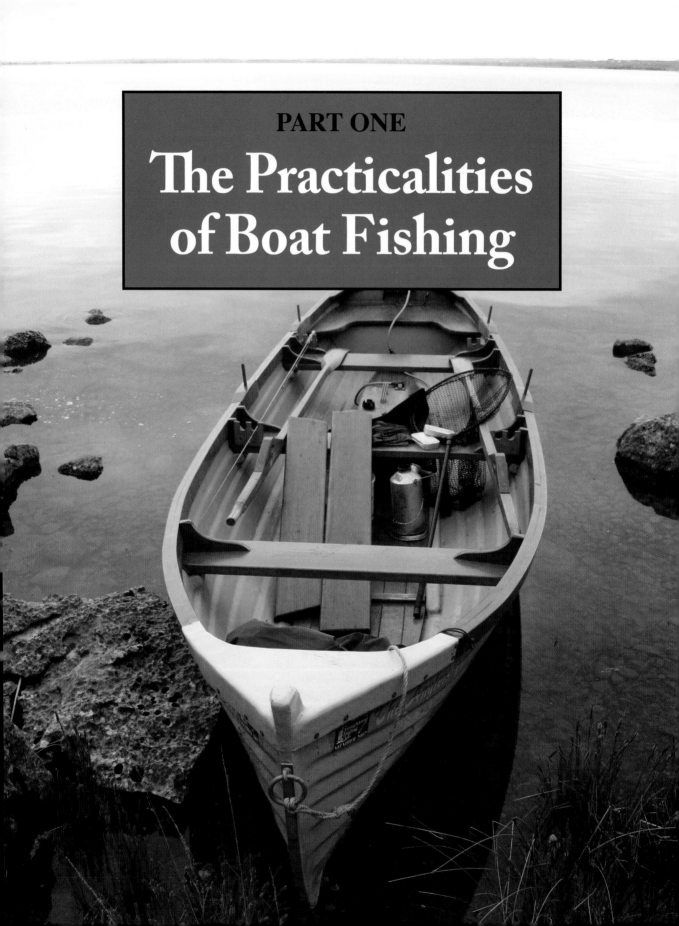

PART ONE
The Practicalities of Boat Fishing

CHAPTER 1

Boat Fishing Basics

I enjoy bank fishing, particularly on the larger fisheries where one is free to roam in search of fish. Working down a shoreline, systematically covering new water, can be a very satisfying and absorbing way to fish. Time becomes immaterial as I slip into an easy casting rhythm, leisurely searching the water for a feeding fish before taking a step forward following each cast. Not only do I find this style of fishing relaxing but it can also be very productive at times, particularly when the trout move closer inshore.

However, fishing different reservoirs from the shore can also be heart-breaking and it soon became obvious to me that to achieve consistent success one had to be prepared to go afloat. To any observant angler, the disparity between the catches of bank and boat fishermen over the duration of a season is quite clear and at certain times there is nothing a bank angler can do to offset this imbalance.

When conditions are against the bank fishermen there is little hope of any sport, no matter how far one can cast or where one fishes. I remember days on Grafham when the trout would not come within 100 metres of the shore and we, the poor bank fishers, looked forlornly on as the boat fishermen took fish after fish.

Haphazard stocking policies don't help the situation at all. It can be either feast or famine depending on the season or when the next injection of fish are stocked to liven things up. For bank anglers there is always the early season bonanza when a glut of fish can be taken following the main pre-season stocking. However, the easy harvest doesn't last long and invariably there follows a lean period until the weather warms and the trout start to move on the surface.

In late May and June there is the chance of some sport if the conditions are good and of course there is always the evening rise to raise our hopes. However, July and August can be desperate months, unless there is a summer stocking, until the fish move inshore again in September. As much as I love fishing, I do go to

Above: Green Island on Corrib, looking towards Ben Levy.

5

catch fish. If I was to achieve that aim and catch fish consistently then I felt there was no alternative but to leave the bankside and go afloat. Besides, messing about in boats looked like fun, certainly preferable to suffering another blank day on the shore.

BOATS – THE BEGINNING

Boat fishing presented me with a set of new problems to solve. On each visit to a fishery, the problem would change with the conditions and the season. To anchor or not to anchor, slowing the boat's drift or using a boat's drifting bias to fish a particular drift effectively were factors that I had never encountered or had to consider before. I soon realised that success wasn't guaranteed just because I had chosen to fish from a boat.

We did catch more fish, which was the reason for going afloat. However, our success was purely because we were over more fish. There were occasions when we could and should have performed better, if only we had a better understanding of boat handling. Our failure to make the best of certain situations through our lack of experience fishing from boats was, to say the least, frustrating. My boat handling skills were going to have to improve. I needed to learn the fundamentals of boat fishing so that, given a certain situation, I could fish with confidence no matter what the weather conditions.

Knowledge and confidence grew, but it took time and experience. At first we used to habitually anchor because that is what the majority of the other boats were doing. We did not give due consideration to the prevailing conditions or how to position the boat to take advantage of those conditions. It didn't take long for the penny to drop. I soon realised that these factors were important and that they could make a significant improvement to our catches. Armed with this knowledge, we began to capitalise on the advantage of being afloat. Fishing from boats had far more to offer than I imagined and I was eager to learn more.

Northampton Style

The 1970s was a period when the majority of boats on English reservoirs and lakes were anchored, with only a few drifting Northampton Style, bow to the wind, fishing lures on the swing. With the exception of Chew, one rarely saw boats drifting broadside with two anglers fishing a short line in front of the boat, akin to the traditional fishing of Irish or Scottish lakes. This was a style of fishing that appealed from the moment I first saw the method employed.

Traditional Style

But none of my friends fished this traditional style, so I had no experienced, old hand to learn from. I was very much in the dark. Opportunities to fish while on holiday in Scotland or Ireland were seized, particularly if there was an invitation to fish with an experienced angler or local boatman. Fishing traditional style, short-lining with a team of wet flies, for this was the way one fished from boats on wild waters, was great fun and productive too. While out on these trips I would try to take in as much information as possible but when it came to methods, they seemed pretty basic and were not as complex as the reservoir techniques.

Tackle would consist of a longish through-action rod of cane or fibreglass, a floating line and a team of three or four wet flies spaced evenly apart on a fairly short leader. A short line was then fished in front of the boat. Some anglers would fish a short cast using the rod action in one continuous lift and a hand haul to move the flies. The length of the cast was limited to the working length of line that could be fished with the one movement. This kept the flies high in the water and on its day – preferably one with warm, balmy overcast conditions – it was effective. But the method itself was very restrictive.

Other anglers would favour a slightly longer cast which required a number of hand hauls before the rod was raised to lift the flies to the surface. This latter method, which was more versatile, allowed the angler to fish the flies through the upper layers and it was this technique which I adopted. A more productive method, it was this style of pulling flies, albeit on a short line, that has evolved into the modern loch-style methods we have today. Surprisingly, some of those early days resulted in superb bags of fish but I know now that luck played an important part. Never spurn luck!

Looking back, conditions always seemed to be perfect and the plan simple: just align the boat on a drift and fish a team of three traditional flies on a short line through the upper layer of the water. The method was simplicity itself. Casting a short line, pulling the flies back with smooth pulls followed by a long steady lift brought fish charging through the waves to seize the flies. Sometimes the final draw would entice a fish up from a deeper lie to make a head-and-tail rise over the top dropper.

Traditional drifting style was not only novel but great fun compared with the static boat fishing techniques we had adopted for the small reservoirs. Not only was it enjoyable, it was also effective for the wild browns. So I reasoned: if the method could take wild fish, why not reservoir trout? Also, with so few boat anglers drift-fishing broadside at this time on the reservoirs, traditional methods might give me an edge. It was worth a try.

The early attempts met with mixed results for several reasons which at first I did not fully understand. It was obvious that if I was to avoid further frustration, I needed to reassess my approach. Why was it that wild uneducated trout responded so well to the traditional tactics, but whenever I used similar methods on the reservoirs, my results were mixed? There had to be other factors involved.

Troubleshooting

I tried to rationalise where I was going wrong with my traditional approach. Firstly, I needed to consider the waters which, to my knowledge, were best suited to traditional boat fishing methods. To improve my confidence, a free-rising water was a necessity, which automatically ruled out one of the fisheries that I was familiar with and fished quite a lot at the time. Datchet, a deep reservoir, held some stunning trout but they required a more specialised deep water approach as the fish were poor risers. This and the haphazard stocking policies on some of the other waters could explain some of my early poor results.

As Rutland had yet to open, we were left with Chew, Draycote, Grafham, Farmoor and Pitsford. Of these, Chew was arguably the best water around for good quality surface sport but all these reservoirs could, provided you chose the right time to go, produce superb top-of-the-water fishing. And of course this was another point which I had in my eagerness overlooked. What was the best time of year or season for traditional wet fly fishing on the surface?

Some fisheries produce good surface fishing earlier than others but in the main the richer lowland reservoirs do not produce well until mid-May or later,

The author with a 5lb rainbow from Rutland's South Arm.

unlike some of the wild brown trout lakes that I fish where good surface fishing can be had from late March onwards. Grafham never really used to get going until June but once the fish began moving on the surface, the sport could be memorable. So here again we had simple fundamental principles to learn that anglers now take for granted.

Old-style traditional boat fishing on the surface of rich lowland reservoirs that are predominantly stocked with rainbow trout is largely a waste of time before the waters have warmed sufficiently to encourage the fish to the surface. On many reservoirs this doesn't happen until mid-May, even with the mild winters and warmer springs.

It is now common knowledge that throughout the season fish will move up and down through the layers. If we want to catch early season fish, we just fish with the right density of sinking line. But, when I started boat fishing on reservoirs, modern top water fishing was still in its infancy and when it came to sunk line techniques from a drifting boat, methods that we now take for granted, were only just being developed. We may have lacked an armoury of different methods, the depth of knowledge and the written information that many of our contemporaries now have access to. But our understanding or lack of it was more than compensated for by a vast pool of untapped grown-on fish on which to concentrate our efforts.

It should be remembered that the common tactic of the day was to fish lures, so an angler applying a thoughtful approach to imitative top water methods enjoyed a tremendous advantage. These fish provided some wonderful fishing and when Rutland opened in 1977, an opportunity presented itself which I feel may never be repeated. With my improving techniques and a huge stock of over-wintered trout, Rutland in the 1980s provided me with some of the finest surface fishing I have ever experienced on any reservoir in England.

There were several unique events in stillwater trout fishing that I regret having missed. One was Grafham in its early years and the other was Datchet, a water which I knew well but one which I neglected to take advantage of when it produced some superb grown-on trout. The downside for me of the Datchet fishing was that it was a deep-method water and this did somewhat reduce the interest.

However, in the Eighties I was fortunate to have experienced something unique, fishing Rutland with small imitative flies for a pool of seasoned trout that had basically from the time of stocking not been exposed to any angling pressure other than that from lure fishermen.

Anglian Water now stock Rutland with larger fish and there is a sizeable stock of trout in the reservoir. However, these fish are subjected to much greater pressure from anglers fishing small imitative flies over the well-known lies. Because of greater fishing effort

and angler awareness of modern imitative techniques, the fish do not survive as long, and they are also educated to the danger of small flies much earlier. This restricts the pool of uneducated grown-on trout, further compounded by the small fly methods used by the competition anglers. They not only fish the competitions but also practice with flies that meet the size restrictions imposed on them by competition rules.

Also many of the anglers who now fish the reservoirs are well-informed about the areas which hold the better quality fish. Add to this the problem of cormorant predation and here are, I feel, the principle reasons why we will not see the type of fishing we experienced in the 1980s again. Even though I feel the reservoirs are now better managed.

BOAT DRIFTING

What I learnt about boat craft and surface methods on the reservoirs could also be applied to wild fishing. My fishing in Scotland and particularly in Ireland benefited as a result.

Although the basic principles are fairly easy to grasp, even some experienced anglers do not make the most of their opportunities through a lack of understanding about boat craft. It still amazes me even now, with all that has been written about boat fishing, when I see a boat poorly handled on the drift.

The majority of fibre glass boats drift with a bias towards the stern. This means that as the boat drifts with the wind, it doesn't drift in a straight line but moves diagonally across towards the stern side. If you line a boat up to drift a line between two marks, this movement from bow to stern becomes most noticeable, so when lining up your drift you have to compensate for this sideways motion.

The action of the boat as it creeps sideways when drifting forward with the wind is called 'crabbing' – so as the boat drifts forward it also crabs across the waves. Not all boats behave the same. This crabbing action is worse with some boats than others but it does seem to be an inherent fault with fibre glass boats.

Drifting Bias: the engine

A boat with a drifting bias is a common problem, which is made worse when the angler on the engine fails to switch the boat around through 180° to use the drifting bias of the boat effectively. This usually happens when the angler who is on the engine prefers fishing one side and therefore is not giving due consideration to his partner or to the prevailing conditions. Most right-handed anglers on the engine prefer to position the boat with the engine on their left-hand side. This avoids the engine interfering with their casting action but also gives them the advantage of the easier casting angle 9 to 12, provided they are prepared to cast over their partner's head.

Traditionally, casting over one's partner's head would have been regarded as unacceptable. If this arrangement has been agreed to allow for these considerations, then that is fine. But every effort should still be made by the angler operating the engine to put both rods over the fish.

Recently I even read a recommendation that competition anglers should fish with the engine (ie. the stern of the boat) on the left hand side so as not to interfere with the drift of other competition boats. Although this may seem logical for competitions, it does not mean that every angler in a drifting boat has to do the same. As a pleasure angler, I would find this very restrictive. The boat is a drifting platform and should be positioned to give both anglers the best opportunity of taking fish.

If we were bank fishing we would give careful consideration to the best position from which to fish off the shore. Depending on the wind direction, there will be favoured spots along any given shoreline and we try if possible, providing another angler hasn't already taken the position, to select the most likely spot to produce fish.

The same applies to boat fishing. We position our platform to both anglers' advantage wherever possible and if this means positioning the boat with the engine on the right hand side then you do that. If you are on the engine you do not position the boat with the engine on the left hand side and take that position every time: unless either the other rod has declined that position or you are selfish. There are no set rules as to which way round you position a boat, so if other boats out on the water have positioned their craft with the engine on the left-hand side then they are perfectly free to do so but if you feel that positioning your craft the opposite way round gives you an advantage, then you are free to do likewise.

I would always look at the prevailing conditions and position the boat accordingly, to take advantage of them. I would not look at what other boats were doing

A brace of over-wintered rainbows from Draycote reservoir.

9

and follow the pack if I thought they were not covering the fish properly. Whether you fish with the engine on the right or left is irrelevant when it comes to other boats drifting nearby. What you must not do is drift down onto or across another boat's drift: this would be bad form.

It isn't always easy to line up a boat's drift to cover a pod of fish which are known to be holding over a certain mark, and guarantee that both rods will have equal opportunities of rising trout. But with careful consideration of the boat's line of drift and the way the trout are moving around over the lie both rods over the course of a day should enjoy success.

Boat Partners and a Fair Drift

To give an example I remember an early June day on Rutland sharing a boat with my business partner in Wychwood Tackle, Bruce Vaughan. We are both right-handed and the only concession was that Bruce preferred to cast over the outside of the boat as he didn't like casting over his left shoulder or over the angler adjacent to him.

At that time we regularly fished Rutland. The

fishing was as near to wild fishing as you could ever hope from a stocked water and the most productive areas were over shallow water particularly at the extremities of the two arms. This meant that the best line was invariably on the inside, casting towards the shore. Very rarely did we drift over open water. Consequently, the angler on the inside had more opportunities to cover fish. Realising this, no matter who was on the engine, we would try to split the day so that both had an equal share of the inside line, or if a concentration of trout had been located, position the boat so that both rods could fish effectively.

Now on that June day, the wind was north-west and very cool (10°C) for the time of year. Considering the conditions, we elected to begin up the North Arm under Burley drifting from the trees towards Tim Appletons. It proved to be a good decision as there was a huge concentration of fish over the shallow before the dead trees. The problem was, the wind blowing slightly onshore. Therefore if Bruce remained on the engine casting over the outside of the boat, he would always be on what in most situations would be the favoured inside line.

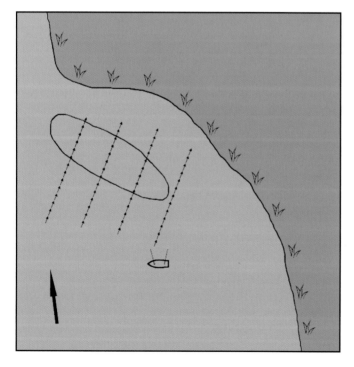

Diagram 1 shows how the bow rod is favoured during each drift when the boat 'crabs' to the stern.

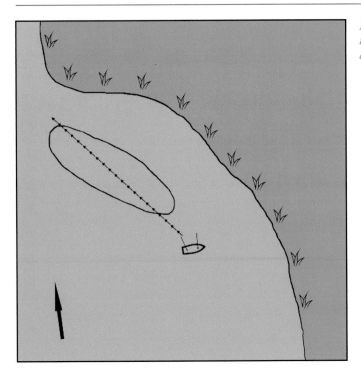

However, on this day it was working against him as the boat crabbed inshore, leaving me to cover the majority of the productive water as we systematically worked down the shore. This is illustrated in Diagram 1 (opposite page). I could see what was happening and explained to Bruce that we needed to turn the boat around so that the engine was on the outside. The majority of boats, especially moulded fibre glass boats, drift with a bias towards the stern and we could use this bias to offset the effect of the slight onshore wind, thus holding the boat parallel to the shore for much longer. See Diagram 2 (*above*).

Seeing that my suggestion made sense, Bruce agreed so that is what we did and as Bruce did not like casting over my head we swapped positions. I went on the engine and turned the boat through 180°. Performing this simple manoeuvre would not only offer an equal opportunity to both rods to cover the fish-holding shallow, it would also allow them to fish the holding area for longer. Opposite this shallow was an old green bucket that had been washed up by the winter storms and whenever we drew alongside the bucket, action was assured. We had a great day fishing small imitative flies to moving fish catching a large number

of trout, and once our desire to catch had been satiated, we left. It was uncanny the number of times we passed that magic marker with both rods bent double as we simultaneously played fish.

Had we left the boat drifting with the stern on the inside, I would most certainly have had the best of it, covering most of the productive water, thus depriving the other rod of an equal opportunity.

Of course it is a different matter when the fish are well dispersed, drifting open water and most of the action is falling to one rod. If this happens then the less successful angler should try to emulate what the successful rod is doing as closely as possible. However, skill or method count for little if one rod covers the best water as can happen with confined lies or inside lines. Therefore, when drifting over shallow, productive lies, it is important to position the boat so that both rods may have an equal chance of covering fish.

Shallow Drifting

Trout feeding over shallow water take well and often it is the first fly they see, provided it is well presented, that deceives them. If you share a boat with a fellow angler, gamesmanship should never come into play by intentionally making the fellow rod sharing the boat ineffective. In *A Man May Fish*, Kingsmill Moore exposes this sort of behaviour when he asked the squire, the owner of the Big House, what he thought of a famous classical scholar who came from the neighbourhood. "Not much," the squire replied "He always tried to take the inside cast."

I think that sums it up nicely.

There are other situations where the bias drift of a boat can influence the results but they are not so critical as when drifting shallow lies. For instance when drifting a calm lane, a selfish angler on the engine could pull the boat off before the rod in the bows has had a reasonable chance to cover both sides of the calm lane. Without a boatman to hold a steady line, it is very often difficult to position the boat so that both anglers can cover a calm lane simultaneously. It is therefore much fairer to allow the boat to drift across the lane so that the anglers in the stern and the bow cover both sides of the lane before pulling across and repeating the drift again.

This way the boat will make a zig-zag course down the calm lane and once a concentration of fish have been discovered then the productive line should be drifted again, hopefully offering opportunities to both anglers. The same applies when the fish are tight in to confined lies such as weed beds or features, particularly at the back-end of the season when the fry pack in to any cover they can find. Then very often there are only a limited number of chances of taking trout from such lies. Knowing this, a considerate angler aware of the drifting bias can position a boat so that it crabs into a confined lie, offering both rods the best opportunity of a fish.

POSITIONING THE BOAT TO TAKE FULL ADVANTAGE OF CONDITIONS

Just as the weather is forever changing, the versatile angler will also adapt to the conditions of the day. We have to adjust if we wish to maintain consistent results. With experience and an adaptable approach, the answers will come. There are no set rules that the fish will follow but there are situations where they behave in a characteristic manner and we can use the information to our advantage.

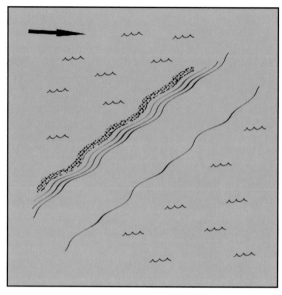

Diagram 3: The shaded area shows the favoured line of the feeding fish – on the windward side of the calm lane where the surface food tends to collect.

For instance when fish are taking surface fly, such as spent egg-laying adult flies, these spent flies will collect in certain areas, depending on the wind strength and direction. The calm water in the lee of an island, downwind of the main hatching area, is a classic.

But what are the effects of a calm lane on windblown terrestrials or adult flies? We are not talking here of emerging or hatching flies but a fly that is blown onto the surface of the water and encourages the trout to feed on the surface. In situations such as these, the bulk of the food will collect on the windward side of the calm lane and therefore the majority of the surface-feeding trout will favour this side of the lane. See Diagram 3 (*above*).

The same pattern will emerge for any surface-borne organism – snails for instance, when they rise to the surface, will collect on the windward side of a calm lane and the trout swim up and down this margin. How many times, when bank fishing, have you fished into a wind that is slightly onshore and observed the fish feeding on the far side of a wind lane that inclines slowly inshore? Very often these fish can remain tantalisingly out of reach as it is difficult to punch the line through the calm air above the lane and present your flies on the far side.

Anglers who haven't experienced trout moving to a fall of surface fly would not be necessarily be aware of the influence of the wind and its effect on the fish. This would be particularly true of a lot of reservoir anglers who are aware of the strategic importance of a calm lane but in the main they would be fishing for trout that are feeding on emerging or hatching insects. Such food tends to collect along the edges of the lane or in the calm water itself and because of this the trout tend to move through or along both sides of the lane. Thus they do not favour a particular side, unlike the fish moving to surface food only. With experience an angler will know how the fish respond to situations such as these and will concentrate on the productive areas but this can only come from being observant and adjusting to the conditions.

DO NOT DISTURB THE FISHING WATER

One of the simplest manoeuvres, yet much overlooked, is that of avoiding disturbing the water that is going to be fished before setting up the boat for a drift. Why so many anglers underestimate the importance of this task

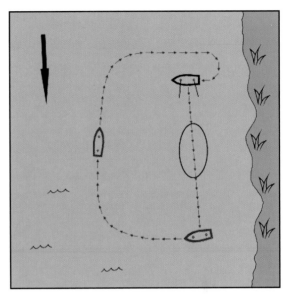

Diagram 5: If it is absolutely necessary to turn the boat through 180 degrees (so that the fishermen are facing correctly downwind) then ensure that the boat has been taken as far upwind as possible before turning downwind through the turn.

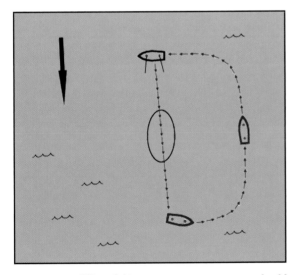

Diagram 4: When fishing over open water, one should always approach the drift from the correct side, thus avoiding having to turn the boat around – an activity which unecessarily disturbs the water.

is a mystery to me. Yet I have shared a boat so many times now with knowledgeable fishermen who seem to give the matter of lining up the boat without disturbing the fishing water for the next drift little or no thought whatsoever. The most common fault is motoring up too close to the water about to be fished. Always give the fishing ground as wide a berth as possible, particularly when fishing for wild trout.

At least the anglers will then be fishing water that is undisturbed by the motion of the boat, from the moment the boat comes to rest. Although blindingly obvious, turning the boat upwind is a mistake I have observed many times, particularly when lining the boat up in the confines of a small bay: but there is no excuse for making this mistake over open water. The two fishermen are then faced with water that has been disturbed by the motion of the boat, which no self-respecting trout would enter. They then have to wait for the boat to drift through the disturbance before they can start fishing (*see* Diagram 6). With a little thought this can easily be avoided.

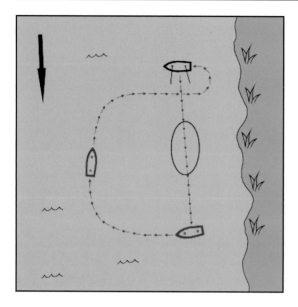

Diagram 6: You will be fishing disturbed water at the beginning of the drift if you manoevre the boat in this way.

When fishing sinking lines, the position in the boat can affect the depth of presentation, even when both anglers are using identical outfits. This only becomes noticeable if the depth of the fly's path is critical. A drogue will offset this problem as it slows the boat down and corrects much of the bias drifting, so the boat drifts in a slower and straighter line. But without a drogue, the angler in the stern will be forced to recover line faster than his neighbour in the bow because he not only has to compensate for the quicker forward motion of the boat but also the exaggerated sideways movement as well.

This sideways movement is pulling the stern angler's line into his neighbour's water and he is thus forced to recover line, whether he wants to or not. The angler in the bows will be drifting down and away from his flies.

What this means in effect is that if the stern rod were to cast his line well to his left, he has the opportunity to fish his flies deeper if he so wishes and will always cover the trout first. The bow rod cannot do this, as he would be casting into the stern rod's water, but he can, by using the arc created by the sideways movement, fish a more attractive line and hang his flies for longer around the side of the boat. It depends on the season and the prevailing conditions which method will be the more successful.

They all have their day.

Below: Several boats drift towards the shore of the South Arm at Rutland Water in a comfortable wave.

ANCHORING

When it comes to anchoring most anglers do not give enough thought to positioning the boat to obtain the best results. They think anywhere will do. They just simply drop anchor and hope for the best, with no consideration at all to the prevailing conditions or the area to be covered by their flies. Boats are not allowed to anchor in most competitions so we are talking here about pleasure or sport fishing with a friend or invited guest. Anchoring and gamesmanship or coveting the best areas shouldn't be an issue. Yet there are times when most of the action, whether intentional or not, may come to one angler only.

This may happen if the boat is positioned to cover a fish-holding feature that favours the successful angler's side. In such situations, the anchor position can be adjusted to suit both anglers fishing similar methods and then hopefully the catch rate will even out. When anchored on a single rope, the boat will swing (or yaw) back and forth over a given area, allowing both rods an equal opportunity to cover fish. A boat, when tethered by a fixed rope, yaws back and forth like a pendulum and the distance of the swing produced by the yawing

effect will be dependant on the length of rope and the wind speed. See Diagram 7 (*below left*).

There are times when it can be advantageous to use the yawing action to cover a wider arc of water by intentionally anchoring on a long rope. I have used this ploy when fishing onto a windward shore, particularly during the early part of the season. The longer the rope the greater the length of shore line I can cover on the swing. So, when trout are feeding on midge pupae that are being carried back towards the boat on the undertow of the waves, this can be a very effective fishing technique. Once I have exhausted a given area, the boat can also be made to swing further in the direction of the bow by adjusting the fixing position on the boat nearer to the bow end. So, from the same fixed anchor position, the rods can then cover fresh water. If

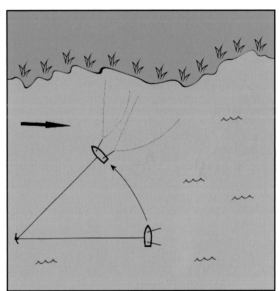

Diagram 8: When fishing from an anchor it is possible, by adjusting the point of its attachment to the boat, to 'steer' the boat nearer to where you wish to fish.

I want to maintain the boat's distance from the shore I would need to lengthen the rope to compensate for the change in swing. These little ruses avoid lifting the anchor to reposition the boat – which causes unnecessary disturbance and frightens the trout.

When anchoring a boat to fish down a shoreline along which the wind is blowing (Diagram 8, *above*) the same principles of adjusting the length of anchor

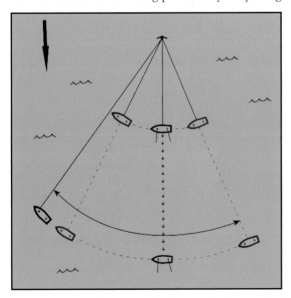

Diagram 7: Yawing action of a boat tethered to a fixed point. The longer the 'tether' the greater will be your coverage of the water.

A fine Draycote rainbow with well-formed fins indicating that it has had time to adapt, grow and gain condition since it was stocked.

rope or the position on the boat to which the rope is fixed are useful ploys that can improve the catch rate. With a good wind blowing along or slightly onshore, it is preferable to fish with the bow of the boat pointing towards the shore with the rope attached to the gunwale off the middle of the boat, just as we would in the downwind position. Both anglers can then fish downwind covering the water within the arc created by the yawing action of the boat. Once that water has been thoroughly covered, then adjusting the position of the rope so that it is attached closer to the bow end will exaggerate the swing inshore at an angle, giving both rods a good line to fish and fresh water to cover.

The rod in the stern has the more favourable position in this instance, as he can swing his flies through a wider arc but the bow rod has the advantage of fishing into the shore. Many times I have used this method of anchoring a boat on reservoirs such as Rutland and Draycote to good effect. On Farmoor fishing the windward shore using a long anchor rope can be very effective as the fish are induced to take on the slow swing created by the yawing movement of the boat.

FISHING WITH ONE ANCHOR

I prefer fishing with one anchor. It is simpler and avoids excessive disturbance but there are days when it may be necessary to keep the boat even more stable, in a fixed position. Fishing from a stable platform allows the angler more control over his presentation but there are also fishermen who find it difficult to control their presentation from a yawing boat. Lack of control over the fly line when it is out on the water is a failure on the part of the angler who isn't allowing for the swing of the boat. If control over the fly line isn't maintained throughout the retrieve, the line will just meander across the surface of the water, thus making a natural presentation impossible.

FISHING WITH TWO ANCHORS

For those anglers who find control over the line difficult, or in situations where a slow natural presentation is a problem, then it is advisable to use two anchors. To position the boat, two anchors are dropped simultaneously, one from the bow end and the other from the stern end of the boat, as the boat drifts downwind over the anchoring position.

The fixing points for the anchor ropes should be kept as far apart as possible with one rope attached towards the bow and the other towards the stern end of the boat. Keeping the fixing point of the ropes apart will help stabilise the boat and this can be further improved by spreading the anchor positions.

To spread the anchor positions it is essential to

16

motor the boat at low revs across the wind over the anchoring point and then drop first the stern anchor and then the bow anchor at least three lengths of the boat apart. Cut the engine just before lowering the bow anchor and pay out rope until the forward momentum of the boat ceases. This will ensure that the anchors only start to dig in once the boat is pushed downwind. With the anchor points spread, rope is recovered until the desired position is achieved. To avoid damage to a boat when attaching an anchor rope or a drogue rope to the gunwhales of a boat it is advisable to attach the rope to a G clamp rather than the rowlock or the thwart seats.

When anchoring, wind strength doesn't deter me so long as it remains constant. In, fact we have had some very good days in big winds that would have made drift fishing uncomfortable and ineffective. If I was given a choice of weather conditions for catching quality over-wintered fish in April or May, I would choose the third day of a period of strong winds blowing from the same direction.

Wind direction or temperature would not bother me so long as both conditions had remained steady for several days. Some of my best bags have been taken following a weather pattern of strong, raw, easterly winds – conditions that many anglers would say were all wrong for a good day.

And where are the fish in such conditions? Close in on the windward shore feeding hard on midge pupa or daphnia. It is important when fishing the windward shore in such weather that the water doesn't colour up, as not all waters produce well in these condition. But on those that do the fishing can be superb.

If you are going to fish imitative patterns in a big wave it is essential to anchor to obtain the best results. In a strong wind a good anchor is a necessity to hold position and can make all the difference between a good day and a poor one.

An anchor that will hold in any wind is essential. If the anchor slips, a lot of valuable fishing time and a great opportunity to take a good bag of fish could be wasted. There are times when at the end of a day's fishing I curse the weight of my anchor and although I may stop taking it with me once the weather warms and we start drifting in earnest, I most definitely wouldn't be without it during the early season fishing.

THE DROGUE

As the weather warms and the fish become more active, and move towards the surface, a mobile approach is preferable to the sedentary methods of fishing from an anchored boat. There will still be the odd day when an anchor may be necessary but these will be few and far between as the season progresses from late spring into early summer. Mid-May to late June can provide the cream of reservoir fishing and there is no finer way to enjoy the full potential of traditional flyfishing than from a drifting boat. Although I have experienced some superb days fishing at anchor I find it hard to compare them with a good day drift fishing which to me is the very essence of our traditional sport.

CONTROLLING DRIFTING SPEED

With drifting, it is essential to have control over the boat and to be aware of how the craft drifts to maximise the full potential of a drifting platform. Controlling the speed of the drift is essential and is best achieved by the use of a drogue – which are available in many shapes and sizes. The other point to be aware of is the 'drifting bias' and how much the boat crabs across the wind, as discussed earlier.

Once familiar with the way a boat moves before the wind it should be possible to line up a drift and determine the line the boat will follow over a given distance. Even on long drifts a good angler should be able to determine the position where his craft will finish and line it up so that the drift covers productive water. This can be so important when, for instance, a pod of fish have been discovered in a tight area over open water and we need to follow the same line again.

If there are no obvious features to pinpoint the location of the fish then you are reliant on remembering the line you have just drifted to cover the same water again. So always try to remember landmarks or bank-side features that were used to line up the original drift.

Also, when on a long drift over open water you can save a lot of time if you know the line that you were drifting by not going back to the beginning of the drift, covering what was unproductive water.

Controlling the speed of a drifting boat relative to wind strength is at times essential: the stronger the wind, the greater the need for speed control. Modern stillwater trout anglers are now aware of this and appreciate that slowing the speed of the drift down can improve results. It was the success of competition anglers controlling the speed of the drifting boat that created an awareness among reservoir fisherman of the importance of this tactical manoeuvre. As with many new innovations, the anglers fortunate enough to know the benefits of using a drogue well before they became popular, experienced a tremendous advantage in certain situations.

OLD-FASHIONED DROGUES

When I first began reservoir boat fishing, anglers rarely used a drogue and those that did invariably made their own from sheets of square canvas. Some of these early drogues were made with a hole in the centre which served no functional purpose, but no one ever seemed to ask why the hole was necessary. Even when drogues became commercially available they still sported the ubiquitous hole in the centre and we blindly fished with similar designs until well into the late Eighties.

The big disadvantage with the conventional drogues was the single main running line which was attached to a swivel or ring. To this ring or swivel was connected four short lengths of cord, each of which was connected to a corner of the square canvas sheet. As a means of slowing the boat's drift, these drogues fulfilled that function. But when it came to pulling the drogue back into the boat at the end of a drift, they were absolute drudgery, because with a single main line one had to haul against the drag of the opened drogue. This was made worse in a strong wind as one had to contend with the increased drag created by a faster drifting boat. And if we were drifting onto the shore we had to start hauling the drogue back much earlier than we would have liked because of the time it took to retrieve it.

A NEW DROGUE DESIGN

These disadvantages became irritating particularly if we were drifting onto a productive shoreline we wanted to fish out, to the very last moment. With the conventional design this was impossible as the drogue took too long to haul in. Something had to be done.

In 1989 Bruce Vaughan and I were fishing the north arm on Rutland when, after several seasons of trying to find a solution to the problem, the answer came to me. It was staring me in the face. In fact it was actually falling out of the sky but I didn't realise this immediately. The seeds had been sown a few weeks earlier at an air display to which I had taken my eldest son. While at the display, the RAF Falcons made a parachute drop and as I watched the descent through a pair of binoculars it became apparent that one of the team members was finding it difficult to hold the formation line. His animated hand movements could clearly be observed as he worked hard pulling the cords to bring himself back into line with other members of the team.

At the time it did not dawn on me that here was the solution to our drogue problem. But while fishing with Bruce on Rutland, another air display was taking place at a nearby airfield, and it came back to me. The wind was blowing from the south and it was around mid-day when the RAF Falcons made a drop from a Hercules aircraft that had passed overhead. The parachutists disappeared over the back of Burleigh in a perfect descent. Watching them come down I recalled my earlier observation and how hard that team member had worked to bring his chute into line.

The Eureka Moment

I don't know what brought my thoughts around to the drogue; perhaps Bruce had cut his hand on the drogue cord. He had a habit of cutting his hands and drawing blood on the drogue cord, anchor rope or the pulley cord of the outboard, an act that would always have the pair of us roaring with laughter at the sight of his blood-splattered hands. Anyway for whatever reason, suddenly I wasn't looking at a chute with a man attached pulling on more than one cord, I was looking at a drogue.

And it wasn't the square drogue with a single cord attached to a swivel with four cords connected to the four corners of the square. Instead it was a rectangular drogue with a continuous length of cord each end of which was attached to webbing loops which in turn were attached to the two corners each side of the drogue. So instead of a single cord stretching out from the boat to the drogue we would have two, and by pulling on one

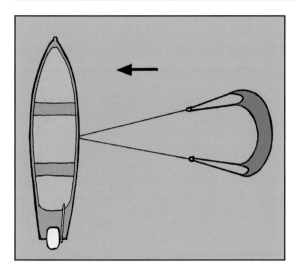

and held position much better than the conventional square design. When we came to the end of the drift, one sharp pull on one of the cords collapsed the drogue and it could be quickly hauled in. There was none of the drudgery of hauling against a dead weight and we could fish the drifts right out with confidence, allowing the boat to drift right into the marginal shallows before putting our rods down.

We were so pleased with the results that only minor alterations were required to the original prototype design. Having established that the drogue worked without any hidden problems we launched this unique design as a commercial product through Wychwood Tackle and called it the Para Drogue (*see left*).

It has proved to be a huge success throughout the nineties and is one of the most popular drogues used by English boat fisherman, requiring only one alteration (in 1998) when we increased the size from 60" width x 40" height to 72" width x 50" height. We increased the size because modern stillwater techniques demanded

of the cords the side would collapse allowing the drogue to be dragged in with little resistance.

Good in theory but would it work in practice? I had a prototype made which was 60" width x 40" height and we were on Rutland the following week using this new prototype drogue. As a first trial with a prototype design, the drogue could not have worked better. Being rectangular in shape, the drogue dug in

A rainbow, with colourful gill marking, comes to the boat at John Barnes' fishery, Oxfordshire.

slower drifts and the larger size met this requirement admirably. The larger-size drogue slows the boat's drift to such a level that the angler can fish the slowest of retrieves for nymph techniques with confidence.

No Point in the Hole

I must admit that, at first, I had reservations about the design concept as the image of anglers struggling with the two cords conjured up all sorts of horrors in my mind. However we received positive feedback from anglers all over the country and surprisingly enough the one aspect of the design that caused the most consternation was the omission of the central hole. We explained that the object of a drogue is to slow the boat's rate of drift down and therefore it is essential to present as large an area of resistance as possible. Putting a hole in the middle would only reduce the drag factor.

Most people went away happy with our explanation but occasionally you would get someone who couldn't accept it despite the fact that they themselves could give no rational reason as to what function the hole served. They had always used a drogue with a hole in the centre, and that's how they thought it should remain.

Surprisingly, the two cords presented few problems so it would seem that when using the drogue most anglers used their common sense and didn't get in a tangle. The one thing to remember after pulling on one of the cords to collapse the drogue is to make sure that the two cords remain separate.

To achieve this, simply keep pulling the cord and let it fall into the boat, then pull in the drogue and drop the drogue onto the cord or lay it on a thwart board or the side of the boat then pull the other cord in and lay that on top of the drogue.

To set the drogue up at the beginning of a drift, just grab the top cord and the drogue and throw it over the side. The remaining cord will follow and once the drogue is at full extension it will dig in and bellow out.

SAFETY

In this chapter I have covered:

- slowing the boat's drift
- anchoring
- drifting bias and using that bias to advantage
- setting the boat up for a drift without disturbing the water to be fished
- observing conditions when applying boat craft

Experienced boat fisherman will be aware of these points but anglers new to boat fishing or beginners will be well advised to try and understand these fundamentals if they are to take advantage of fishing from a moving platform.

Life Jackets are Essential

Lastly, for anyone considering going afloat, always remember to wear a lifejacket. You will see from the photographs in this book that I wear a life jacket and have done so for at least twenty years and I am indebted to Vaughan Lewis, a very good friend, for making me aware of self-inflating lifejackets that inflate to a minimum of 150 Newtons when immersed in water. They take very little time to put on and do not inconvenience the angler with bulk or weight so there really is no excuse for not wearing one.

This harness-type of lifejacket is far more versatile than a lifejacket that is incorporated into an angler's jacket or coat. The harness type can be worn over any type of clothing, from shirt sleeves to full foul-weather protection gear.

It is surprising even now how many anglers I still see out on the water or in magazines not wearing any form of life-support system and yet these same fishermen will gladly spend 3 to 4 times the cost of a lifejacket on a rod. They obviously place a higher value on the fishing tackle they use than on their lives.

Facing page: Drifting into Rainbow Corner at Draycote reservoir in promising conditions.

CHAPTER 2

Of Lines and Leaders

In the early days of the modern stillwater trout fishing revolution, sinking lines fell into three distinct categories: fast, medium or slow sinkers. The fastest sinkers were invariably lead-cored which, as their name suggests, sank very quickly and, apart from the Aquasink, were quite crude to cast.

The Wet Cel II was probably the most popular medium sinker and still is a well thought-of line for mid-water fishing. Examples of slow sinkers were Wet Cel I, Cortland or a pale brown slow sinking line from Garcia.

Many fishermen possessed a fast or medium sinking line for deeper fishing but anglers were slow to recognise the potential of the slower sinking lines, so it took some time before they became widely used.

The main problem with the slow sinking lines for imitative methods, was that they sank too quickly and therefore sank below the taking zone of the fish, making slow retrieves (so essential when fishing nymphs) impossible. With the growing popularity of small stillwaters and the insatiable hunger of modern fly anglers for new products, a new generation of slow-sinking lines, called the intermediate or incorrectly-named neutral-density lines were produced.

Once anglers realised what they could achieve with an intermediate line, these lines very quickly became popular, particularly with the competition fishermen.

As the stillwater trout market is heavily influenced by what the competition anglers are using, it was only a matter of time before the majority of stillwater anglers owned an intermediate line of some sort.

BRANDS OF INTERMEDIATE LINES

There are a number of different brands of intermediate lines available today and the sinking rates vary slightly from brand to brand, which can cause confusion to prospective purchasers. Not only do the sinking rates vary but because some of the lines are made from different compounds, the way the line behaves to drag, undertow, water pressure, temperature and the flies on the leader can affect the sinking rate of the line in practice. It is these variables that cause confusion and frustration to some anglers, when the fisherman next to them is bagging up using an intermediate line and yet they cannot touch a trout when they fish an intermediate line themselves. Usually, it isn't the angler's fault.

In situations such as these, where only one fisherman is catching using an intermediate line, it will be found on closer inspection that the success of one fisherman will be attributable to the brand of intermediate line used. The important point to remember here is that not all intermediate lines of different brands have the same density or sinking rate. So if someone you are sharing a boat with or standing next to is catching well fishing with an intermediate line and you have changed to an intermediate yourself, using similar flies, and feel you are over fish but are still not getting any takes, you need to discover what make and weight of line your companion is using. If the lines are different then you need to understand how both lines behave and see if you can compensate for the different sinking characteristics of the line you are using.

Understanding how different makes of intermediate lines behave can only be achieved by fishing with several makes of line and building up experience over a period of time. Once you have an understanding of how the lines behave, you can then determine whether to carry more than one line or to just settle for a line that suits your style of fishing.

One of the early PVC intermediate lines that proved popular with small stillwater anglers well before intermediate lines caught on with the competition fraternity, was the turquoise line from Scientific Angler. Similar to a slow sinker this was quite a fast sinking PVC intermediate line that penetrated the surface film quickly, even in a flat calm. Once the line had penetrated the surface film, there was no shadow and anglers found this advantageous on small clear waters. In addition the flies could be fished at the cruising depth of targeted fish with faster retrieves that fresh stock fish find so attractive. The disadvantage with this line, as with all the faster sinking intermediate lines, is that it does not hold up in the water with the slower retrieves necessary to fish imitative flies on the larger lakes and reservoirs.

SLOW-SINKING INTERMEDIATE LINE IMPROVES PRESENTATION

When fishing imitative flies from the bank or from an anchored boat with a slow retrieve, a method which is so effective during the early season, I favour one of the slower-sinking PVC lines to hold the taking depth through which the fish are cruising. One of the best slow-sinking PVC intermediate lines I have used for this style of fishing, but sadly is no longer manufactured, was a salmon pink line made by Masterline. This line had a very slow sinking rate and had to be cleaned well with detergent before use to get it to cut through the surface film.

The effectiveness of these slower sinking PVC lines made an impression on me several seasons ago when the clear intermediates came onto the market. Bruce Vaughan and I were fishing Draycote early season from an anchored boat into Rainbow Corner in a north-easterly wind. We were fishing onto the windward shore over a huge concentration of trout that were holding around 10 feet down. For several trips we had been fishing with the new clear lines catching plenty of fish.

However, on this occasion I began with the Masterline slow-sinking intermediate and was into fish from the very first cast, whereas Bruce who was fishing with identical nylon and fly patterns was struggling to get a take fishing the clear line. As we were using similar leader arrangements and fishing a very slow retrieve it was clear that Bruce's flies were sinking through and below the fish.

It wasn't until I persuaded Bruce to change to the slower sinking line which I knew he had that his catch rate increased. This was a classic example of the improved presentation with the slower sinking line and a slow retrieve being just what the fish wanted.

This fine, silver, over-wintered rainbow – from Draycote reservoir – shows the white veining on the tail and anal fins, and the translucent edges to the ventral fins.

PENETRATING THE SURFACE FILM

A big problem with intermediate lines, particularly the slower-sinking lines, is penetration of the surface film. For the first few casts many of the lines are slow to cut through the surface film but as they take on moisture (and all plastics will absorb a degree of moisture, particularly the clear lines) penetration of the surface film will improve. There is nothing worse than watching your line lying on the surface struggling to cut through the film. This is even more annoying in a flat calm when the line either refuses to cut through the surface film, or takes an age to sink. Productive fishing time can be lost if the line refuses to sink, so to avoid this problem it is advisable to clean the line well with detergent before use. Either carry a small plastic bottle of liquid detergent or cleaning agent with you and clean the line before you begin fishing, or clean the line the night prior to your trip. This will avoid frustration and wasting valuable fishing time on the day you are fishing.

CLEAR INTERMEDIATE LINES

The introduction of a clear intermediate line several seasons ago by Scientific Angler in their Mastery Series of lines was a clever piece of marketing and these lines have proved very popular.

Today there are a number of different brands of clear line available and several manufacturers now produce clear lines with different sinking rates but whichever brand of clear line you choose, they all sink faster (particularly once they have taken on moisture) than the designated slower PVC lines. If you ignore the hype and concentrate on the sinking rates and utilise the way the line behaves to your advantage, you will catch more fish than placing all your faith in the fact that the trout cannot see the line.

Best for Small Stillwaters

Because of their faster sinking rates and better surface penetration, the clear lines are more suited to fishing small stillwaters and for fishing from drifting boats. They will not hold a level as well as the slower sinking lines with very slow retrieves but on the majority of small waters this will not be a problem.

From a drifting boat it is essential to get down to the trout before the boat has drifted over the line, and in windy conditions the clear lines have the advantage; whereas the slower lines would more suitable in moderate or light winds. There would be windy days during the season when even with a drogue out, the slower sinking lines would not have sufficient time to attain the correct depth to begin fishing effectively before the boat has drifted over the line. So if you can't anchor, it would pay to carry at least two intermediate lines of different densities.

When buying an intermediate line, do not worry whether the line is clear or coloured. With a sinking flyline, go for an unobtrusive colour. Rather, I would suggest that you consider the sinking rate before you purchase, and chose a sinking rate suitable for your style of fishing. If you are going to fish a number of different waters, both large and small, then you are going to require lines with different sinking rates. A little thought before you purchase could avoid the frustration of the earlier scenario of fishing adjacent to an angler who is catching many trout on intermediate line, and achieving a presentation you cannot duplicate with your line.

MONOFILAMENTS FOR LEADERS

Some flyfishermen do not like to admit it, but luck plays a significant role in flyfishing success. However, over a period of time the luck factor will even itself out. And if we were to analyse a table of results over a given period, the better anglers with superior water craft and technical ability would appear at the top of the results list. Confidence and skill are enhanced by using the latest equipment or techniques and good anglers have a knack of quickly accessing productive innovations. There is a speedy exchange of information and if a novel idea is successful, it is difficult to keep it under wraps for long. The high success rate of good flyfishermen, anglers who consistently catch more trout, cannot solely be attributed to a certain method or product, as that advantage will quickly be eroded by common awareness. What good anglers do is apply these innovative methods or techniques more consistently, at the right times, and not only that but they also know where to fish and in what conditions or season to apply the techniques.

Fishing Competitions Influencing Tackle

Many of the recent improvements in modern stillwater fishing have emerged through the competition scene. Over the last twenty years there have been many new developments which have undoubtedly improved our fishing. A lot of fly anglers now place great store on competition results and if a method or item of tackle is attributed to a good result in the competitions then the word quickly gets around. Today's fly anglers cannot complain about not having access to a lot of very useful information and very good products to fish with.

We now have fly lines of every conceivable density, with a wide range of sinking rates, chemically sharpened hooks, the very latest high modulus carbon fibre rods and large diameter, wider Arbor

reels. These are products which have been designed to improve the fisherman's confidence, help him perform and ultimately catch more fish. The same can be said of the developments in leader materials. We now have standard nylon, the thinner copolymer monofilaments and fluorocarbon specifically packaged and marketed for flyfishing.

Fluorocarbon leader materials have been well received, but are they really the panacea that some fishermen obviously believe? Although fluorocarbon had been around for some time before it became popular in this country, the success of the Bewl team in two major competitions in 1996 certainly drew a lot of attention to the product and was instrumental for the sudden increase in demand for fluorocarbon leader line. Anglers at the time willingly paid the extra money for fluorocarbon line in the hope that they could emulate the results of the Bewl team.

We will never know if Bewl's success was solely due to the leader material or simply down to a team of very good anglers working to a winning plan under the prevailing conditions.

Clear Monofilament

Fluorocarbon is a significant development in leader material without doubt but I would consider clear nylon as the most significant development in flyfishing, particularly for fishing in or near to the surface. Fishing evening sessions on Farmoor reservoir convinced me of the huge advantage clear or pale tinted monofilaments have over the darker monofilaments for surface fishing. In 1974 we experienced tremendous evening rises on Farmoor I but the fish were proving difficult, or so I thought. Although I was catching a few fish I wasn't making any real impression on the numbers of trout that were rising and I felt that it was my fly patterns that were at fault.

So I went down the route of tying up new patterns of nymphs, but when it came to the actual test of deceiving the fish my new flies met with the same indifferent result. No matter what pattern of fly I tried, the results were basically the same. I was convinced that pattern of fly was the problem, but was it?

At the time I was using a well-known and respected brand of nylon, Maxima Chameleon – a superb all-round line – and I hadn't for one moment considered that the colour of my leader line could be

A beautifully marked brown trout about to regain her freedom. As always, when releasing trout, they should be handled as gently as possible, with wetted hands and quickly returned to their own world.

responsible for the trouts' refusal. I tried dropping to finer leaders and this showed a slight improvement but it wasn't the answer. I would never have considered that my leader could have been at fault until one evening when fishing with a friend. The fish dutifully rose as usual and I was expecting another tough evening in warm, light wind conditions. But my friend surprised me: he began to catch trout, and by the end of the session, a lot of trout.

Although we were fishing with similar fly patterns, I hardly touched a fish. My friend couldn't account for the difference in our results. But I couldn't let it go. I felt that there was something amiss with my set up and it was something other than my flies. As we were both fishing floating lines I dismissed the fly lines, so that just left the leaders.

It had to be the nylon, I suggested. My comment met with much laughter. But we had been fishing in close proximity to one another, and he had kept me informed as to which flies were catching. I had never

thought of asking what breaking strain (BS) of nylon he was using. It was five pound, while I was using three pound nylon. But it transpired that my friend had gone to the local tackle shop for Maxima, as usual, only to find they were out of stock, so he had bought instead a little 25-metre spool of tippet material, a brand by the name of Kroic.

When he held out the spool I could read the dimensions of the nylon on the label, and not only was he fishing with a line that was stronger than the line I was using, but the 5lb tippet material was also a thick line for its stated BS. Diameter therefore of the leader nylon was definitely not the reason for the trout refusing my offerings: the problem was something else. My friend's nylon was a pale grey.

At the time I did not consider line colour to be significant but I did sense the answer was connected to that little spool of monofilament.

To test the theory I purchased two spools of the nylon in different breaking strains and fished with the

25

new nylon the next evening. The results were a revelation. My catch rate soared! My catches were such that I became intrigued as to why the new line should make such a profound difference when fishing to rising trout. Like many of the problems we encounter when fishing, the answer didn't immediately appear obvious. It is easy to see it now, but we are now well aware of the importance of clear nylon for top water fishing.

Line Colour is Important

Line colour was never a consideration then and it took a long time before anglers realised the benefit of using pale nylons. The improvement in catch rate was baffling. Then, the day after my second or third session with the new nylon, I laid the old darker-coloured nylon alongside the new line and held them up to the light. The sky was bright with a light cloud base. Side by side, the only significant difference (if we ignore diameter) was the colour. Now the penny was beginning to drop: the dark coloured line stood out like a sore thumb, whereas the lighter line seemed to blend in with the background light.

The breakthrough had been made. Rising trout would no longer present me with the same difficulties again and I enjoyed some wonderful surface fishing. Pale-coloured nylon seemed to be the answer to a lot of my problems, and from then on I fished with pale-coloured or lightly-tinted nylons. Brands which I used then were Racine, Kroic and Bayer. Remember, this was 1974, and I believe it took the majority of fly fishermen 10 years or more to catch on, but by then newer, more technically-advanced monofilaments were coming on to the market.

Although there will always be times when trout can prove very difficult, at least I now knew that the colour of my nylon wasn't the cause. With a little persistence and ingenuity it is usually possible to sort out a tactic that will work even in the most difficult of situations.

FINE DIAMETER COPOLYMER

I regard clear nylon as the most significant development in flyfishing over the last 30 years. Anglers using clear or pale-coloured nylons for fishing in or near the surface, before this simple factor became common knowledge, enjoyed a tremendous advantage over their counterparts. But by the mid-1980s the word was well and truly out and the advantage had been lost.

However, in 1985-86 a finer copolymer line came on to the market, with all the advantages of added strength and finer diameter.

Like the fluorocarbon lines of today, this finer diameter copolymer became very popular even though it was more expensive than the standard monofilaments. The problem was that the majority of anglers bought purely by breaking strain and didn't give the diameter of the line any consideration. So, coupled with a finer, low-stretch nylon and poor knot technique they quickly lost faith in the product.

Clear nylon is the most significant development in flyfishing over the last 30 years.

But those who sensibly persevered quickly discovered the benefits of the line for fishing dries or surface nymphs and again they had an advantage in some situations over those who had lost faith. However, with the advent of carbon rods with softer tips for fishing the smaller flies on light lines, the popularity of copolymers slowly returned and the line has enjoyed a renaissance for top-water fishing.

DIFFERENT MONOFILAMENTS

A big failing with anglers is that although they are aware of the many different brands of monofilament available, they fail to recognise that these different brands can be: standard nylon, copolymer or fluorocarbon. And the decision of which brand of leader material to choose can be made even more confusing if a brand offers two or even all three types.

It pays to know which type of monofilament you prefer, so if your favourite line is unavailable, you can choose another brand which offers a monofilament with similar properties to your old one.

All three types (standard nylon, copolymer and fluorocarbon) have different characteristics. The angler who is well aware of the different properties of the three types, and who uses the characteristics of each line to suit specific applications, can benefit greatly.

SURFACE FISHING

On paper, fluorocarbon does appear to offer advantages over the other monofilaments, but I am not convinced that it will replace all other leader materials. Forget about the refractive index being similar to water, or other technical claims suggesting that fish cannot see the line. Remember Chameleon? This was a line they also could not see. But if you can see it, the fish will see it also.

What is important, particularly for surface fishing, is that the line isn't obtrusive; that it is lightly coloured, or clear, so that it appears less visible against a light background. A less visible line will not deter the trout from the fly. Fluorocarbon does appear to take on the colour from its surroundings when fished sub-surface and when held against a darker background, the line does appear less visible to the eye. This absorption of background colour does offer an advantage for sub-surface work as the light intensity diminishes with depth. So for fishing nymphs, particularly deep nymph or sunk line work, fluorocarbon would be an obvious choice.

When held up to the light, especially against a sky with a light cloud base, the advantage is not so obvious. Try a simple experiment to prove this. Take a standard mono, copolymer and a fluorocarbon of the same diameter and hold them up to the light and observe. Providing all test samples are either clear or a lightly tinted colour, you will observe that it is difficult to differentiate between the three types. Held against a light background, if I were highly critical, I would suggest that the fluorocarbon looks slightly darker than either the standard or copolymer mono.

Because there is little difference between them, I favour the copolymer with its lighter density and higher strength to diameter, for the majority of my surface fishing, even though it tends to twist and kink like the devil. Being denser than the other types of mono fluorocarbon is fine for fishing sub-surface, but when fishing on the top this factor can be a disadvan-

A well-conditioned rainbow from a large stillwater fishery – like this one from Draycote – will fight with incredible gusto and strength.

tage. When fishing a team of dries from a drifting boat they can, in windy conditions, drown the flies quicker because the leader is pulling them down. Not only this, a drowned leader (if it is well down) can cause excessive drag when lifting off. This drag from the well-sunk leader will not only cause a delay when trying to lift off quickly to cover a rising fish, but it can also pull the fly down and out of the trout's mouth, when you strike. After the fish has risen to the fly, and returns to its holding depth, will whisk the fly away from the trout.

With their denser composition, it might be thought that fluorocarbons would offer an advantage in flat calms or light winds, penetrating the surface film as the leader alights on the surface of the water. But this isn't so: working against the flies' air resistance, fluorocarbon would have difficulty penetrating the surface film, if the presentation is good.

It is possible to make the line cut through the surface film once the flies have alighted on the surface by easing the line gently, to pull the leader in. The line can be coaxed through if a little tension is applied but this can also be achieved, albeit to a lesser degree, with the other monofilaments if they are well degreased. It isn't surprising that in a flat calm the line fails to cut through the surface film.

Remember the classroom experiment in your school days to test the surface tension of water by dropping a needle on to the surface? The needle floated indefinitely if it did not penetrate the surface film, so what hope have we of penetrating the film with a monofilament, no matter how dense it is, with flies attached?

FLUOROCARBON & BREAKAGES

Fluorocarbons are stiffer than other monos, which is good when using droppers, as they are less prone to kinking or twisting. In 1995, I fished with fluorocarbon for the first time as a result of having seen an impressive tank test at an international angling trade show. I was delighted with the line on first impressions, particularly as it was less prone to twisting or kinking. But then I experienced a number of unexplained break-offs while playing fish hooked on droppered leaders over open, snag-free water. This was on leaders which previously had accounted for several trout.

So I began a number exploratory tests in an attempt to try and determine why the break-offs were occurring. The breakages always occurred at the dropper's knot, so it was here that my attention was focused. When joining two lengths of monofilament, or when I wished to form a dropper, I always used the water knot. I made up several leaders for testing and the knots even with some pretty vigorous pulling, produced no obvious faults. However, when I pulled two ends apart – the dropper tail and the main leader section – (a good test for seeing how prone a line is

to knotting weakness) the line parted well below the stated breaking strain. Other monos break well below the stated BS when subjected to this test but they do not break as readily as the breaks I was experiencing with fluorocarbon. As I always attach my fly to the tail that hangs downwards from the water knot, this weakness to reverse pull should not have been a problem – but it was. With a straight even pull there isn't a problem – in fact the knot strength was very good – but what happens when the direction of pull changes? The fluorocarbon line is considerably weakened, more so than either copolymer or standard nylon.

I rarely find problems tying knots in any of the three monos and hold a strong belief that if you moisten and pull the turns of the knot up smoothly and firmly, you can always expose a weakness before a fish will. With a firm steady pull when tying the knot, the line will part just as the turns of mono tighten or bed down, if there is a weakness. I was confident about my knots, so why should fluorocarbon break as it did with fish in play?

Danger in Weed Beds
I knew the line was fine when subjected to a straight pull, but was considerably weakened when the angle of pull changed direction. This weakness under changing direction of pull made fluorocarbon less reliable than other monos.

The fluorocarbon weakness may never be exposed when playing fish over open water, if you can maintain a straight, even pull, but what happens when you hook a fit, mature trout that changes direction quickly, or if the dropper momentarily gets caught up on weed? The two tails are then drawn apart and the angle is such that it considerably weakens the line with fatal consequences.

This would explain why anglers are sometimes so easily broken by large fish when fishing floating fry patterns using 8lb fluorocarbon close to weed beds.

Change in Direction Causing Breaks
Again, a similar scenario could occur when fit fish are hooked on droppers using fast-sinking lines. A trout hooked on a heavy sunk line could easily break away as it changes direction deep in the water, leaving the angler – through no fault of his own – with an unexplained break-off. This seems to happen more

often with the superfine brands of fluorocarbon than it does with some of the coarser types.

Many anglers are convinced that fluorocarbon makes a difference to their catches and will fish with it to the exclusion of the other leader materials. But if they were to analyse their catches at the end of the season, I wonder if they would consider that in some situations they may have been better off using one of the other monofilaments?

For sub-surface fishing with a single fly, fluorocarbon undoubtedly offers a distinct advantage. Much the same could be said when fishing sub-surface with a team of flies over open water. However, if there are snags around, or if fishing deep sunk line tactics, the angler should take this into consideration and make a risk assessment as to the best course of action.

Personally, if I felt I had to use fluorocarbon, I would avoid the superfine brands and keep droppers to a minimum. I use fluorocarbon for my sub-surface work with a floating line but if I have any doubt at all about the area I am fishing – and I'm thinking particularly of rocky, shallow areas where larger-than-average

wild trout may lurk – I would use standard nylon.

For my surface fishing I would opt for either the copolymer or standard nylon, particularly on wild systems that contain big trout which are hard won. Copolymers can be the very devil to fish, but they do hold up better in a wave, and they have excellent strength for their diameter, which are big advantages.

Flyfishing for salmon can be particularly hard on leaders, especially when using the heavier flies. A standard nylon will take the rough and tumble and would be my first choice. I have caught many salmon using quite crude leaders and the heavy nylon definitely balances the heavier flies better.

And at no time have I felt disadvantaged using a line that may be a bit coarser in diameter for a given breaking strain, than the higher tech monofilaments, for wild migratory fish.

For low clear water or where the fish have been subjected to a bit of angling pressure, I will use fluorocarbon with a single fly for migratory fish. But these would be the only conditions where I consider fluorocarbon necessary for salmon.

A quartet of rainbows from Farmoor, totalling 16 lbs.

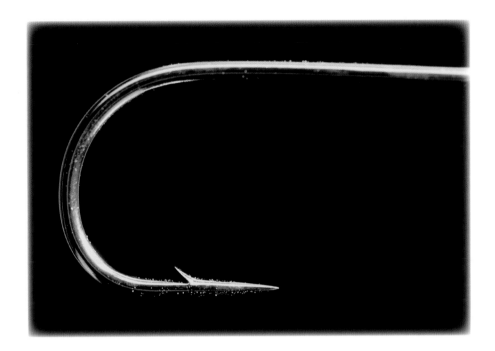

CHAPTER 3

A Word about Hooks

Listen to a group of anglers talking and you can confidently predict that at some time during the course of the conversation, fishing tackle will be discussed in great detail. Tackle gurus have a sponge-like capacity to absorb all the marketing hype about a new product and will, if offered an opening, pontificate endlessly on the subject. They regurgitate every detail about the product; from the material with which it is made to the application it was designed for, and they will then either praise, criticise or suggest some improvement to the product.

Viewed with an open mind, there is nothing wrong with these observations, and if we are to progress, improvements in tackle design are the way forward. Angling is blessed with a preponderance of clever fishermen who know how to improve well-established products to suit their own fishing styles.

Occasionally, a totally original idea is developed. Tackle manufacturers then become aware of the modification or improvement and produce the successful idea commercially. This is how a lot of new products find their way into the retail shops. Compared to twenty years ago, anglers now have a wide range of excellent fishing tackle to choose from, catering for the specialised branches of our sport.

CHOOSING THE SHAPE

Hooks are the pet subject of many fly fishermen, particularly fly tiers, and for all the different patterns we currently have for flyfishing, it still appears that we do not have sufficient designs to cater for all our needs. I find it amusing that there are still fly fishermen craving a certain design of hook that is not available through the retail shops. Listening to some of them talk, they appear more concerned about design and shape than any other aspect of the hook. This appears to be the pet gripe of fly tiers in particular who want to tie flies of a specific shape and length.

I basically require six different hook styles to cater for all my trout fishing, and that includes doubles which I now rarely use other than for seatrout or salmon. Depending on the fly I am tying I would choose from the following: a straight round or sproat bend standard length hook (fine, medium or heavy wire), a 3X long shank nymph hook (medium wire), a sedge hook with a reverse bend (medium wire) or the double straight round or sproat bend (medium wire). Five of the hook types are made from medium or heavy wire and they cater for all my wet fly requirements.

The fine wire hook is specifically for dry flies and this is the one hook that has in the past given me the most problems. Where I have found this hook wanting, particularly the fine wire hooks imported from Japan, is in terms of strength. It is this weakness of certain fine wire hooks that has cost me more wild brown trout on dry flies, than I care to remember.

Unfortunately, it wasn't until the 1994 season that I eliminated this particular problem, after much trial and error. It was the loss of three incredible brown trout one evening when spent gnat fishing on Lough Sheelin that drove me to find a solution to the problem of soft, springy, fine wire hooks, losing me trout because of the hook springing or gaping.

DIFFERENT WIRE GAUGES

There is no question about the quality of Japanese hooks. In the mid-1980s I worked for a company that began importing hooks from Japan and they were without doubt the finest hooks I had ever seen, comparing well with the British and European hooks we had been using up until that time. They beamed quality: the consistency of shape, point length, point sharpness, neat cut and depth of the barb. And the eyes, perfectly formed with no gap where the end of the wire butted up against the shank of the hook.

For consistency they were unequalled; every one a perfect clone. With ground and chemically-etched needle points, these hooks were obvious winners and so they proved to be for coarse and game fishermen.

I never for one moment questioned the strength of these hooks, for at that time most of my fishing was with heavy or medium wire hooks. I tied all my flies on the new imported hooks and enjoyed some wonderful wet fly and nymph fishing.

Working with Brian Leadbetter, we designed fly hooks produced from different wire gauges, and as competition fishing was becoming popular, anglers soon became aware of the advantages of fly hooks made from different weights of wire. For the first time, specifically-designed hooks became available, made from different thicknesses of wire that complied with competition rules, so that anglers could fish with flies tied on heavier wire hooks to make their flies fish deeper. The range of different-density sinking fly lines were not available then and competition anglers could not add lead to their patterns to make the flies fish deeper. So they compensated for the lack of ballast in their fly dressings by using flies tied on heavy wire hooks; and heavy wire wide-gape hooks became fashionable.

The majority of hooks were made from medium or heavy wire (medium or heavy wire: thickness of wire relative to size of hook) for both coarse as well as flyfishing. Fine wire hooks were used for more specialised branches of the sport such as dry fly on rivers, light line or coarse match fishing where small, fine wire hooks were matched to light lines and rods.

However, not all the small hooks were made from fine wire: some of the specialist and match hooks (down to size 22) were made from heavy wire when hook strength was important and anglers wanted to fish small hooks on stronger lines. So, unless you were incompetent and fished a fine wire hook on heavier tackle for big, hard-pulling fish, the question of weak hooks never arose. Most of my coarse fishing was for big fish, and if I wanted to fish with small hooks (for tench or barbel for example) the hooks would have been made of heavy wire. It was easy to mask and counter the weight of the hook with the bait, particularly when bottom fishing.

HEAVY WIRE HOOKS

Heavy wire hooks for this type of fishing weren't detrimental to success; in fact quite the opposite, because the heavy wire hooks were never likely to open up whilst playing big, hard-pulling fish. While it was easy to overcome the weight of the wire when bait fishing, it was a different matter when it came to fishing flies on or in the surface film on the large stillwaters.

FINE WIRE HOOKS

As dry fly fishing on stillwaters became more popular and consequently more anglers used dry flies tied on fine wire hooks, losses through hook failure became a regular occurrence. Some of the more experienced fishermen that I spoke to about the issue of losing trout through hook failure did realise what was happening, but accepted the losses as they were moving so many fish.

Boats pulled up on the sailing club's slipway at Farmoor.

In England we were blessed with some very well-stocked fisheries where dry fly, although still in its infancy, was a very productive method, so losses through hook failure were tolerated. In fact anglers were even pushing back into line the points of hooks that had gaped when the trout were coming thick and fast. They never for one moment questioned the soft, springy characteristic of the fine wire Japanese hooks – they just accepted it as the norm for all fine wire gauge hooks.

So successful and popular was dry fly fishing that many thought it was more essential to fish the fly in the surface film – and risk the hook gaping – than to fish with a heavier wire hook that would inevitably sink the fly if there was a reasonable wind blowing, and take it below the surface.

Another disadvantage with the heavier wire hooks was that they required more fly dressing to keep them afloat to compensate for the weight of the hook. This over-dressing would in certain situations cause the trout to come short. Short rising is a common problem. One of the chief reasons for trout rejecting a dry fly is when the fly is fishing too high in the water, particularly in light winds. This is why anglers who overdress their dry flies experience a lot of splashy rises but very few confident takes, resulting in a hooked fish. Ideally, what we require is a fly that will remain afloat with a lightly-dressed body that sits on or just in the surface film. To achieve this, a fine wire hook is essential.

Hooks Bending – Even with Rainbows

Another feature of the English reservoirs such as Rutland, Chew, Grafham etc, was the abundance of rainbow trout stocked, in relation to brown trout. It wasn't cost-effective for the fisheries to stock the slower growing, more expensive brown trout. So those fisheries that did put in a small stocking of browns, did so only to add some interest and variety to the fishing but the rainbow remained the backbone of the stocking. Therefore our stillwater fishing in England centred on the rainbow trout, a fish which, weight for weight, I consider fights better than the brownie.

Now the point I wish to make isn't about the fighting qualities of the two fish, but that rainbows, particularly those which grow quickly in the richer fisheries, do not have such a hard bony mouth as wild brown trout. Yet even though we were fishing for trout with softer mouths than wild browns, we were still experiencing problems with hooks gaping. The problem of the hook springing or gaping was never really questioned, however, even though the hooks were at fault for losing fish. This was because at the time, free-rising fish were plentiful. There was always another free-rising rainbow coming up the wind lane. If the conditions were right, dry fly was so effective that anglers accepted the failure of fine wire hooks as the norm. I put up with it on the reservoirs, but as I began to catch increasing numbers of wild brown trout on dry fly, I began to have serious reservations.

In June 2000 I took a bag of fish from Rutland that weighed nearly 33lbs on dry flies and nymphs. Most of the fish were caught on fine wire hooks and yet although these were big rainbows, the hooks did not fail me. That bag of trout would have filled me with immense pride and satisfaction 10 years earlier. Yet although I was obviously pleased to have caught that bag of fish, it didn't have quite the same meaning any more. I knew that most, but not all of the fish, had been stocked earlier that season at between 3-5lbs and that they had just mended well. This for me detracted from the significance of the capture. But with the capture of wild fish, the significance can never change.

> *A slack line loses more hooked trout than any other cause.*

The class of trout I caught from the reservoirs on imitative techniques was down to a specialised approach and to sheer dedication. The reward has to be there. And eventually, the challenge of pursuing wild fish from wild fisheries provided that reward. To lose wild brown trout, particularly the hard-won larger fish, because an item of tackle was at fault was just unacceptable. The fine wire hook issue had to be resolved.

Why Anglers Lose Trout

With the wild fish, not only did I have the problem of the hooks gaping and remaining open, but also of the inexplicable losses while playing trout that were apparently well-hooked. We all lose fish. It is inevitable that some trout will come adrift during play but you have a good idea when a fish is well-hooked and when a fish should have been landed. If a well-hooked fish escapes in open water and neither tackle nor knots have failed, the loss will be down to one of two factors, both of which are angler error: either the fisherman has put too much pressure on the fish, thus breaking the nylon cast; or he hasn't put sufficient pressure on the fish, which allows the trout, through a lack of line tension, to eject the hook as the fish changes direction. Of the two faults, I would say the latter is the more common. I feel this is because some anglers want the fish so badly, they are afraid to put too much pressure on the trout and therefore fail to keep the line tight at all times whilst the fish is in play. Playing trout with too much caution will inevitably lead to more stress being put on the fish through playing it for too long. But worse for the angler, he runs the risk that with light pressure, whenever the trout changes direction the pressure will ease further and the hook will drop out. If a firm pressure is maintained throughout the fight, then this is unlikely to happen and the trout will be brought to hand much sooner.

MY UNACCEPTABLE FISH LOSS ON CORRIB FOCUSES MY MIND

I knew that the losses I was experiencing were not due to poor technique in playing fish. Nor were they due to bad luck. Something was amiss, and in 1993 the issue came to a head. While on holiday in Ireland fishing the mayfly, I had four good days on Lough Corrib taking 46 wild browns mostly on dry mayflies. The biggest fish was just over 5lbs, with 2 more over 4lbs, so I was obviously very pleased with my four days' fishing in the west even though I had lost several good fish.

Losses through trout throwing the hook, or a poor hold tearing free, are part and parcel of the game, and they seemed but a small irritation when compared to the quality of sport I had enjoyed. We then went on to Sheelin for three days, and on the first evening I took a good trout of 5lb 14oz on wet fly. This was a good start and I was on a high. The next day, conditions were perfect, with a warm south-westerly blowing that dropped off in the evening. I took four fish to 4lb 12oz on wet and dry flies, but during the evening we experienced an immense fall of spent gnat and I lost three huge trout of between 6-9lbs. It totally took the edge off what had been a good day and an exceptional holiday.

A cracking Corrib brown trout – my first of 5 lbs from that lough.

When I think of the 1993 mayfly, my mind is always drawn to those three lost fish. All the fine trout that preceded them seem lost in a mist, their capture eclipsed by that final hour. The three fish were hooked and lost in play, I could understand losing one, perhaps grudgingly even two, but to lose all three was nothing short of unbearable. It could not have been clearer at this point that something was amiss, and as we motored back up the lake in the growing darkness, I vowed to myself that no matter what it took to solve the problem, I would find a solution. It would never happen again.

I was using a mayfly/nymph hook with a 3X longshank for most of my dry mayflies and although I was aware at the time of the problem with the fine wire Japanese hooks, the mayfly hook pattern that I was using wasn't made from a particularly fine wire gauge. Therefore it was hard to believe that the hook was at fault. True, they had gaped slightly but they still maintained a good spring when I tested them with my thumbnail.

But when I put a little extra pressure on the hook they then would open up in the same way as the fine wire hooks I had been using for my dry bits and emerger patterns. I remember discussing the problem of the hooks with Nick Carberry of Rooksbury Mill, saying that the paying rods on his fishery who were used to catching rainbows between 4–7lbs, referred to this hook as the distant release hook because of the self-same problem! This was with stocked rainbows, so imagine the problem with wild browns. Even if the hooks were not gaping, they were failing to penetrate the hard bony mouths of the large wild browns because of the springy nature of the wire.

On striking a rise, if the point hit bone, the hook would spring rather than remain straight, thus creating an angle and deflecting the point, making it harder for the point of the hook to penetrate the mouth of the fish.

If a fish remained attached after the initial deflection of the point, it would inevitably escape as the point had failed to penetrate the tough tissues of the trout's mouth. Also, although the point would return to a straight or nearly-straight position after impact, it was probably only lodged lightly in the fish's mouth and escape was just a matter of time.

The overall quality of Japanese hooks is second-to-none but the price for ignoring a problem with the strength of the finer wire hooks for dry fly fishing was now too high to pay.

We do not experience the same problems with wet fly fishing, because usually with wet fly there are no sudden shocks. Many of the fish hook themselves and we just tighten into them and because of the way they take, the hook usually finds a good hold in the fish's mouth, pulled in against the momentum of the take and the tightening of the rod. There is a smooth, progressive increase in tension.

With dry fly, on the other hand, we strike the rise to pull the hook into the fish's mouth with a fast sharp rod movement. The impact shock is therefore much greater than with wet fly. And because we are striking the rise, the problem is further compounded because there is a greater chance of the hook point hitting bone at the front of the mouth rather than being drawn into an area that will give a better hold, such as the corner of the fish's mouth.

Because of these sudden shocks the stress on the hook is much greater with dry fly and if there is a weakness with the hook, then dry fly fishing is more likely to expose it. This I have learned to my expense, but after the 1993 mayfly experience, this was an expense I was determined to live without.

HOOK TEMPER

Many of the hooks imported from Japan were made by a small number of manufacturers. So, after trying a number of brands of imported fine wire hooks with the same results, I began to question the quality of Japanese steel and the hook manufacturing process used by these companies. I needed expert advice, and someone suggested that I talk to an English manufacturer about the issue of wire strength.

As there were only two companies making hooks in the UK, my enquiries soon led me to the Sprite company, owned at that time by Vince Green. Sprite was a small company, a hands-on business that was absolutely dependent on Vince. He was very knowledge-able about the manufacturing of fish hooks, and though he was reluctant to criticise fellow hook manufacturers, he did enlighten me.

Talking to Vince about the apparent lack of strength of the Japanese fine wire hooks was a revelatory experience, and although I took some convincing he was adamant that the hooks had not been tempered properly. He maintained that in order to produce consistently strong hooks it was essential to get the tempering temperature right and this has to be adjusted for each batch of hooks made. This is because the carbon content for each batch of wire can vary slightly and therefore subtle changes of tempering temperature would make a significant difference where strength was concerned.

He proved the point conclusively that hooks of the same wire gauge could be made stronger by making up some hooks in identical wire gauges to the imported hooks. These hooks which I tested were indeed stronger and our tests suggested that the hooks could be as much as 23% stronger. The difference in response to increasing pull was very interesting. When Vince's hooks finally began to spring open after being placed under increasing pressure, they would give only a small amount and then break, unlike the imported hooks that gave at around 23% less pull (than Vince's hooks) and then continued opening. Although Vince's hooks did break, they consistently required a stronger pull to make them open than did the imported hooks.

At first I had reservations about the hooks breaking but there is a huge difference in strength between a hook which breaks when tempered correctly and a hook which breaks because it has become brittle through over-tempering and will snap easily. A hook which is tempered correctly may, when subjected to severe stress, eventually break but it will also be considerably stronger than a hook which is under-tempered and just straightens out. For a lot of my fishing, both coarse and fly, I used hooks of medium-to-heavy wire and although I did not know it at the time, these hooks were under-tempered but because of the coarseness of the wire, this weakness was never exposed.

In fact we used to fish hooks in some very heavy wire gauges for big fish to prevent them opening. But I wonder now whether we fished with hooks of unnec-essarily heavy wire gauges, because they were never tempered to their maximum strength. Certainly where bait fishing for big fish was concerned, there was no harm in fishing with a hook produced from a heavy wire, as this gave a good buffer and there were ways of masking the thickness and weight of the heavier wire. However, when fishing dry fly, fine wire hooks were essential and the weakness of poor temper was exposed. There was very little buffer because of the fine wire, and therefore the hooks, if soft, would just open up or spring sufficiently to prevent good penetration of the point.

JAPANESE TEMPERING FAULTS

I asked Vince why he thought that so many of the imported hooks were never tempered to their maximum strength. He sad that the tempering process was one of the final stages of hook manufacture and there was a lot to lose if a mistake was made with the tempering, so most of the bigger producers would always err on the side of safety. Thus they would work to a fixed table of furnace temperatures and the hooks were always likely to be slightly under-tempered to avoid running the risk of getting the tempering temperature wrong and producing brittle hooks.

But because the carbon content of the wire varies from batch to batch, the temperature will always require some slight adjustment. For me, this was an important discovery.

Now, for all my dry fly fishing I use fine wire hooks produced by Sprite without experiencing any of the problems that I previously encountered. I have so much confidence in these fine wire hooks that I can play fish firmly and bring them to the side of the boat just as quickly as I would with the heavier wet fly hooks. Problem solved.

Unhooking a classic Corrib brown trout, showing the heavily-spotted livery typical of these fish

CHAPTER 4

Choosing the Right Flies

A failing I find annoying in many of the older angling books about traditional styles of fishing, is the lack of detail regarding fly patterns. This oversight is frustrating, particularly when trying to learn more about a water that I have not previously fished, or where I lack experience fishing for a specific species of fish such as salmon, seatrout or wild brown trout.

The first book I read on reservoir fishing by T. C. Ivens appealed because it covered both lure (Attractor) and nymph (Deceiver) tactics. This book turned out to be a real gem, as not only was it an informative book about stillwater flyfishing; it also covered the tackle and flies in detail. You felt there could be no mistake regarding the size, shape and colour of Ivens' flies because he listed the dressings in full and there were good colour plates to support them. As an angler who had just taken up stillwater flyfishing, this book proved to be most helpful.

In addition to this there were articles appearing in magazines which were informative about modern fly patterns and methods. Although mainly concerned with lure fishing, there were the odd gems which gave one the confidence to experiment and develop new fly patterns. It was from this base that I created my own style of imitative flies for stillwaters. Certainly from the mid- to late-1970s, when most anglers were fishing lures, I felt that my imitative flies gave me an edge that boosted my confidence when fishing on the reservoirs and that proved a great asset when I graduated to waters such as Rutland in the 1980s.

Although I enjoyed many of the early books about traditional fishing, a common failing, I felt, of their authors was a failure to explain fully the correct colour, shape or the exact identification of the patterns they found successful. For example, I have seen so many different shades of claret, wing profiles (proud, low, rolled or folded), gold or silver ribs, hackle colour, wound or beard hackles and tail tippets that if I were told that a Mallard and Claret was successful on a certain fishery, it would mean very little other than the fly had some form of claret in its dressing. The identification of shape and colour was never in doubt in Ivens' book and the same could be said of Kingsmill Moore with his description of the flies used for Irish brown trout and seatrout. Like Ivens, he tied his own flies and this obviously helped when describing his patterns and therefore left the reader in no doubt, particularly when he was referring to colour.

The fly bought in London might bear little resemblance to the fly of the same name bought in Perth or Dublin. I make this point because, whilst knowing the name of the fly is obviously helpful, it is of greater benefit to know the exact colour, shade and shape. One of my favourite authors, Sidney Spencer, devoted a number of chapters to flies. But in many instances, I don't know if the flies he mentions were fully dressed or simple spider patterns.

With flies, the important factors are shape and colour.

Without colour plates and a detailed explanation about the dressings, he failed to make the point clearly. I may be wrong, but I feel convinced that his beloved 'Dusty' was not a Dusty Miller with a pink hackle, but a Silver Wilkinson, probably incorrectly named by some shop proprietor or professional fly tier. Although I found this irritating, Sidney Spencer's books still remain among my favourite titles. Reading such evocative writing, about a style of fishing that I myself find so enjoyable, from an age when the sport had more innocence and mystery than it does now, gives me much pleasure.

I know that reading older books has helped enormously with the development of the flies which I now use, particularly the flies for wild fish. Along with the information gleaned from modern books, and articles, this has given me the confidence to try various methods of tying flies, and to mix colour. Many of my early attempts to tie successful imitative flies met with mixed results, but over a period of time a pattern would develop, which with subtle changes has led to the stillwater flies I now fish. With a lot of my flies, the important factors are shape and colour.

The way they are dressed will reflect how or at what depth I want them to fish in the water. My buzzer patterns, for instance, have taken time to evolve, but now the same colour fly could be tied with a wing; without a wing; or with a wing and hackle. This gives me three permutations for each colour, and depending on the depth, or stage of the insects' lifecycle the trout are feeding on, the tying I use will change. For example, if the trout are feeding on the pupa well down in the water, I fish either the wingless or winged buzzer; if they are feeding on the emerging pupa or drowned adults, I fish the hackled pattern. A hackled fly not only holds up in the water better, but the hackle also represents the legs and wings of the emerging or adult insect.

The other advantage to tying a series of flies in this style is that it gives me a number of opportunities to offer a similar fly, of the same colour, under different weather conditions. For example, on cloudy days in early spring, when the trout are feeding well down in the water, the addition of the white wing can make a distinct difference to the pulling power of the fly, and it will on occasions easily outscore the wingless fly of the same colour. The white wing can prove a great attractor to the fish, and this eye-catcher, particularly under low light levels, I believe improves the catch rate of the fly.

Exaggerate the natural to trigger the trout

Although I would not advocate going to the extremes of exact imitation, I do believe that mimicking or exaggerating certain features can improve the attractiveness of a fly. Trout are easily deceived by a well presented fly, even if it isn't a close copy of the prey item they are feeding on. Providing the pattern is suggestive of food, and there are sufficient triggers to encourage the fish into a feeding response, then it is highly probable that the trout will take the fly.

In fact, I believe that they find a caricature, or an exaggerated resemblance of a food item, of similar colour to the prey they are feeding on, more attractive! In many instances they take it in preference to a close copy or even the natural food. This is why many of the general imitative patterns which I tie incorporate the features which I consider important and wish to mimic. The nymphs for example, would have a tail, a slim body and a thorax, all general features that are found in aquatic nymphs but exaggerated just a little.

By dressing a fly in this way, I have hopefully incorporated a number of triggers that will stimulate a fish into taking the fly into its mouth. If the representation was that of an emerging pupa, I would still retain the nymphal shape but I'd include a hackle or a wing or even a heavily-dressed tail that represents the shuck of the hatching insect. They may appear similar, but by tying flies in this way I can cover various stages of the insect's life cycle and therefore fish balanced teams.

Imitating three stages of same fly

For instance, if I was fishing over water approximately 10 feet deep and wanted to cover the three stages larva, pupa and emerging fly, I would fish a Pheasant Tail on the point, Grey Buzzer on the middle dropper and a Dog Fly, Magnet Nymph or Dark Olive Midge on the top dropper.

However, if I wanted to fish deeper with representations of the larva and the ascending pupa, I would substitute the Magnet Nymph for a buzzer pattern and shorten the length between the droppers, particularly the point to middle dropper.

If I wanted to fish the upper layers, I would retain the hackled fly on the top dropper, change the middle dropper for a hackle pattern and substitute the point fly for a winged buzzer pattern or a point fly tied on a lighter wire hook.

The flies may not be exact imitations but it is important to be aware of what stage in the insect's lifecycle we are trying to represent and apply some thought to the way the flies are dressed and how they are presented. So when tying a fly we should consider the depth in the water we want the fly to fish and the shape of the organisms we are hoping to mimic and then tie the flies in several colours. Black, brown, grey and olive should cover most situations.

To avoid any risk of confusion about the flies I use, I have included the fly dressings along with colour photographs of the most successful flies for each of the fishing disciplines which I cover.

A 12 lb springer, taken in early April, from the Bangor Erris on the River Owenmore

41

Grey Duster

Ginger Bits

Hare's Ear

Dark Brown Bits

Claret Bits

Fiery Brown Bits

Orange Bits

Red Bits

Olive Green Bits

Cluster

MY FAVOURITE DRY FLIES

DRY FLIES for reservoirs and lakes

GREY DUSTER
Hook: Fine wire
Body: Light grey seal's fur
Hackle: Badger two to three turns.

GINGER BITS
Hook: Fine wire
Body: Ginger seal's fur
Hackle: Ginger or honey dun.

DARK BROWN BITS
Hook: Fine wire
Body: Front ⅓rd & rear ⅓rd dark brown seal's fur, middle ⅓rd black seal's fur
Hackle: Furnace or coch-y-bonddu.

HARE'S EAR BITS
Hook: Fine wire
Body: Hare's fur mixed with a little ginger seal's
Hackle: Red game

CLARET BITS
Hook: Fine wire
Body: Claret seal's fur
Hackle: Red game

HOT ORANGE BITS
Hook: Fine wire
Body: Hot orange seal's fur, the colour of burnt orange, dull rather than bright
Hackle: Red game

FIERY BROWN BITS
Hook: Fine wire
Body: Fiery brown seal's fur
Hackle: Red Game

RED BITS
Hook: Fine wire
Body: Brick red seal's fur
Hackle: Red game

OLIVE GREEN BITS
Hook: Fine wire
Body: Olive seal's fur
Hackle: Red game

CLUSTER
Hook: Standard fine wire
Body hackle: Grizzle, with red game wound in from half way

DRY FLIES and emergers

POST HACKLE GREY MIDGE
(Klinkhamer variant)
Hook: Fine wire grub hook
Rib: Black thread
Body: Canada goose or grey goose herl
Thorax: Peacock herl
Hackle: Grizzle **Post:** White polyester

POST HACKLE OLIVE MIDGE
(Klinkhamer variant)
Hook: Fine wire grub hook
Rib: Olive green thread
Body: Canada or grey goose herl
Thorax: Dark olive seal's fur, with hare's back fur
Hackle: Furnace **Post:** White polyester

POST HACKLE OLIVE
(Klinkhamer variant)
Hook: Fine wire grub hook
Rib: Orange thread
Body: Hen pheasant tail
Thorax: Hare's fur
Post: Yellow polyester
Hackle: Honey dun or ginger

GINGER HOPPER
Hook: Fine wire
Body: Light ginger seal's fur with a hint of olive
Legs: Knotted pheasant tail fibres
Hackle: Ginger or furnace.

CLARET HOPPER
Hook: Fine wire
Body: Claret seal's fur
Legs: Knotted pheasant tail fibres
Hackle: Red game or Greenwell

CHOCOLATE DROP
Hook: 2X long nymph hook
Body: Dark chocolate coloured seal's fur
Wing: Dark deer hair with butts left facing forward
Thorax: Same as body
Hackle: Red game or furnace

HARE'S EAR SEDGE
Hook: 2X long nymph hook
Body: Hare's fur
Wing: Deer hair with butts left facing forward
Thorax: Hare's fur mixed with fiery brown seal's fur
Hackle: Furnace or coch-y-bonddu

FIERY BROWN SEDGE
Hook: 2X long nymph hook
Body: Fiery brown seal's fur
Wing: Deer hair with butts left facing forward
Thorax: Same as body or dark brown seal's fur
Hackle: Red game

GREY MAYFLY
Hook: Long nymph hook
Tail: Grey squirrel tail
Body: Grey seal's fur
Wing: Grey squirrel tail
Hackle: Badger or honey dun clipped underneath

GINGER MAYFLY
Hook: 2X long nymph hook
Tail: Grey squirrel dyed yellow
Body: Light ginger seal's fur
Wing: Grey squirrel dyed yellow
Hackle: Honey dun or pale ginger

GREEN MAYFLY
Hook: 2X long nymph hook
Tail: Grey squirrel dyed yellow
Body: Medium olive seal's fur
Wing: Grey squirrel dyed lime green or yellow
Hackle: Furnace or coch-y-bonddu

DADDY
Hook: 2X long nymph hook
Body: Grey seal's fur
Legs: Knotted pheasant tail fibres
Wing: Badger hackle points
Hackle: Cree

Post Hackle Grey Midge

Post Hackle Olive Midge

Post Hackle Olive

Ginger Hopper

Hare's Ear Sedge

Claret Hopper

Chocolate Drop

Brown Sedge

Green Mayfly

Grey Mayfly

Daddy

Ginger Mayfly

SOME ESSENTIAL MIDGES AND MAYFLIES

NYMPHS and buzzers

HARE'S EAR
Hook: Nymph Hook Size 10-14
Thread: Black
Tail: Guard hairs from hare body fur
Rib: Oval gold tinsel
Body: Dark fur from hare's ear
Thorax: Same as body fur well picked out
Wing Case: Canada primary feather

PHEASANT TAIL
Hook: Nymph or standard hook size 10-14
Thread: Black
Tail: Cock pheasant centre tail fibres
Rib: Copper wire
Body: Cock pheasant centre tail
Wing Case: Pheasant tail
Thorax: Dark fur from hare's ear well picked out

CLARET NYMPH
Hook: Nymph or standard hook size 10-14
Tail: Red game cock hackle fibres
Rib: Gold wire
Body: Claret, fiery brown and black seal's fur mixed
Wing Case: Pheasant tail
Thorax: Same as body fur well picked out.

C & G NYMPH
Hook: Nymph or standard length hook size 10-14
Tail: Ginger cock hackle fibres
Rib: Flat gold tinsel
Body: Light ginger seal's fur
Wing: Hen pheasant centre tail feather. Leave wing butts on larger sizes to represent breaking wing case.
Thorax: Ginger and cinnamon seal's fur mixed and well picked out

DIAWL BACH
Hook: Standard length or grub hook size 12-14
Tail: Red game
Rib: Copper wire
Body: Peacock herl
Hackle: Red game beard.

OLIVE NYMPH
Hook: Standard length size 12-14
Tail: Light ginger mixed with yellow cock hackle fibres
Rib: Gold wire
Body: Light olive seal's fur
Wing: Bronze mallard
Thorax: Light olive mixed with a little yellow olive seal's fur
Hackle: Greenwell

MAGNET NYMPH
Hook: Medium wire standard size 12-14
Tail: Badger cock hackle fibres
Rib: Copper wire
Body: Canada goose herl
Thorax: Peacock herl
Hackle: Well marked badger

GREY BUZZER
Hook: Sedge hook size 10-14
Rib: Silver wire
Body: Canada primary feather
Wing: White cock hackle fibres
Wing Case: Canada goose primary
Thorax: Canada goose primary
Breather Filaments: Butts of the wing fibres clipped short

OLIVE BUZZER
Hook: Sedge hook size 12-14
Rib: Gold wire
Body: Canada goose primary for the thorax
Wing Case: Canada goose primary
Thorax: Olive seal's fur
Breather Filaments: Butts of the wing fibres clipped short

FIERY BROWN BUZZER
Hook: Sedge hook size 12-14
Rib: Black floss
Body: Fiery brown seal's fur
Wing Case: Cock pheasant centre tail
Thorax: Fiery brown & black seal's fur mixed
Breather Filaments: Butts of wing fibres clipped short

BLACK BUZZER
Hook: Sedge hook size 12-14
Rib: Black silk
Body: Dark Canada goose primary feather
Wing Case: Canada goose primary
Thorax: Peacock herl
Breather Filaments: White cock hackle fibres

EPOXY BUZZER
With or without a rib, a good deep water pattern.
Hook: Sedge hook size 12-14
Rib: Pearl lurex
Body: Black tying silk
Wing Buds: Hot orange floss
Thorax: Tying silk

Hare's Ear

Claret Nymph

Pheasant Tail

C & G Nymph

Diawl Bach

Olive Nymph

Magnet Nymph

Olive Buzzer

Grey Buzzer

Fiery Brown Buzzer

Epoxy Buzzer

Black Buzzer

SOME FAVOURITE NYMPHS AND BUZZERS

DOG FLY
Hook: Sedge hook size 12-14
Rib: Silver wire
Body: Canada goose or grey goose herl
Wing: Badger hackle fibres
Thorax: Peacock herl
Hackle: Badger

PEACOCK & BADGER MIDGE
Hook: Sedge hook size 12-14
Rib: Pearl lurex, silver wire over
Body: Peacock herl short flue
Wing: Badger hackle fibres
Thorax: Red seal's fur
Hackle: Badger

HOT SPOT MIDGE
Hook: Sedge hook size 12-14
Rib: Pearl lurex, silver wire over
Body: Peacock herl short flue
Wing Buds: Hot orange floss
Thorax: Peacock herl
Breather Filaments: White floss

HACKLED AMBER NYMPH
Hook: Sedge hook Size 12-14
Rib: Gold twist
Body: Ginger seal's fur
Wing: Hen pheasant centre tail
Thorax: Hot orange seal's fur
Hackle: Red game cock hackle

SEDGE PUPA
Hook: Sedge hook size 12-14
Rib: Oval gold tinsel
Body: Ginger seal's fur
Wing: Hen pheasant tail. Butts left long tied sloping back over thorax
Thorax: Rabbit guard hairs from the back fur mixed with ginger seal's fur

DARK OLIVE MIDGE
Hook: Medium wire standard size 12-14
Tail: Red game hackle fibres
Rib: Gold wire
Body: Canada goose primary
Thorax: Dark olive seal's fur
Hackle: Red game cock hackle

DAMSEL NYMPH (Gold Head)
Hook: Nymph hook size 10-12
Tail: Olive marabou

Rib: Oval gold tinsel
Body: Olive marabou
Hackle: Red game cock hackle
Thorax: Fur from hare's ear

MONTANA NYMPH (Gold Head)
Hook: Nymph hook size 10-12
Tail: Black marabou
Body: Black marabou
Rib: Silver wire
Hackle: Black cock hackle
Thorax: Lime green floss

THE BUG
Hook: Medium wire size 10-14
Tag: Hot orange floss tied front & rear
Rib: Flat gold tinsel
Body: Guard hairs from rabbit back fur

WET FLIES

All tied on medium wire standard length hooks size 10–14 unless stated otherwise.

CLARET BUMBLE
Tail: Gold/yellow cock hackle fibres
Rib: Gold oval tinsel
Body: ⅔rds claret seal's fur, ⅓rd fiery brown seal's fur
Hackle: Claret palmer body, black shoulder.

GOLDEN OLIVE
Tail: Gold/yellow cock hackle fibres
Rib: Gold oval tinsel
Body: Golden olive seal's fur with just a hint of green
Hackle: Golden olive palmer body, light ginger front, bronze mallard shoulder.

KATE McLAREN (variant)
Tail: Gold/yellow cock hackle fibres
Rib: Flat silver tinsel
Body: Black seal's fur
Hackle: Black palmer body, red game front, bronze mallard shoulder.

Dog Fly

Peacock & Badger Midge

Hot Spot Midge

Hackled Amber Nymph

Sedge Pupa

Dark Olive Midge

Damsel Nymph (Gold head)

Montana Nymph (Gold head)

The Bug

Claret Bumble

Golden Olive

Kate McLaren (variant)

MORE USEFUL MIDGES AND THREE WET FLIES

WET FLIES *continued*

GINGER OLIVE
Tail: Ginger cock hackle fibres with a few bronze mallard, mixed
Rib: Gold oval tinsel. **Body**: Ginger seal's fur
Hackle: Ginger palmer body, bronze mallard shoulder

DARK OLIVE (dropper)
Tail: Red cock hackle fibres
Rib: Gold oval tinsel
Body: Dark olive seal's fur
Hackle: Dark red game or furnace palmer body, bronze mallard shoulder

DARK OLIVE (point)
Tail: Red cock hackle fibres
Rib: Oval gold tinsel
Body: Dark olive seal's fur
Wing: Bronze mallard
Thorax: Dark olive seal's fur or peacock herl
Hackle: Furnace

MEDIUM OLIVE
Tail: Red game and bronze mallard, mixed
Rib: Oval gold tinsel
Body: Medium olive seal's fur
Hackle: Light red game palmer body, bronze mallard shoulder

HARE & GREEN PALMER
Tail: Red game and bronze mallard mixed
Rib: Oval gold tinsel
Body: Dark hare's fur and dark olive seal's fur, mixed
Hackle: Red game palmer body, bronze mallard shoulder

FIERY BROWN PALMER
Tail: Red game and bronze mallard mixed
Rib: Oval gold tinsel
Body: ⅔rds fiery brown seal's fur; ⅓rd black seal's fur
Hackle: Red game palmer body, bronze mallard shoulder

CLARET & SILVER DABBLER
Tail: Red game and bronze mallard, mixed
Rib: Flat silver tinsel
Body: Claret seal's fur
Hackle: Red game palmer body, bronze mallard over

DARK WICKHAM'S
Rib: Gold wire
Body: Flat gold lurex
Hackle: Red game palmer body, furnace shoulder
Wing: Optional. Dark hen pheasant tail

INVICTA PALMER
Tail: Gold/yellow cock hackle fibres
Rib: Oval gold tinsel
Body: Yellow seal's fur
Hackle: Red game palmer body, blue jay beard
Wing: Hen pheasant tail tied as a shroud.

SILVER INVICTA
Tail: Golden pheasant crest
Rib: Silver wire
Body: Flat silver lurex
Hackle: Red game palmer body, blue jay beard
Wing: Hen pheasant tail

MALLARD & CLARET (point)
Tail: Golden pheasant tippet
Rib: Oval gold tinsel
Body: Claret seal's fur
Wing: Bronze mallard
Thorax: Claret seal's fur
Hackle: Red game

BIBIO
Rib: Pearl lurex, silver wire over to reinforce lurex
Body: ⅔rds black seal's fur, ⅓rd red seal's fur
Hackle: Black palmer body, soft furnace two turns shoulder

Ginger Olive

Dark Olive (dropper)

Dark Olive (point fly)

Medium Olive

Hare & Green Palmer

Fiery Brown Palmer

Dark Wickham

Claret & Silver Dabbler

Invicta

Silver Invicta

Claret & Mallard Nymph

Bibio

MY FAVOURITE TRADITIONAL WET FLIES

SALMON & SEATROUT FLIES

CLARET BUMBLE
Hook: Standard length or low water salmon
Tail: Yellow over hot orange cock hackle fibres
Rib: Flat gold tinsel
Body: Rear half, claret seal's fur; Front half, fiery brown seal's fur
Hackle: Claret palmered; black front; blue shoulder

KATE MCLAREN (seatrout)
Hook: Standard length
Tail: Yellow cock hackle fibres
Rib: Flat silver tinsel
Body: Black seal's fur
Hackle: Black palmered; brown shoulder

PHEASANT & YELLOW
Hook: Standard length
Tail: Yellow cock hackle fibres
Rib: Flat silver tinsel
Body: Yellow seal's fur
Wing: Hen pheasant wing
Hackle: Red game

TEAL BLUE & SILVER
Hook: Standard length or double
Tail: Hot orange cock hackle fibres
Body: Flat silver tinsel
Rib: Silver wire
Wing: Teal or silver mallard
Hackle: Blue

SILVER STOAT
Hook: Double or treble
Tail: Yellow cock hackle fibres
Rib: Silver wire
Body: Flat silver tinsel
Wing: Black squirrel tail
Hackle: Black

SILVER THUNDER STOAT
Hook: Double or treble
Tail: Yellow cock hackle fibres
Rib: Silver wire
Body: Flat silver tinsel
Wing: Black squirrel tail
Hackle: Hot orange

NINJA STOAT
Hook: Double or treble
Tail: Yellow
Rib: Flat silver tinsel
Body: Rear half, red floss; front half, black floss
Wing: Hot orange bucktail or squirrel tail or arctic fox
Hackle: Badger

SQUIRREL & GOLD
Hook: Double or treble
Tail: Red
Rib: Gold wire
Body: Flat gold tinsel
Wing: Grey squirrel tail
Hackle: Black

THUNDER & LIGHTNING
Hook: Single, double or treble
Tail: Yellow cock hackle fibres
Rib: Gold oval tinsel
Body: Black floss
Wing: Black squirrel with bronze mallard over
Hackle: Hot orange palmered; blue jay or guinea fowl throat

BELTRA BADGER
Hook: Single, double or treble
Tail: Yellow cock hackle fibres
Butt: Silver wire
Rib: Silver wire
Body: Flat silver tinsel
Wing: Red squirrel with grey squirrel over
Hackle: Lemon yellow palmered; blue throat

GOLDEN OLIVE (salmon)
Hook: Single
Tail: Yellow cock hackle fibres
Rib: Flat silver tinsel
Body: Lime yellow coloured seal's fur
Hackle: Lemon yellow palmered
Wing: Bronze mallard tied over

STOAT'S TAIL
Hook: Single, double or treble
Tail: Golden hackle fibres
Rib: Flat silver tinsel
Body: Black floss
Wing: Tip of stoat's tail or black squirrel
Hackle: Black

Claret Bumble

Kate McLaren

Pheasant & Yellow

Teal Blue & Silver

Silver Stoat

Silver Thunder Stoat

Ninja Stoat

Squirrel & Gold

Thunder & Lightning

Beltra Badger

Golden Olive

Stoat's Tail

SOME USEFUL PATTERNS FOR SALMON AND SEATROUT FROM A BOAT

PART TWO
The Reservoirs

CHAPTER 5

Reservoir Trout Fishing

The English reservoirs could never be classified as *wild* stillwater fisheries, but they do provide an opportunity to fish for trout that, as they mature, are the nearest equivalent to wild fish we have. The grown-on or over-wintered trout which have matured and put on weight in the larger richer fisheries are superb specimens. These fish are not only pleasing to the eye but they are also very challenging and rewarding to catch.

Fishing methods have improved and anglers are now more tactically aware, so the pressure on the mature stock of some of the better reservoirs has increased. Moreover, the numbers of good quality, over-wintering or acclimatised trout have been affected by water quality, and the effects of cormorant predation.

The water supply reservoirs have enjoyed mixed fortunes over the years, and with no new major reservoir planned to open for some time, we are left with

what one could term 'established fisheries'. The growth potential of trout from the fertile land over which the established waters were flooded has long been exhausted.

All the better waters are mature, chemically-rich fisheries, and it is the composition of the water pumped into these impounded systems that will determine if the stocked trout flourish or struggle to put on condition. The water is continually being recycled, and as consumed water is replaced, the composition of the nutrients within the reservoir alter. It is the fluctuations of draw down, and changing chemical enrichment of the incoming pumped water, that affect the balance of the ecosystem.

This is why the fishing can vary so much from one season to the next. Impounded man-made reservoirs are volatile environments that are continually changing. One good season on any particular water does not necessarily mean that we will enjoy similar good fortune the following year. If sufficient fish survive angling pressure and cormorant predation, and the water is of high quality, the angling will be superb.

When I first began stillwater trout fishing, the limit bag was the yardstick for a successful day. Anglers then were conditioned into thinking that success was measured by the number of fish one brought in at the end of the day. Thankfully attitudes have changed and "limititis" isn't so common-place today. Most modern anglers are now aware of the difference between recently stocked, or grown-on acclimatised trout. These over-wintered fish are the trophies which the more discerning trout fishermen target during a day's fishing. Anglers who fish for the mature trout desire more from their day's sport than just another limit bag of stockies. The emphasis is on quality. Fishermen now purposely set out to catch the better trout, and with the right approach, they can succeed.

SMALL STILLWATER FISHERIES

On well-managed, small-water fisheries where high stock densities are maintained to give consistent sport, a good catch is the norm. And without doubt a lot of small fisheries give good value for money for a visiting day rod. To satisfy the demands of today's market, small put-and-take fisheries have had to improve the quality of their stock.

The fish are now bigger, sport full tails and fins and are blemish-free. There are many small-water fisheries scattered all over the UK, that provide anglers with local stillwater trout fishing. Indeed there are fishermen who specialise in fishing small waters only and there are those who would not feel comfortable boat fishing on the larger fisheries, particularly a wild lake. Anglers new to the sport of flyfishing will more than likely catch their first trout from a small-water fishery and learn much about flyfishing tactics that will stand them in good stead when they move on to the larger or wilder fisheries.

Also there is no doubting the consistency of small fisheries when one considers catch returns: indeed word quickly gets around if they are not giving a fair return. So, for the price of a day ticket, anglers all over the country have access to waters where they can confidently expect to catch trout, and if bringing a bag of fish home at the end of a day's flyfishing were the sole object then one would be quite happy to fish purely on well-stocked small-waters. However, it is the limitation of such waters and that missing vital element of wildness which I find detracts from the satisfaction of making a good catch.

ROOM TO HUNT

I like catching fish; I always have, but I don't need easy fishing or a large bag of trout to take home to make my day enjoyable. My greatest pleasure comes from hunting good fish over wide expanses of water where they have room to lose themselves. One then has to study the varied topography and take into account the prevailing conditions, the time of year, and what the fish may be feeding on.

On the larger waters there will be variables that simply do not exist on smaller fisheries. Doing this consistently is my aim. A good trout in difficult conditions, or a small bag of quality fish when weather, a hatch of fly, or the mood of the fish conspire to produce a good day, are infinitely more satisfying than a cricket score of lesser fish.

Denis O'Keefe summed it up nicely when he was trying to tell me why he liked boat fishing on the big loughs of Ireland. It had been a difficult day's fishing on the Corrib and trout were hard to come by. With very little fish activity to distract him, he had obviously given the matter some thought when he suddenly turned and remarked, "You know Dennis, it isn't a fish in the boat that really matters; it is the hunt." I fully understood the point Denis was making. This concurred with my sentiments also, for without the hunt, the reward does not have the same value.

Although wild waters will never be as consistent as the heavily stocked put-and-take fisheries, the challenge of fishing for wild trout will always give me greater satisfaction. However, living in central England until the year 2000 did limit my opportunities to pursue truly wild fish with a fly rod. To restrict

Anglers new to the sport of flyfishing will more than likely catch their first trout from a small-water fishery.

myself to fishing solely for wild trout would have confined my fishing to a few precious weeks a year. Luckily, I discovered the delight of fishing the larger reservoirs, and the sport they had to offer. Fishing the larger reservoirs for fit, grown-on trout was an alternative to the wild fishing that I found both interesting and rewarding to pursue. The waters were big; I had room to hunt. The flyfishing bug had bitten! Grafham, Rutland, Draycote, Datchet and Farmoor were all major reservoirs that opened over a ten-year period, starting in the mid-1960s. A new fishing era beckoned; the stillwater revolution had begun.

EARLY DAYS

In the early 1970s I became very interested in flyfishing, but could no longer find the quality of trout I desired from my local rivers. This was as a result of over-fishing, abstraction, pollution and mismanagement. Sadly, the rivers were in decline and were but a shadow of the fisheries that generations of game fisherman had once known. In 1971 I fished for reservoir trout for the first time at the newly-opened Draycote Water, and caught a brown trout on my second visit. This early success was all the encouragement I needed, and although I never consistently caught big numbers of trout during that first or indeed second season, I did catch enough trout to keep me interested. What did help was the size of the trout; mainly browns up to 4lbs, and all good fish.

Over the seasons to come, stillwater flyfishing would dominate my fishing year. Although I fished the rivers for trout, grayling, seatrout and salmon, stillwater flyfishing became my passion. It was on the reservoirs where vast tracts of fertile water were stocked with trout that I found an interest that was a near-equivalent to the wild fishing I loved. The mature grown-on trout of the large reservoirs, in the 1970s and 1980s were outstanding, and I feel that the quality of this fishing will never be repeated.

MATURE OVER-WINTERED TROUT

Educated, over-wintered trout must rate among some of the most difficult fish to catch on a fly, particularly near the surface and with small flies. Mature trout will not tolerate clumsy presentation, poorly-tied leaders or noisy boat handling, and it's no use getting some of the basics right if the chosen water is incapable of supporting over-wintered fish. So first establish which waters are capable of producing grown-on, quality fish, and indeed which waters, due to water quality, during the coming season will offer the best opportunity of producing good trout. Since rainbows form the bulk of the sport, we need to identify waters that are sufficiently large and fertile to support a reasonable head of over-wintering stock, which can grow quickly and survive for several seasons.

Unlike the browns, the rainbows are voracious, open-water plankton feeders, focusing on the zones where the density of food is greatest. Cropping the zones, they prey upon daphnia, ascending or suspended larvae and pupae of various insects, following the fauna up and down through the layers.

Small stillwater fisheries produce big fish and provide a lot of fun but they do not offer the same range of challenges as the truly wild waters.

With an abundant supply of food, stock rainbows rapidly put on weight. Then, in late-summer/early-autumn, they switch to fry feeding which runs well into winter, and continues until the cold water temperatures slow down their food intake. If the fish have made good, healthy growth then a proportion of the stock will survive and over-winter.

Rainbow trout, in particular, are grazers and thrive when suspended food is in abundance, but they do not forage as well as the brown trout. If there is a shortage of planktonic prey they can fail to make good growth, simply lose condition and burn themselves out. Rainbows *are* capable of feeding on the bottom of lakes and reservoirs or finding a food resource when the pickings are thin. But they only do well if there is an abundance of food. Unlike brown trout, rainbows, with their high metabolic rate, lose condition faster if food is scarce, and will not survive the winter if they do not make condition in the autumn months.

Rainbows lose their condition faster than browns.

Browns are capable of holding condition and surviving for longer on meagre pickings, and should food abundance improve then they are quick to take advantage of this change.

Farmoor Browns

I remember a year class of browns on Farmoor reservoir; these fish would have been between 20 and 23 inches in length, and rose well to surface flies. They were very lean and were obviously struggling to find food. The following season those browns were different animals. They had obviously found richer feeding, and fish which would have struggled to make 5lbs the previous season, were now full with firm bodies and good shoulders. In mid-May of that year, the evening before travelling to Ireland for my annual mayfly trip, I took a fish of 7lb 6ozs that measured just over 23 inches. The fish was in superb condition. Its body was firm, tight as a barrel, totally different to the flaccid, lean creatures we were catching the previous season, and an excellent example of how capable brown trout are of improving condition after a period of poor feeding.

In a large reservoir like Rutland, with its deep water and stable water temperatures, the rainbows, if the water quality is right, will over-winter well, (although they didn't fare so well to begin with when Rutland first opened in 1977). There was no repetition of Grafham's heady start, with reel-screaming runs from large, fast-growing rainbow trout. Much to everyone's surprise, superb quality brown trout made the headlines. The browns obviously found the clear water and rich bottom-feeding to their liking, but as with all newly-flooded reservoirs, the water could not sustain this early harvest. If "catch-and-release" had been an acceptable practice at that time, what might the quality of the sport provided by those early brown trout have been?

However, rod pressure took its toll and as the marginal bottom food became exhausted, the remaining browns sunk away to deeper waters, and the rainbows were left to provide the surface sport. Initially they were disappointing, but in the 1980s as the reservoir matured and the biomass built up (which suited the cruising grazers) Rutland rainbows began to prosper and pack on weight.

Wary of Lures

Also, the vast majority of anglers were using lures and many were still unaware of the advantages of fishing with clear nylon, particularly when fishing in the upper layers with small flies. The fish soon became wary of lures, this is why a sizeable population of over-wintering fish built up and grew on, relatively unmolested. The shallows at the top end of both arms supported a tremendous stock of first-and-second-winter rainbows, and the majority of these fish grew on to a size range of 3 to 5lbs. They provided some of the finest top-water flyfishing that I have ever experienced at any reservoir in the UK.

With imitative methods, that were fine-tuned on waters such as Farmoor and Draycote, I enjoyed some wonderful sport with grown-on, naturalised fish. It would have been a poor day had we not returned with at least a brace of grown-on fish; trout that exceeded 3lbs, in peak condition. These fish fought well with reel-screaming runs ending in a bar of silver leaping at the end of a long line. 60 to 80 yard runs were not uncommon, and very exciting.

Mid-May to early July would provide the cream of the surface fishing for first- and second-winter fish. Then if conditions were at all favourable, one would be targeting fish moving on the surface. Fishing cannot

Late evening in Rutland's South Arm. A fish at last, before the long motor back to the fishing lodge.

get any better than this. To see the tail and dorsal fin of a big fish, leisurely rolling; and then covering the rise with a fly in the hope of deceiving the trout, is pure joy. The moment the hook was set the water would explode, and the fish would scream off, taking the fly-line to the backing. Those fish swam so fast that the line would actually make a hiss as it cut through the water, and for a brief period following the strike, they were difficult to control. In fact, one rarely had control, as they careered in all directions at breakneck speed. These were super-fit grown-on fish in peak condition, which had put on most of their weight in the reservoir.

RUTLAND'S DECLINE

Sadly, it was not to last, as the fishing crashed in 1990-91, and the demise of Rutland as we knew it happened very rapidly indeed; too quickly to attribute solely to cormorant predation, as many would have us believe. There was no slow build-up to the problem: the water just crashed, and within 12 months, the over-wintering population had been decimated.

Had cormorant predation been solely responsible, there would have been a gradual decline of first- and second-winter fish as the predation built up. But the older trout disappeared almost completely, leaving just thin, under-nourished stock fish; and a few of the larger second-winter, or older resident trout.

Fish Failing to Thrive

Concerning the survival of stock fish, I can't help feeling that the cormorant played a similar role to that of the mink in relation to the disappearance of the water vole. The water vole was already in difficulty when the mink came along; mainly through loss of habitat. With a lack of marginal cover, the mink found the voles easy prey, and all but finished them off. The voles disappeared from many areas which they had historically inhabited for generations; leaving just a few isolated pockets, in which suitable habitat gave them cover from mink predation.

What happened to Rutland was either due to disease or a change in the water quality. Whatever the case, the fish did not grow and were always vulnerable to cormorant predation. I can't help but feel that what happened to Rutland was in some way linked to a change in water treatment policy by Anglian Water Services; but it may have been purely coincidental that the implementation of a new treatment process, on both Rutland and Grafham, should occur at the same time as the decline of the two reservoirs.

In 1989, Anglian Water Services was under tremendous pressure to combat the build-up of blue-green algae. They closed the reservoir for part of the '89 season, owing to possible links with the deaths of some dogs and sheep, which might have contracted toxic poisoning after ingesting algae.

In May of 1990, Anglian Water Services implemented a programme to slow the algal growth, by reducing the available phosphate. It may be purely coincidental that the food chain collapsed in both Rutland and Grafham (both of which were being dosed with ferric sulphate) at that time. The daphnia disappeared altogether, and the fish put on no weight, and were in poor condition.

Rutland's magnificent over-wintered rainbows were no more. With poor growth rates, the stock fish remained vulnerable to cormorant predation for a long time, and I would say there were seasons where they made very little growth, if any at all. It is doubtful that the stock which survived until the end of the season would have made sufficient weight or condition to survive the winter. First-and-second-winter stocks were definitely not surviving in the same numbers as they were before 1990. We did see little windows of light, such as late '92 and spring of '93, when good rainbows remained inshore, feeding hard; despite being subjected to a lot of bank pressure.

Although angling pressure on certain areas was intense, the fish remained inshore, feeding over the freshly-flooded margins; flooded due to the reservoir re-filling after a long period of draw down. In a balanced fishery, these educated trout would have left the margins once they had been fished over, and yet they remained, despite the presence of anglers.

To catch these fish from a boat, you had to anchor close inshore, which in some areas was not possible because of the 50 metre exclusion zone. The main body of the reservoir was devoid of fish so drifting open water even at the top of the two arms was a waste of time until the inshore feeding had become exhausted. What we experienced in the late season of '92 and the spring of '93 was unnatural behaviour, and the trout would not have remained inshore for so long, had there been reasonable feeding offshore. Why should we have experienced this increase in over-wintered trout, if cormorants were totally to blame for the wipe-out of stock during the two previous seasons, and subsequent seasons up to 1996?

LARGER STOCK FISH

From 1996, to overcome the problems of poor growth and cormorant predation, Anglian Water Services stocked with larger fish. On my last two visits to the fishery in June 2000, I took two heavy limits; one of 30lbs plus on buzzer-nymphs and dries. My last limit from my favourite reservoir, weighed over 33lbs; the heaviest bag of trout I have ever taken from Rutland, and although the fish were well mended, and had been in the reservoir for some time, they were not the same class of trout we caught there 20 years' previously. That era has passed.

Angling pressure on stock is now such that, even with good water-quality over a sustained period of time, and no cormorant predation, it is highly unlikely that the stock will ever reach the levels we enjoyed in the 1980s. One has only to fish the reservoir after a major flyfishing competition, to understand the effect on the reservoir's stock. Even on a large water such as Rutland, the fishing slows dramatically following one of these events. I understand from friends that the 2002 season at Rutland was an indifferent one as well; with the fishing falling off as the season progressed. Again the fish appeared to be failing to put on weight, and this time, water-quality and the infestation with a gill parasite called '*Ergasilus sieboldi*' were held responsible. The parasite has probably been in the water for years, but has only now become a problem because of the poorer condition of the fish. This decline in condition could stem from a lack of food due to decreased water-quality. The fishery is well managed, Anglian Water Services' fishery staff are second to none, but the problems are, I feel, out of their control.

It is highly unlikely that the Rutland stock will ever reach the levels we enjoyed in the 1980s.

BIGGEST FISH

I find it ironic that in 1990, when the reservoir developed problems, I caught my largest brown trout from the top of the north arm on a traditional fly. At 11lbs,

11lb Rutland brown – my biggest to date.

it was the largest trout of the season from Rutland. The method I used was very dear to me, but it was one I was beginning to think would never produce a fish of the calibre that it did. I experienced the magic of the take unfold before me from the moment the fly touched the water: the tell-tale movement; the bow-wave behind the fly; the acceleration as the fish moved forward to take the fly; and the rise, just as the fly was breaking through the surface film, right beneath the boat. A truly unforgettable take. It came at the end of a difficult day towards the end of the season, to a top-water method: a fitting epitaph to one of the finest periods of reservoir fishing I have ever experienced.

The following is an article I wrote for *Trout and Salmon* in November 1990 describing that eventful day, and I think it shows just how difficult the fishing had

become towards the end of the season of 1990. I had not even covered a moving fish until four in the afternoon; this was on a day of reasonable fishing conditions, and at a good time of year.

THE GREMLINS DEFEATED

If I had to restrict my fishing to one trout water in England it would be Rutland Water. Since opening day in 1977 – when John Everard and I had caught superb limit bags of browns before breakfast – the reservoir has been kind to me. I would find it difficult to recall a day when Rutland hasn't offered me at least one chance of a good fish. If such opportunities are missed, the reservoir cannot be blamed. Even when the fishery is in one of her sulkier moods, there is always the possibility that somewhere, something is going to happen. I never lose faith, because sooner or later the reservoir may awaken from her slumber. Then, she shows fish that would make even the most critical angler concede that Rutland holds some truly magnificent trout. It is the quality and numbers of the over-wintered stock that draws fly-fishers from all over the country.

On September 8, Rutland was having an off-day. The morning began with our usual pre-fishing conversation with Roger Thom, after which Bruce Vaughan, my fishing partner, and I left for the fishing grounds, feeling a little subdued. Roger wasn't too optimistic about our chances. He was obviously disappointed, as the Benson & Hedges Final was imminent, and he understandably wanted the fishing to be on top form. We commiserated, and headed for the south arm. There was a moderate north wind blowing, so we began a long drift from the Bunds.

Midway through the drift, I raised a heavy fish to the top dropper which came adrift after a few moments' contact. I felt annoyed with myself: the fish had taken well, and I should have boated it. We continued drifting towards Lax Hill. With the reservoir so low, the bottom was visible all the way and the water between three and eight feet deep was perfect for our style of fishing.

Bruce raised a good fish in the bay at the foot of Lax Hill, but the trout missed the fly and didn't come again. A few moments later I took a nice, clean fish of around 2lb on the middle dropper – one of this year's earlier stock fish. We finished the drift with no further action, so I swung the boat around and tried a new line, on to and along the point of Lax Hill. As we approached the remains of an old submerged hedgerow, I hooked and lost two good fish in succession. I could not believe my ill luck; this was never going to be an easy day, and opportunities would be rare.

We tried the drift again, but the fish were having none of it. They had either moved or were keeping their heads well down. It doesn't take a lot to upset established trout in shallow lies, particularly in the autumn, so it pays to move on when you have covered an area.

An overdue lunch break was now called for. We had agreed to rendezvous off the point of the Hambleton Peninsula with some anglers practising for the Benson & Hedges, but we were already late and the point was thirty minutes away. So we took our break in Manton Bay, then went in search of 'Fiery' Brown and company before moving on to the north arm. We found them fishing Sailing Club Bay, but they had nothing to report, save for several abortive follows from fish to sunk line tactics on the lift. The other two boats in the team had taken one fish apiece. All had found the fishing dour. Rutland really was out of sorts, and it looked as if we were in for a real struggle.

Rutland's North Arm

However, there was still the north arm, and one spot in particular, where we had previously located a concentration of brown trout.

As we arrived at the top of the north arm, the wind shifted to the west and dropped in strength to leave a nice ripple. Under the changed conditions I decided to try nymphs tactics, and on a long drift towards the tower we duly found at long last a few moving fish. At four o'clock I had my first opportunity to cover a rising fish, which took my Grey Buzzer the moment it touched the water. But this fish came adrift on its first run. I shifted uneasily on my seat. All was not well at my end of the boat. Bruce, meantime, had neither raised nor seen a moving fish within casting distance and he too, was having a desperate time of it. In such situations there is nothing one can do except keep on trying.

Thirty minutes later, I spotted another fish which rose 25 yards downwind of me. I covered the trout with my tail fly, a Pheasant Tail, and it took on the drop. A good solid take. This trout was well

hooked, I was confident of landing it, but again, for no apparent reason, the hook hold gave.

The air temperature began to drop as evening approached, the wind strengthened, and what few fish were rising went down. We decided the time was right to try a drift over the plateau, where a few weeks earlier we had found a concentration of browns. On that occasion white lures on a fast sinking line, duly brought me browns to 3lb 14oz and I pulled several more, before losing a very heavy fish that I felt certain was not a rainbow. Thoughts of that big fish haunted me as we quietly motored up to start the next drift. By then, only two other boats were down the arm, and the area we were going to fish hadn't been covered for some time. With luck, one or two of the better fish would start to move.

There was something menacing about the way this fish was following

For this drift I went back to my traditional outfit and tied a white mini muddler on the top dropper, a silver invicta on the middle dropper and a wormfly on the point. We scanned the water for moving fish. A big trout made a leisurely roll on Bruce's side of the boat. He didn't see it, but I told him the position and he covered the area.

The fish didn't respond. We were now over the plateau but nothing moved, so we continued casting and retrieving. With no boats anywhere near us, we had the area to ourselves. The perfect way to end the day, I thought, just the quiet swish of our rods and the rhythmic sound of the water lapping gently against the side of the boat.

I found myself soaking in the atmosphere, when my attention was suddenly drawn to the end of my line. Down in the ripple, a bow-wave had appeared behind my tail fly. The trout didn't rush forward to grab the fly, it just kept its distance behind. There was something menacing about the way this fish was following: it just kept coming without altering speed.

"Don't drop away below the fly," I begged. "Just a few more yards, and I will make you an offer you can't refuse."

The fish continued to follow into the lift zone without changing pace. Now I made my move – long, steady draw on the line, simultaneously raising my rod hand. The flies accelerated. First the bob, then the middle dropper broke surface, and, with my rod hand at full stretch above my head, the wormfly broke through. The trout rushed forward, a small neb emerged and went down. With what movement I had left, I struck. "I'm in!" I cried.

The trout sounded and just hung there: solid, unrelenting power. It was obviously a brown. It held position in front of the boat before deciding to run towards the bow and under Bruce's line. I piled on the pressure, but could not turn the fish, so I casually passed my rod around Bruce who hadn't cleared his line and started to play the trout over the back of the boat. The rod was bent double, and the line sang to the strain of our tug o' war.

I desperately wanted a glimpse of my adversary, but he was having none of it. I play fish hard, even on light tackle, but I could make no headway with this one. It began to dawn on me that this could be something special. At no time did the trout take more than 20 yards of line, yet it was a full 15 minutes before we actually saw him for the first time. We estimated his weight at 8lb, and a quick glance at my watch told me it was five past six.

Four minutes later, the fish made another pass of the boat. He looked absolutely magnificent in the clear water. I was transfixed as he swam majestically, almost casually, away; there was something surreal about this pass. We could clearly see the depth of the trout's body and the breadth of his back.

Suddenly, I felt anxious. I had been playing this trout, hard, for some time and it occurred to me that the gremlin might not have left the boat.

One other boat came in closer to watch the final moments, but thankfully remained at a respectable distance. By now my right arm was tiring, and to keep the pressure on I brought my left hand up to support the rod. Slowly but surely the trout grudgingly gave ground and his runs grew shorter. He came to the top and wallowed. Impatient, I tried to manoeuvre him into the net, but the fish wasn't yet ready, and rallied. How I wished this trout would give up! Even in the final act of the drama I was expecting the hook-hold to give and disaster to reign. But the fish surfaced once more; and this time I slid him over the waiting net.

Triumph at last, the sweeter for the wait. Bruce lifted the trout into the boat and we looked on in awe, absolutely speechless. For a few moments we said nothing, then Bruce broke the ice. "Well done," he said, grinning, and shook my hand.

A double-figure brown had been an ambition of mine for a long time. I was beginning to think it was an impossible dream to take such a fish off the top with a traditional fly. Ever since I was a small boy, when I lost a large brown trout on the River Evenlode, such fish have held a fascination for me. On a day when I met those two imposters, triumph and disaster, my dream finally came true: an 11lb brown trout on a floating line from a drifting boat. I cannot ask for more: my cup is full.

I feel that typifies how difficult the fishing had been at the time. Good fish were there to be taken, but you had to hunt them out. However, if I had boated all the heavy fish I lost earlier in the day, I would have had some bag of quality trout! At the time I knew the reservoir intimately as we were fishing Rutland most weeks from May until the end of September. So I had a good idea of which areas held fish, in particular the heavier trout which were our target fish. We concentrated on these drifts to the exclusion of the popular areas that were producing higher numbers of smaller fish.

Good fish were there to be taken, but you really had to hunt them out

On my red-letter day, those areas which reputedly held more trout had failed to fish well. 'Fiery' Brown's team came in with two fish between six rods even though they fished some of the more productive areas.

Benson & Hedges Competition

With the Benson & Hedges competition only two days away, most of the anglers fishing were practising for the competition and were concentrating on the areas that held a greater stock of trout rather than risk an all-or-nothing gambit over the shallows at the top end of the two arms. To prove they were no slouches, 'Fiery' Brown's team featured in the shake-up for one of the top places at the end of the competition, and as for my day? I came in with a brace, one of them a big fish, and I was delighted.

RESERVOIR METHODS

The tactics that we used on Rutland Water will catch trout from most stillwater fisheries, certainly the larger waters. When it comes to methods, I feel this is a matter of personal choice. I have tried and taken trout on just about any legitimate fly method, from the indicator, to fishing with a lead line on the rudder.

We have to come to terms with the fact that there are times when, if one doesn't go deep with a sinking line, and fish either a lure, or a booby, then the bag will be light. Early and late season on Farmoor reservoir for example, when the trout have gone deep and dropped down beyond the second ledge, beyond the reach of most conventional tactics, the booby or deep lure would produce a lot of fish, provided that you could cast far enough to reach them.

Although I have taken some big bags of trout using such tactics, they are methods which do not appeal to me. Given a choice, I would always prefer to fish imitative methods with nymphs or dry flies, but even I admit that there are days when one is wasting time using such methods.

On days such as these we have to make a tactical decision: we either persevere with a method which

we prefer, but isn't suitable on the day; or we employ common sense, and use a tactic that will produce fish. No matter what method we choose to use, a good understanding of the trout's behaviour, and water craft, will always be important factors that determine how successful we are over a given period of time.

If the conditions allow, I would always favour drifting, and given a choice my day would be a soft day, one of light wind with plenty of moving fish to target. Quite a contrast to those wild days, so loved by hardened wet fly anglers. Wild conditions will mask deficiencies of presentation and technique and this is when the wet fly can be so effective.

The action of wind and wave help hide poor entry and any flaws in the presentation and if there is a hatch of fly or if the trout are well on and prepared to chase then the wet fly will dominate. Wild conditions will excite the trout, but the big disadvantage with strong winds is that they play hell with the slower presentations required for the imitative methods.

This does not mean that you cannot take fish on nymphs or the dry fly in such conditions. On the contrary, I have taken some excellent bags of trout on dry fly on wild days, but squally winds limit the time for which one can maintain a good presentation, and this impacts on the effectiveness of the method. However, windy or not, the methods we employ on the reservoirs are equally productive with wild trout, and the imitative tactics that we use on fisheries such as Draycote, Farmoor, Chew and Rutland will catch trout on most wild lake fisheries. We just have to make allowances for such things as lower stock numbers and the feeding behavioural patterns of wild brown trout as opposed to those of the stocked rainbow.

Don't Anchor for Wild Trout

I wouldn't recommend anchoring for wild brown trout because in most situations this would be detrimental to sport, although there are occasions when pushing the boat gently in, onto a rocky shallow or shoreline, or dropping a mud weight, can be advantageous to avoid spooking surface-feeding fish. There are always exceptions, but in the majority of situations, anchoring for wild fish is not advisable, whereas on the reservoirs, anchoring can be very productive, particularly during the spring and the back-end.

It should be remembered, however, that on the reservoirs we are fishing over a much greater density of confidently-feeding fish, leisurely milling around, and on some waters a mix of both rainbow and brown trout. Even though the wild trout will be feeding on much the same type of fauna, there are fewer of them and they cover a wider area much faster than the stocked reservoir fish. All you will do by anchoring is create a fish-free zone around the boat. With wild trout, employ the methods that are successful for catching reservoir fish, but don't anchor: use a drifting boat, and your day will be far more productive.

EARLY SEASON FISHING

For most early spring reservoir fishing, I fish imitative flies from an anchored boat and would feel confident using just a handful of different fly patterns. Restricting me to two or three patterns for point and four or five patterns for droppers wouldn't overly concern me even if the fish were preoccupied on daphnia or buzzer nymphs, the two most important early-season prey foods.

Location is the most important single factor at this time of year, as the trout tend to be tightly packed, particularly on the bigger waters. Once fish have been located it is then essential to ascertain the most productive taking depth. When that's been established you must concentrate on holding that depth for as long as possible with a slow retrieve.

I cannot emphasise the speed of line recovery too strongly. It is important to maintain contact with the fly throughout the retrieve and to keep that fly moving as slowly as possible through the taking zone. The optimum taking zone may be only a narrow band within the water column, no greater than 2 to 3 feet deep, even though you may be fishing over water 12 to 15 feet in depth and could possibly cover an area the size of a football pitch.

Keep that fly moving as slowly as possible through the taking zone

With increasing day length and rising temperatures, spring for many trout fishermen heralds the beginning of a new season. Not only that, but chironomid (midge) activity will increase rapidly and by mid-April, most of the early hatches of buzzer will have reached their peak. Historically, many of the traditionalist lake fishers would have looked to midsummer for the best hatches of fly but by late June the heavy hatches of chironomids are over.

The big advantage with the heavy hatches of buzzer is that they rise in such numbers from the bottom muds that they pull the trout off the daphnia, which is good news for the imitative fly fisher as it offers the opportunity to present the trout with either a larval, pupal, or if the conditions are right, an emerging or adult imitation.

Cold Weather Tactics

In cold and breezy weather, look for the fish well down in the water where they will be gorging themselves on the pupae, waiting for an improvement in weather conditions, before ascending to the surface to hatch. With the slightest sign of an improvement in weather conditions, particularly a rise in temperature combined with falling wind strength, the pupae ascend to the surface and hatch in such numbers that they will attract the trout to the surface even on the earliest of spring days. Be alert and watch for these conditions, for they will provide the earliest opportunity for fishing to rising fish.

Action is Sub-Surface

Most of the feeding activity during the early season will be sub-surface, and as there will be no surface activity to give away the whereabouts of the fish without prior knowledge or experience of fishing the water, you will have to trust the local advice or have confidence in your own ability to choose the right area. In the early season, if I haven't moved a fish within 30 minutes, I move on, unless confident that I am over fish but haven't found the correct taking depth. Location is the key to success, particularly on the larger waters, so do not be afraid to move if the fish are not forthcoming.

Gauge the Taking Depth

Once fish have been located, it is important to determine the most productive taking depth. This is easily ascertained, by changing the amount of time we allow the flies to sink. Once the most productive depth has been established, it is then important to hold the flies in the taking zone with a slow retrieve for as long as possible.

This is easier if conditions will allow you to fish with a floating line, providing the trout are not too deep. In a side wind or where drag can be a problem, I would opt for a slow intermediate line. In most situations, you will be fishing with the wind on your back, which is ideal for the floating line and fishing downwind. Fishing thus allows for greater control over your

retrieve and improved presentation. Early season trout are not in the mood for dashing around chasing food; they just cruise through the zooplankton taking in food items. This is why it is important to fish the flies slowly, allowing the trout plenty of time to come onto the flies and take them in, as they swim by.

I firmly believe that for stocked reservoir fisheries, within reason, the pattern of fly is much less important in early Spring. Concentrate on the location, depth and speed of retrieve, for this is the formula that will bring success.

Concentrate on the location, depth and speed of retrieve

Ideally, I look for water between 8 to 12 feet deep over known fish-holding areas, and if the wind is blowing along or on-shore, so much the better. The boat should be anchored well upwind from the holding area and then, by slowly paying out the anchor rope, allowed to drop down onto the outer fringe of the fish-holding area.

Start with the Outer Fringes

I prefer to begin fishing over the outer fringes first, and if I am getting takes, hold that position until the offers from fish slow down. Once this happens, lengthen the anchor rope by another 10 metres or so, allowing the boat to drop deeper into the holding area. This manoeuvre, of lengthening the anchor rope, will normally improve the number of takes again, and the same manoeuvre can be repeated as activity falls off.

Dropping the boat deeper into the hot spot, in a series of moves, allows the angler to pick off the trout patrolling the outer fringes. This avoids disturbing the main concentration of fish, and with each drop, the anglers are fishing new water again.

On a good day, if covered correctly, these early season hot spots can produce prodigious numbers of trout, and if catch-and-release is allowed, you will have to make a decision, according to your conscience, when you think it appropriate to stop fishing.

Early Season Tackle

My leaders for fishing over water up to 12 feet deep with a floating fly line, are made up from either 6 or 7lb clear copolymer or 5lb fluorocarbon. For deep nymph

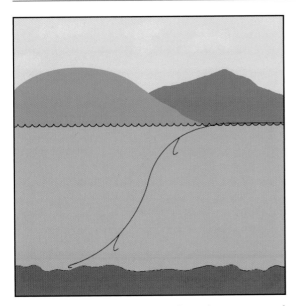

Diagram 9: Ideal leader set-up for early season nymph fishing. The middle dropper is in prime position for trout cruising just off the bottom.

flies attached to the tail that comes off the top side of the knot, towards the fly line. They do this so that the dropper fly hangs away from the leader and is perhaps a little less likely to tangle, but an angler who insists on committing such an act of folly will lose fish through knot failure, because it will constrict and ultimately break the nylon. The name of the game is to put trout in the boat.

It is difficult enough to hook them. The last thing you want to do is lose fish through failure of your tackle, particularly as it could so easily be avoided.

Many reservoir anglers fish with heavy wire hooks and epoxy-coated flies to achieve depth. Because I fish a floating line, I much prefer to fish with a leaded or weighted fly on the point. With a weighted pattern, tied on a medium wire hook as an anchor fly, and nymphs tied on medium wire hooks for my droppers, I can achieve depths up to 12 feet comfortably using a floating fly line, providing I do not have to fish across a strong side wind.

> *I much prefer to fish with a leaded or weighted fly on the point*

fishing, my first choice leader would have a distance from point fly to first dropper of 4 feet and 6 feet from the first dropper to the top dropper, with a further 10 feet from the top dropper to the leader butt or fly line connection (*see* Diagram 9, above).

An alternative to this leader set-up would be to space the droppers an equal distance apart, leaving between 5 and 6 feet between each dropper, with 10 to 12 feet to the flyline (*see* Diagram 10, right).

I would nearly always fish long leaders, at least 20 to 22 feet in length. However, if the conditions, such as bright sun and light wind, demanded more length between my top dropper and flyline, I would increase the distance between these two points, but not the working distance between the flies.

I prefer the water knot for tying up my leaders, making three turns through the loop before tightening. When attaching droppers, to avoid strangulation of the nylon, always attach the dropper fly to the knot tail that hangs downwards towards the point end of the leader. This is particularly important with the copolymer or fluorocarbon nylons, which are less tolerant to knot deficiencies than standard nylon. I still see ill-advised anglers fishing with their dropper

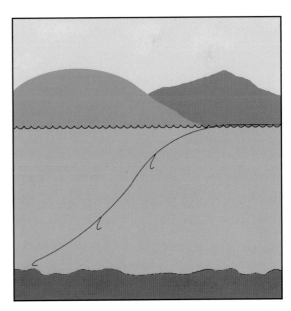

Diagram 10: How the flies would fish with a weighted fly on the point. Good for searching the layers to find the productive zone.

I was involved with the concept of producing heavy wire hooks, to achieve depth, but this was a modification produced for competition anglers, who are not allowed to use any form of weight in the dressing of their fly patterns.

For pleasure fishing, I am faced with no such constraint, so I much prefer to tie my flies on less obtrusive medium wire hooks, and with the ballast in the point fly, I have more control over the way my flies fish. I just vary the amount of lead wire used in tying the pattern, to achieve varying sink rates – a far more flexible method.

If the trout are holding around ten feet down, I usually find that many fish will come to the point or first dropper. The first dropper, allowing for the angle of the leader and the length of the dropper, will be fishing between two to three feet above the point fly. These two flies, will take the majority of the trout if they are holding deep. The top dropper is more of a guide, an indicator to inform if the fish are migrating towards the surface, but it will always take the odd fish when fishing over a concentration of trout.

However, if I begin to take a succession of fish on the top dropper, this tells me that the trout are either higher in the water than I first anticipated, or that they are lifting in the water with the zooplankton. This movement of the trout towards the surface, following the lifting blanket of zooplankton, very often occurs on

The author unhooking a Draycote rainbow.

mild, spring days, particularly in the late afternoon.

The zooplankton rising in the water column is caused either by daphnia lifting towards the surface with falling light levels, or the buzzer pupae rising towards the surface, possibly to sense if the prevailing weather conditions are suitable for hatching.

If the trout move towards the surface, I change the point fly to an unleaded pattern and increase the length of my leader between point fly and first dropper to 5 or 6 feet, the same distance as between first and top dropper. I can achieve a much flatter presentation, with the droppers an equal distance apart and an unleaded fly on the point. This allows me to hold the flies higher in the water, with all three flies in the taking zone. (*see* Diagram 11, below)

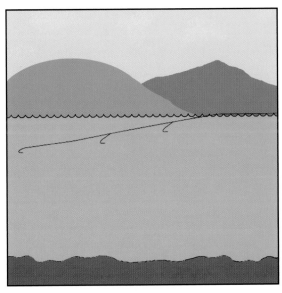

Diagram 11: This configuration of leader set-up, with the droppers spaced an equal distance apart, is also the type of leader I use with an intermediate line, where again the flies come through on a flatter plane but lower in the water. This is a good configuration for presenting all three flies in the taking zone. The depth at which the flies fish would be dependent on the density of intermediate line, the length of time the line is allowed to sink before commencing the retrieve, and the speed of retrieve.

If your flies are fishing below the trout, they are fishing ineffectively, so it is imperative to keep them on or just above the trout's holding level. As the fish are mobile, moving up and down through the layers following the food, it pays to be flexible, adjusting to the fish's movements. So if the offers slow down with flies higher in the water, revert back to the deeper fishing set-up with a leaded fly on the point and search out the deeper water.

During the early season, the trout can be tightly packed along some shorelines, so once you have located them, never move away until you feel the area has been exhausted. Failure to induce a response with the deeper method indicates that the trout have moved or they have gone off the take. Either way, a move is in order if you want to continue catching.

Sometimes the fishing will slow and then pick up again, but very often, particularly if they have had a lot of fishing pressure not only from your boat but from other boats around you, you are better off moving, provided you have searched out the depths methodically. If trout are not forthcoming, then it is advisable to move and try another area.

The Induced Take

When fishing inshore areas, where trout are holding their position just over the bed of the lake, the sacrificial nymph, which is simply used to drag along the bottom, can be a deadly way to present the first dropper. This induces the trout to take the dropper fly as it lifts in the water, just off the bed of the lake.

This is achieved by allowing the point fly to deliberately catch on bits of weed or to scrape along the bottom of the lake. Once resistance is felt via the point fly, you ease off the tension just a little. This allows the dropper to fall lower in the water as the leader sags. By recovering line slowly, the tension increases and as the sag of the leader curve straightens, so the dropper rises – a great inducement to any passing trout.

This inducement can be repeated many times throughout the retrieve. I have taken some very good trout using this method. It is a good tactic for catching mature, educated trout. It is essential to have the wind on your back for this method, as you have more control over your floating line. The aim is to make the dropper lift, just when the point fly grounds itself on the bottom. Side winds are not so conducive to this method, as they create a bow in the line that puts drag on the flies, so the leader is under tension all the time. The induced take is all about increasing, then slackening that tension.

Watch That Line!

The takes from early season trout are usually confident draws on the line that can be felt by hand, but once you have located the fish, it is advisable also to watch the line for indications. Watching the line for takes, with plenty of fish around, will provide valuable experience for later in the season when the takes are not so confident that they can be readily detected by hand.

Watching either the end of the fly line, the curve in the line or where the line enters the water from the rod top, will indicate a taking fish and it may surprise some anglers how many indications they may observe, but not feel by hand, before the trout has ejected the fly.

The takes from early season trout are usually confident draws on the line that can be felt by hand

Although I do not think fly pattern is as important as some would have us believe, I do need to have complete confidence in the flies that I fish. I try to keep my selection as simple as possible.

Later in the season when the trout have been subjected to angling pressure or if they become preoccupied, a greater range of flies will be necessary to cope with specialised feeding. However, for most early season situations, endless rows of different fly patterns are not the answer to catching trout.

Keep fly selection to a few proven general imitative patterns, and if you are not catching, I will be surprised if the choice of fly is the problem. If I am not catching fish, I would be looking to the area I had chosen, the depth at which I was fishing, or my retrieve for the fault; not in my fly box for the answer.

MY RECOMMENDED EARLY-SEASON FLIES

* Point flies such as the Pheasant Tail, Hare's Ear or patterns with mobile tail made up of marabou, in both weighted and unweighted versions, size 10 or 12 standard, or 3X long shank hooks should cover most early-season situations.

* Goldhead flies with mobile tails are very effective when there are a lot of stock fish around, and the Tadpole or the Damsel dressings with their seductive tail movement are excellent fish-takers.

* I have great faith in the Pheasant Tail for point position, but this fly could be any one of a number of different patterns, provided you have confidence in the pattern – *that is all that matters*. What you will find on these early sessions is that the first fly you tie on will invariably catch you fish, and give you confidence in the pattern. And because you have taken a trout with the fly, it will become your first choice, and so you use it again and again!

* Watercraft will outperform fly selection any day, and this is even more so with naive early-season trout.

THE DROPPERS

These require a little more thought but again, keep the selection as tight as possible. The fish will be feeding on chironomids in one form or another, or daphnia.

If they are feeding on daphnia, they can be induced to take a buzzer pattern. Daphnia is too minute an organism to impersonate with an artificial imitation. However, daphnia-feeding trout do respond to movement and colour, and they will take nymphs if they come on to them. So it pays to concentrate on the one form of food we *can* imitate and fish with buzzer imitations.

The early season midges tend to be dark in colour; thus any dark buzzer pattern will suffice with or without wing buds. I have great confidence in a dark grey pattern made up from Canada goose herl with a silver rib or a midge tied up from peacock herl with a short flue and a pearl rib, or flies with a Canada goose herl body and different shades of seal's fur or peacock herl for the thorax. The grey midge, the peacock herl pattern and a midge pattern with a darkish olive thorax would be my preferred choice for the droppers. I would tie them in size 12, on either sedge or grub hooks to give the fly a nice curve to the body.

On Rutland and Draycote I have found that a Dark Olive or hackled midge pattern for top dropper, a Grey Midge for middle dropper and either a Pheasant Tail, Hare's Ear or a Diawl Bach for point make an excellent combination.

A hackle fly for the top dropper can either represent a drowned adult or an ascending pupa, fished with a straight-shanked nymph on the point and a standard pupa on the middle dropper gives a balanced team. This type of leader set-up will tell you a lot about the whereabouts of fish because these imitative flies will always take the odd trout, even if they are preoccupied on a particular colour or stage of the insect's cycle.

Fly Colour

Colour preoccupation feeding is rare in the early part of the season. Generally, you will find that several species of midge pupae are ascending at the same time and if you spoon any of the trout you kill, the stomach contents will confirm this. In most cases the spooned contents of the trout's stomach will contain a variety of midge species of different colour and size and daphnia. This proves that the trout are feeding hard on just about anything that is available to them – and in the cold waters of spring the greatest concentrations of food items that are most freely available to the trout, will be chironomids and daphnia.

Some anglers may find that certain colours work better than others, but this I feel is down to personal confidence in the fly, more than a colour preference exhibited by the fish. Very rarely will you find the trout interested only in a specific colour at this time of year. In cold water the trout are active and hungry, so provided your fly is suggestive of food and it is fished sensibly, that is all the fish require as an inducement to take.

Later in the season when large hatches of the olive, ginger or red midges come off, colour preoccupation feeding can be more of a problem. Therefore later in the season it may be necessary to fish a wider range of fly patterns in size and colour to cover all eventualities. But for the early spring fishing a limited number of proven fish takers in several sizes will suffice.

Because the trout feed on all stages of the chironomids cycle, I tie my midge patterns of the same colour without either a hackle or a wing; with a wing; and with both a wing and a hackle in different sizes. This allows me to offer the trout a midge pattern tied to represent the different stages in the hatching cycle. So if one of the flies on my leader is taken in preference to the other patterns and it has nothing to do with the position on the leader, I would obviously change the fly or flies which are not catching to a pattern which is similar to the successful fly.

For instance, when you are fishing sub-surface, the white wing on the winged midge can prove a great attractor, pulling fish to that fly, which is often taken in preference to the standard pattern of the same colour.

Hackled Patterns

Again, when trout are rising or moving just below the surface, the hackled patterns will out-perform the winged or the standard tyings. They hold up better and therefore give a much more realistic presentation, with their slow descent. The dry fly has now largely replaced the position of the hackled flies when trout are rising but I still use the hackled patterns if the trout want the fly just below the surface, or on the drop where they can be deadly. This is a mode of presentation often overlooked for wild brown trout that appear to be rising to surface fly but are in fact taking pupae just below the surface film.

Once trout have been located, take careful note of how the fish are responding to the flies you are using, and then fine-tune your leader set-up to increase the catch rate.

The basics of imitative nymph fishing are straight-forward. Providing colour and profile are a reasonable representation of the flies that are hatching, the rest is down to the angler.

I use the hackled patterns if the trout want the fly just below the surface, or on the drop where they can be deadly

MID-SEASON RESERVOIR FISHING

With warmer weather and higher water temperatures, a mobile approach from a drifting boat becomes more effective. As the season progresses from late spring to mid-summer, we have the cream of top-water sport. Now is your best opportunity to catch acclimatised or over-wintered trout using floating line tactics.

Avoiding Recently-Stocked Fish

Knowledge of the areas frequented by the better quality trout is essential if you wish to avoid recently stocked fish. These areas on popular reservoirs are often well known, and rarely change from season to season. However, there can be exceptions and it pays to be open minded if you want to catch the bigger fish. Always be prepared to adopt a flexible approach to the areas you fish.

Even on smaller reservoirs, there are locations that consistently produce better-than-average trout, but then for no reason at all will come a season when one or more of the known spots fail to produce. I have found this when the wind settles into a certain quarter during the early spring. If it remains blowing in one direction for any length of time, it can have an effect on the movement of the fish, and a big stock of trout can build up and remain where they found a concentration of food.

Once an area holding quality trout has been located, it is then a matter of focusing on them, even if the fishing is slow. You cannot target one of the bigger trout with any certainty, unless they are rising, but you can improve your chances by fishing drifts that are frequented by the quality fish.

Even on what appears to be a featureless expanse of water, good watercraft is essential, and intuitive anglers with the ability to 'read the water' will instinctively find those places that are so attractive to big grown-on over-wintered trout. By taking note and recording all the locations where good fish are caught, a pattern will emerge and spots that consistently produce the bigger fish will become noticeable.

Although the choice of drifts will change with the seasons, our spring and early summer drifts are generally over shallow water. This has the added advantage of the trout responding to top-water methods, for they will invariably see the flies, even if they are feeding hard on the bottom. I have, on rare occasions, seen browns which were cruising just over the bed of the lake, feeding hard on hoglouse or snail, rise up from quite a depth to take a fly. It can be a little disconcerting at first, drifting over shallow, clear water, particularly when the bed of the lake is visible and there are no obvious signs of trout to maintain one's confidence. In such situations, it can be difficult not to let the concentration slip.

Clear, Shallow Water

When fishing over clear, shallow water it is reasonable to assume that if trout were present, you would see them. However, this is not the case. You are looking ahead to the area your flies are fishing, or scanning the water for a rising fish, and only very rarely will you spot a trout ghosting through the water. I have seen trout lift to take my flies when I have been fishing on or near the surface many times, but very rarely have I seen these fish before they have moved up under the fly to take it.

On a bright day if you look down into the water, you may see fish, but then your vision is not obscured by the angle of refraction as it is when you are scanning forward. Even if the water appears empty, be assured if you have done your homework right, the trout will be there.

Although the action can be fast and furious, it very rarely lasts for long

When fishing a shallow drift where the fish lie close to underwater features, do not expect an inexhaustible supply of big trout to queue up to take your flies. Although the action can be fast and furious, it very rarely lasts for long, because it is impossible to avoid disturbing the area once a good fish has been hooked. Occasionally you can ease them out without causing too much disturbance, but more often than not they explode on feeling the hook, careering about the hot spot. The effect on the other fish of a good trout thrashing around in a confined space is obvious, and the drift that at first proved productive very quickly dries up.

This is when it pays to know of a number of such areas, so that you can move onto fresh undisturbed ground once you have taken a fish or two, and the fishing slows. There is nothing to be gained by fishing over trout that have been disturbed and are ignoring your flies – that will simply put the trout down for longer.

There is much to be gained by resting the disturbed area and returning later. The secret is knowing when it is best to move before overplaying a spot. Move too early and you could miss out on extra fish, leave it too long and you end up spooking the fish to such an extent that you put them down for the rest of the day.

Even when I have located good trout over open water, I have seen them quickly put down by too much boat traffic moving over their heads. Stock fish will tolerate a certain amount of disturbance, but mature stock or wild trout are easily put down by over-fishing. When you drift over a good area, the first or second drift is most often the one that produces the best fish of the day. If you want to catch the bigger trout, concentrate on undisturbed water where you know good fish are present, and move on once you feel you have given them a fair trial.

IMITATIVE TACTICS

From a drifting boat my approach to catching the better quality fish with imitative tactics would be one of three methods:
   a) deep sunk nymph
   b) surface or just sub-surface nymph
   c) dry fly
Prevailing conditions and the mood of the fish on the day, would determine which of these methods would suit. Ideally I love to see trout moving, so that I can use the surface nymph or dry fly and, with a little luck, target individual fish.

However, we are not always blessed with ideal conditions and failing any obvious signs of surface movement, we must either assume the fish are well

down or they are just sub-surface but are not showing themselves.

If the trout are well down then we have to get our nymphs down to their level where they are feeding. To fish deep nymph from a drifting boat (unless you are fishing in very light winds) it will be necessary to slow down the boat's rate of drift and cast a long line. So for deep fishing and slow presentations a drogue is essential. When there is no surface movement to indicate the whereabouts of the quarry, anglers have to decide whether they are over fish or if their flies are at the right depth. Having selected your drift, my advice is: always assume you are over fish, then you will have the confidence to find them by fishing the water correctly.

There is nothing to be gained by fishing over trout that have been disturbed and are ignoring your flies

Biggest Mistake

The biggest mistake anglers make when they are fishing at depth is that they fail to feel their way down through the water, maintaining contact with their flies all the time. They make a cast and just let the flies sink. Then when they begin a retrieve, they feel they have no contact or sense of what depth level they are fishing. When they start retrieving, many fail to take in all the slack that has built up and they also fail to compensate for the drifting speed of the boat. There is so much slack and belly in the line that control of the flies has been lost and the files will not be fishing properly. They won't appear attractive to the fish.

For those who can't see the problem, I recommend an experiment with a floating line and a large dry fly. Make a long cast downwind from the boat and do nothing. Because the line and the fly are on the surface, you can see everything that is happening and this will give you a good idea of what happens to your line when the line is sunk. The line gathers as the boat drifts down towards the fly and the faster the boat is drifting, the more the problem is compounded.

This problem of the line gathering is exaggerated the longer you leave the line before starting the retrieve. To gain contact with the fly you then have to haul line quickly and take in all the slack until contact is established, by which time half the retrieve could have been wasted. More importantly if you had been fishing with nymphs you would have missed the chance to take fish on the drop or through the curve which forms as the boat drifts down on to the flies. The only effective part of the retrieve you have left is the lift, which many perform too quickly to attract and more importantly, deceive, fish. In short, from a fish-catching point of view, if you don't deal with the slack, you have wasted the cast.

To overcome this problem of the line gathering, start retrieving your line from the moment the flies have settled on the surface. If your retrieve speed matches the speed of the drifting boat, you'll keep the line straight without moving the fly.

Increase your line recovery speed, and you will notice that you impart movement to the fly: this is what you are trying to emulate when fishing sunk line or deep nymph on a floating line. If performed correctly, the descent of your flies will be controlled and if a trout does take, you will detect a movement of the line or it will be felt in the hand. Your aim is to maintain contact throughout the retrieve, via a straight line.

Once the flies have reached the desired depth you can impart movement to the flies but this only requires a slight adjustment to your retrieving speed: the object is to move the flies as slowly as possible.

IN SEARCH OF THE TAKING POINT

Watch out for the number of takes you get at each of the three stages shown in the box below. If you are observant, you will detect that the fish very often prefer to take at a particular point during the retrieve. They are giving you a clear message.

Concentrate on this stage of the retrieve, to improve the catch rate.

• Sometimes they prefer to take on the drop, which means the trout are in the mood for a falling fly. If so, fish with unweighted patterns, lighter wire hooks including the point fly, or standard nylon leaders. This will slow the descent down, producing a longer, more attractive fall through the water. Long steady draws on the line, or the feeling of increasing weight as a fish moves off with your fly as it is falling, are indicative of trout taking on the drop.

• Fish which take during the movement stage, or through the curve, are felt as much sharper pulls – very often they will make several attempts to take the fly, which will be felt as a series of quick pulls or nips, before you receive a solid take. The takes

If you achieve the following, then your flies will be fishing all the time, producing three stages that are each attractive to the trout:

• Firstly, the controlled descent, which may induce a take on the drop.

• Secondly, if you have maintained close contact with your flies, and given them a suggestion of life by the retrieve, they will have fished through an attractive curve which builds up speed as the boat drifts down onto them.

• Thirdly, we have the lift which, when controlled, can induce those trout which have been following the flies; or it may attract fish which are lying higher in the water, so that they take the flies as they are lifted up.

A happy conclusion to my day at Draycote: 5lb of perfect reservoir brown trout.

are sharper and more distinct through the curve, because the line is under greater tension between you and the fly, and you feel the weight of the fish more quickly compared with that dragging increase of weight when a trout takes on the drop. When trout take consistently in the second stage, you want to get your flies down to them as quickly as possible. A switch to a leaded fly or a heavier fly on the point, fluorocarbon leader if you are fishing standard nylon, or a faster sinking line, could improve your catch rate. It is important to fish your flies in the holding zone for as long as possible to give your imitations a greater chance of being taken by the trout, so do not be over-zealous and use too fast a sinking line, causing your flies to sink through the fish. The aim with

all these presentations is to maximise the length of time your flies are fishing through the productive stage.

• The lift can be the most deadly stage of the retrieve, but arguably one of the most difficult to perfect. By raising your rod arm and continuing the retrieve, you accelerate the flies towards the surface. This lift is attractive to fish, and should be made as slowly as possible. With imitative flies, you will be amazed how slow you can make this lift, and still deceive trout. Even when the flies are in the shadows of the gunwale of the boat, they will still take fish if the lift is maintained. An attractor fished on the top dropper can pull fish into the area of your leader, and then you deceive the fish with one of the nymph patterns that are following behind. Interesting fish in my flies at this stage isn't such a problem, but getting them to take can be. On some days, especially those with a hint of sun, you may notice the flanks of trout flashing as the fish turn over, attracted to the flies lifting from the depths below the boat, but deciding not to take. If you encounter this sort of behaviour, then it becomes a test of whether you can sort out a winning formula. You know fish are following your imitations, but they are refusing to take. So change your flies. Minor adjustments such as changing the pattern of fly, or going down in size may be all that is required to encourage the trout to take.

When fish take on the lift, do not expect confident pulls. Watch the line and leader closely once you begin lifting, and strike at the slightest unnatural movement of either line or leader. If you wait for the pull, you will miss out on a lot of fish during this stage of the retrieve.

Finding the holding depth of trout is the fisherman's biggest challenge

Finding the correct holding depth of trout feeding sub-surface is one of the biggest problems fly fishermen encounter, particularly novices who struggle to locate fish that are not showing themselves. They struggle, not because they choose the wrong locations:

they could be over numerous trout and still catch very few. They struggle because they do not intuitively present their flies at the depth at which the majority of fish are holding.

Actively feeding trout at this time of year, spring to early summer, will be gorging on buzzer and daphnia. So we should be concentrating all our fishing effort in the zones where the food is packed, which is in water between 4 and 12 feet deep. Even if the trout are feeding on daphnia in deep reservoirs or loughs, very rarely will you find them below 12 feet, unless the weather remains warm and bright.

Assuming that our fish are between the surface and 12 feet, somewhere in that 12 feet of water will be a depth band of 2-3 feet that will produce more trout than all the remainder put together. Find that depth band, and your catch rate will improve.

This is where breaking the retrieve down into three stages: drop, curve and lift can prove so informative. Note at which stage of the retrieve the most takes occur, and you will acquire a feel for the depth at which the fish are lying. For example trout that take on the drop or the lift, but fail to respond during the movement or through the curve stage ie. through the majority of the retrieve, suggest to me that the flies are below the fish.

To test this theory, try a few casts either fishing the flies higher in the water by starting the retrieve earlier, or change to lighter flies and note the response. If you start getting more takes, this confirms that the fish are higher in the water, so continue with the new method. But if very few takes are forthcoming at either the drop or the lift stages, but only on the pull through, this information would suggest to me that the fish are deep down in the water. Certainly they are not in the upper layers.

This indicates a need to keep the flies down, and to get them down quicker, by either fishing heavier flies or by changing to a higher density line. But remember, try not to let your flies sink below the trout. You have a better chance of a fish taking a fly which is three feet above the trout, than three feet below.

Homeward bound after a good day on Farmoor.

HIGH SUMMER ON THE RESERVOIR

As the season progresses, surface or near-surface fishing from a drifting boat will become more productive. The evening rise will become a feature too, so if you live close to a good water, a few hours in the evenings can produce superb top-water fishing where you can target individual rising fish.

If trout are showing on the surface, the dry fly in one form or another is usually the most effective method. But if the fish show a preference for sub-surface fly, I'll fish nymphs either just below the surface or pulled with long steady draws. Fishing short evening sessions has taught me much about fishing to rising trout, and how one needs to be flexible to match the mood of the fish.

Rising Trout

When fishing to rising trout, you know where the fish are, perhaps even the whereabouts of an individual trout. So, assuming that you are covering the rise, and you are not catching, you are doing something wrong! Change the fly or the presentation. Evening sessions are short; they teach you to act quickly, or you run out of time. Get it right and you will catch a lot of trout in a short space of time.

Do nothing, and the bag will be light or empty. Change the colour of the flies, the size or the way the flies fish on, in, or just below the surface film. Frustrating as it can be at times, this sort of fishing is a great education, and what you learn while fishing the evening rise, you can apply to day-time rises in much the same way.

Given enough experience, you will recognise certain rise forms and know intuitively what to do when you see trout behaving in a similar way again. If you live close to a good water, and lack confidence or the experience when dealing with rising fish then I would suggest you give short evening sessions a try. Go with the intention of fishing to rising trout only and start your session about an hour before sunset. This will give you about two hours against the clock: great fun, and it will sharpen your mind and your technique.

I always try to keep my ranges of flies as narrow as possible. This helps me to concentrate on the impor-

tant factors for catching fish. For top water fishing I carry a range of:

- Bits patterns of different colours and size to fish the surface film.
- Klinkhamer-style parachute patterns to suspend in the surface film.
- Hackled buzzer patterns to fish high in the water or on the drop.
- Standard buzzer nymph patterns to go deeper.
- Pheasant Tail nymphs and Hare's Ear for good surface-film penetration, and to fish still lower in the water, when the need arises.

I carry these flies in three sizes 10, 12 and 14. Size 12 would be my first choice, then size 10 and size 14, or smaller for the rare occasions when I do have to go down in size. Particularly on dry fly, anglers can struggle to catch and become obsessed with the idea that they either need to change fly pattern, go down in size or fish a finer leader, when none of these changes is necessary.

For rising fish, the two most important factors are presentation and colour, in that order. Hook or fly size are less important factors

I have proved to my own satisfaction time and again that hook and fly size are not important, even when trout are preoccupied on an abundance of tiny fly such as Caenis, and I have caught fish on size 12 or size 14 flies; both imitations that are much larger than the natural.

When fishing dry fly, I very often find that a size 12 Bits will do the damage, providing the way the fly is presented and the colour is to the trout's liking. Keep it simple. In the long run, unnecessary changes will only cost you time and fish.

If the fish want a fly that is hanging through the film, I much prefer the Klinkhamer or parachute flies to the cul-de-canard patterns, although the latter

Caught in late June, this 5 lb Draycote brown trout shows the beginnings of a kype, the slight hook on the extended lower jaw, and the hallmark of a male fish.

are easier to tie. But they are far more trouble when it comes to fishing them. When trout are rising, and I find a pattern that is working, I want to be out fishing again straightaway following the capture of a fish. With the cul-de-cunard patterns, this isn't possible, as you need to clean and dry off the fly before fishing again. In fact, I have found it quicker to snip off the bedraggled cul-de-canard fly that has just caught me a fish and tie on another of the same pattern, whereas with the parachute dressing and the Bits patterns, I simply dip the fly into the water and squeeze it dry. I'm back in business in a matter of seconds! If I'm catching trout quickly, I rarely find the need to reapply floatant to my flies. In fact, I am certain the trout find flies more attractive when they are sitting well down in the water.

DRY FLY ON THE RESERVOIR

Dry fly has now taken over from a lot of the surface tactics, particularly for the more educated trout. The method is simplicity itself, so why over-complicate it? If trout are rising, you have identified the area you are going to fish, and therefore have none of the vagaries of depth, or speed of retrieve to contend with. In fact, dry fly has to be one of the simplest forms of fishing, even if the purists do not like to admit it! All you have to sort out is the colour and how the fish want the fly presented. Do they want the fly on, in, hanging through or just below the surface?

Forget about exact imitation and the size of the food the fish are feeding on: concentrate on the mode of presentation. Fish obviously do not see our artificial flies as we see them. If they did, they would never fall for the deception. So long as our imitation initiates certain triggers, then a confident, feeding fish will take it. With educated trout it can be more difficult to trigger a positive feeding response because these fish may have been conditioned into refusing the presentations that we make with our artificial flies.

If you find that a certain colour is attracting fish but they are refusing to bite, change the fly size, and if that doesn't work go down in leader diameter

If the fish are repeatedly refusing your flies, you have obviously got to make changes if you want to catch them, or move on to easier game. Given time, you will come up with a winning combination if you take the logical steps.

When trout are attracted to, but refusing to take a fly of a certain colour, I would be surprised if the presentation isn't at fault, but if we are confident that the mode of presentation is correct, then going down in fly size or changing to a finer leader diameter or both should do the trick. If this doesn't work, I would definitely move to another area, unless some minor tactic like moving the fly may bring about the desired response. This should only take a few casts to establish.

No Signs of Moving Fish

For fishing blind or searching the water when there are no obvious signs of moving fish, we can adopt a more general approach, and fish a combination of different size and pattern of fly on the same leader to search out taking fish. What I do look out for when fishing blind are feeding preferences. Why continue fishing with three different patterns if one type is pulling more fish? I know anglers who will persist with a leader set-up and make no changes, if one of the flies is catching. If they are getting some success they seem quite content to leave it this way, but if I were pulling fish to a particular fly I would certainly change one of the other patterns, if not both, to see if this would improve my catch rate.

But beware: for I have on occasions found that by changing flies I have undermined the successful pattern. It would seem, in these cases, that although the flies I changed were not taking fish, one of them was certainly attracting fish towards the successful fly.

Strong Summer Winds

I like my flies to sit well down in the water as I feel this induces confident rises. But there is one weather condition where a high riding fly can prove more productive: strong winds. For some reason, a fly that sits well up in the water on a big wave can prove more attractive to the trout than a fly of similar colour and size that is sitting well down in the film.

Why this should be I have no idea but I fancy that the rough conditions impart some subtle movement to the high riding fly without sinking it and this triggers the take. When fish start coming short, it is normally indicative of a slackening in the wind strength. If this happens, I would simply switch to flies that sit well down in the water.

Reservoir rainbows are far more predictable than the wild browns on the larger lakes. Find the right formula with rainbows during a daytime feeding spell and you would expect to make far fewer changes until they go off the feed, whereas with the browns a pattern of feeding may only last a short time before they alter their feeding behaviour completely.

Subtle changes in the weather can affect the way fish rise; certainly a slight increase in wind strength or change of wind direction will put surface-feeding wild brown trout down. There are more changes of weather on the large lakes of Ireland than ever experienced on an English reservoir. But, even on a reservoir such as Draycote, which is about as far inland as you can get, it is surprising how many times in a day the weather changes. Rainbows may go down for a short time following a weather change, but they quickly adjust to the new wind direction and commence feeding again, albeit on a different line! The brown trout, however, very often go down, and stay down unless the wind falls off with the change of wind direction.

A slight increase in wind strength or change of wind direction will put surface-feeding wild brown trout down

No Drogue for Gentle Winds

I rarely use a drogue when fishing the surface in light winds, because I want to cover the drift quickly and reduce the disturbance to the productive area as much as possible. For me, a boat moving freely over rising trout will disturb them less than a slow moving boat with a drogue, particularly in shallow water. Re-fish the drift until the fishing slows, then move on.

With educated fish that are close to shallows or weed beds, you may get two of three drifts before they go down and melt away. Remember those first drifts are likely to be the most productive. Mature stock will not tolerate too much disturbance. If these are your target fish, then go with the intention of catching them. Start fishing with a purpose.

LATE SEASON ON THE RESERVOIR

September and October can be indifferent months. It's a time of year that promises much but can fall flat. A good back-end on the reservoirs is dependent on weather conditions, the density of the remaining stock and how well they have fared throughout the season. But the big autumn trout are out there.

Every season we read reports of big trout that have been taken from various waters – but this doesn't apply to every fishery and it certainly doesn't apply to the majority of anglers fishing for such trout. Yes, it is a period when the big fish become more active, but we are fishing for very difficult trout and we should adjust our level of expectation accordingly. Autumn is never as consistent as the late spring to early summer fishing.

Target the Margins

My approach for late season fish (and I have been fortunate enough to take some large ones) would be to fish the features and the margins, particularly along the edge of weed beds. The fish by this time are well-educated, so we have to consider our tactics very carefully. Also the bigger trout will be in tip top condition and close to snaggy areas. So it is advisable to use stronger than normal leaders to avoid unnecessary breakages. .230mm to .260mm in fluorocarbon or copolymer is what I would recommend.

Disguise the Stronger Leader

The stronger leader does however present a problem in terms of presentation. These fish will have seen plenty of anglers' flies and the slightest flaw will make them suspicious so the heavier line is an obvious disadvantage. We have to make allowances for this. If we present our imitations close to features or along the edge of weed beds, the trout are more confident and willing to take. On occasion the weed beds or such features such as dam walls or towers can be used to disguise the leader, even if we are using stronger monofilament.

Many times I have taken difficult trout by laying my leader on top of a weed bed and suspending my imitation over the edge of the weeds. I have also done this with floating fry on numerous occasions.

If you want to target one of the bigger trout, forget the open water nymph and dry fly tactics which we used earlier in the season. Most of the better fish will by autumn have vacated these areas, and moved inshore, driven by their hormonal changes and a desire for food.

Tactics should be determined by the food on which the trout are feeding. Shallows, weedbeds, the sides of dam walls or towers are food havens for small invertebrates on which trout feed.

Trout on the Fry

However, the one food item that will be high on the list if available are fish fry. Some reservoirs are more prone to fry feeding, and some years are better than others. For example Rutland, Grafham and Draycote produce excellent fry feeding. Farmoor can produce periods of fry feeding, particularly to sticklebacks. Chew never seems to be quite as consistent, but occasionally there is a proliferation of end-of-season fry feeding. These five reservoirs have all provided good autumn days and if one of them was fishing well, I would tend to concentrate my efforts on that water. The fishery that has given me my best returns is Rutland and if this reservoir was fishing well, this would be the water that I would concentrate on most.

Tactics should be decided by the depth at which the fish are lying and the size of the prey food they are feeding on. Sometimes I have find floating fry patterns to be deadly, although it can be difficult to hook the fish. My preference would be for the deer hair patterns over the foam bodied flies. I seem to get plenty of offers to the spun deer hair flies – just simple patterns in white or light brown.

When the trout are looking for food sub-surface, I fish a large nymph tied on a long shank hook suspended below a floating fry. Nymphs with some holographic or pearl tinsel in the dressing are ideal. This duel presentation can be very effective. The floating pattern not only acts as an indicator but can also take the fish which are looking up.

There are days, however, when a suspended pattern will not work; the fish require some movement to entice them to take, and it may be necessary to fish a fry pattern with some soft mobile hair in the dressing. Minkies or patterns incorporating rabbit fur or marabou in the dressing, fished on an intermediate line can prove very attractive to the trout.

It isn't necessary to rip the fly back. In fact, I have never found a fast retrieve very successful when fishing these patterns to trout that are moving to fry. If I were fishing a water where fry feeding is evident, I would be surprised if one of the above methods didn't work.

Last Resort Tactics

As a last resort, I might consider fishing a buoyant pattern on a very fast-sinking line to a feature at depth. This isn't a method I like fishing but if the conditions or the fish demand it, then I will use it. On Rutland, Draycote and Farmoor I have taken some very good trout using this method, fish that I would never have taken had I persevered with a floating or intermediate line. At the end of the season, it certainly pays to be flexible and fish with an open mind.

Avoid the Empty Waters

Fishing short drifts in productive areas or anchoring close to a feature would be preferable to making longer drifts over featureless open water. Do not waste time fishing over empty water. Try to learn the hot spot areas and be prepared to move if the trout are not responding. Trout which are feeding on fry very often betray their presence so if there are no visual signs of fish feeding and no takes are forthcoming, move.

Keep Moving

So if you find a productive area and start catching fish, do not be surprised if it just as quickly dries up. By autumn the larger fish are now pretty wary. They feed for shorter periods and some of these feeding spells can be intense. But catch a fish or two and they can just as quickly go down or move away.

The temptation is to linger in the hope that the fish will return. Sometimes they do but if there are no signs of activity or a recommencement of feeding following a short blank spell, I would recommend you try another area.

The Earlier the Better

Dawn and dusk are the main feeding periods. Of the two, dawn is in my opinion the best, but unfortunately on the public reservoirs, boats at dawn are not allowed. If the bigger trout are your target, go out as early as the fishery will allow. The fish will not have been spooked by other anglers, so there is every chance that they will still be confidently feeding when you arrive at your chosen spot. With luck you may take one or two of the better fish before they go down. Very often my biggest trout are among the first few fish I capture from a chosen area. Avoid making unnecessary noises in the boat and disturbing the area with clumsy boat craft. Present your flies without the fish detecting your presence, and you have a good opportunity of taking some of the better class of trout that many anglers dream of, but very few succeed in catching.

RESERVOIR FISHING: AN EDUCATION

Fishing the reservoirs has been an education to me over the years and I have learnt much about the way stillwater trout respond to different presentations.

Because of the healthy stock densities on most reservoir fisheries, the fishing is more predictable and this gives one the added confidence to experiment, to try new ideas.

Without this reservoir experience, my wild fishing would have been less successful. As much as I enjoy flyfishing the rivers for trout and grayling, I never feel it is quite as challenging as fishing the big stillwaters. We all have personal preferences: mine is lake fishing for trout, and the reservoirs have fulfilled that need for over thirty years. In that time the fortunes of different reservoir fisheries have ebbed and flowed, but when they were good, the sport which they provided could not have been bettered!

81

PART THREE

Wild Fishing

CHAPTER 6

Salmon & Seatrout from a Boat

With the passing of the old year, I look for the early flushes of green among the hedgerows, where the hawthorn has broken bud. Certain hedgerows, particularly those on roadside verges, are always more advanced than the surrounding open country. Those early flushes of green herald for me the approach of a new game fishing year. Pockets of green in a sea of grey and rusty browns burst into life in the same sheltered areas every year. And even though I know these early flushes are premature, well before their growing season, I am always heartened to see them.

Time to check rods, to look in my tackle bag lying neglected since the previous season (where I left it after the last day's fishing). Reels require cleaning, and worn lines replacing. Before making that first fishing trip of a new season, it is advisable to check the contents of one's bag, and to make a list of the items required for the coming season, leaving nothing to chance. Once the bag had been checked, and worn items either rectified or replaced, I then sort through my fly boxes in readiness to start fly tying.

There was a time when I would have tied flies all through the winter, but now with fly boxes full to overflowing, I find it far more satisfying to start tying flies early in the new year, as a build-up to the beginning of a new season. As the hazel catkins lengthen, my fly tying tools come in to play once more to replenish old stock, and perhaps tie up one or two new patterns. It is always interesting to see if a new tying will outperform tried and trusted flies with established form from seasons past.

I find a disciplined approach is required when it comes to deciding the number of flies actually needed for a season's fishing. A choice of too many flies can fuel indecisive actions on the tough days, when, more often than not, the solution doesn't lie in the fly box.

Firstly, I replace patterns that I know work, and once this has been achieved, I then begin tying the new flies: patterns passed on by friends; patterns I have read about in the press; or new creations of my own, based on observations made over the previous season.

The new patterns are all given an opportunity to prove their worth: the successful ones I keep, and the failures are eliminated. If a new fly proves successful, I then decide whether it will replace an existing pattern within the box, because it offers advantages over the older fly, or I add the new pattern to the number of flies that I already carry.

Certain fly patterns breed confidence, and during a fishing season, cyclical hatches of fly, proliferations of fry or daphnia, will always repeat themselves and the flies that worked one season will catch fish in the next when a similar feeding period reoccurs. It stands to reason that flies which were once successful do not suddenly become obsolete overnight.

But we change. We become more confident with the new patterns, and so the older flies are used less and consequently catch fewer fish. Eventually we lose confidence in them, and therefore do not fish as effectively, even when we do give them a try. When we reach a situation such as this, it is best to discard the older pattern, for it has already been replaced in our own minds by the newer dressing, the pattern you now have most confidence in. My aim is to keep the range of flies that I carry as narrow as possible. However, if a new pattern doesn't conflict with any of the existing flies in my fly boxes, I add it to the range. But I am disciplined about new additions.

Time for a break and a brew up of the kelly kettle at Goreport, Lough Carrowmore.

CARROWMORE

With all the flies tied, and necessary preparations complete including an inspection of the lifejacket, the desire to go fishing burns fiercely. Where should you begin a season of wild lake fishing?

I prefer fishing for brown trout, but I also enjoy fishing for salmon, particularly early spring salmon – so I mix my early fishing between the two species.

It is increasingly difficult to find a good water where there is a realistic chance of catching a springer. However, even though the probability of catching a spring salmon, is now much slimmer than it once was, and despite the fact that the duck fly season for brown trout may be well on, I still like to try a few days in pursuit of that elusive early springer.

One is in with a very good chance of an early fish on the Bangor Erris system, comprising Lough Carrowmore and the River Owenmore in north

Remember although the spring salmon are not numerous, in the cold waters of early spring they do take freely

84

west Mayo, on the west coast of Ireland. Prodigious numbers of salmon run this system, which is basically a late spring-summer fishery and although I have taken spring fish from the river, the lough is a much better bet for a springer.

One of the most consistent fisheries for migratory fish that I have ever fished, given fair conditions, is Carrowmore, for spring salmon. Here one can fish with confidence that there are salmon in the system, maintaining the positive attitude so necessary for spring salmon fishing. Remember, although the spring salmon are not numerous, in the cold waters of early spring they do take freely, so try to avoid negative thoughts, fish hard and keep concentrating!

Spring Salmon & Seatrout

Fish entering this system come in through Blacksod Bay and then into Tullaghan Bay, where the rivers Owenduff and the Owenmore discharge their waters. Salmon and seatrout which enter the Owenmore then either remain in the river or run the main tributary, the Munhin river, which is the outflow from Carrowmore lough. The majority of spring salmon and seatrout will run into the lough, where they remain until the spawning season. They then enter the small feeder rivers Glencullin, Bellanaboy or Glenturk to spawn in the headwaters.

Carrowmore lough is a big water approximately 4 miles in length, lying in open moorland with a range of hills, Knocknascollop and Derreens, lying to the west. This is a lovely lough to fish, but the beauty of Carrowmore does not lie solely in the topography of remote moorland: this is a flyfishing paradise, vast tracts of shallow water with a gravel or sandy bottom. It is these extensive tracts of shallow water that make the fish in Carrowmore so free-rising.

The only drawback with all the shallow water is that, in a strong wind, the lough will colour up which has a detrimental effect on the fishing. Ideally you want a period of settled weather when fishing Carrowmore: periods of light-to-moderate winds are far preferable to one of virtual gale, so beloved of many traditional lake anglers fishing for salmon.

The fishing on the lough, and a good length of the Owenmore river containing 17 pools, is controlled by Bangor Erris club, and access is gained through Seamus Henry at the West End Bar in Bangor Erris.

Seamus will take bookings, advise on what fishing is available, and organise a boatman if required. If you haven't fished the lough before, I would suggest that you take advantage of this facility. Until familiar with the lough, a boatman can shorten your learning curve, and show you the productive drifts. This will avoid wasting time fishing unproductive water and is a safe way of gaining knowledge of an unfamiliar water.

Huge Stock of Fish

Although Carrowmore is a relatively safe lough, being close to the sea it can blow up quickly and the shallows where you might ground a boat are not easily seen, owing to the dark nature of the bottom. The river is an easier water to read and the pools are well defined. So a visiting rod would quickly come to terms with the Owenmore river, which although not a prolific spring fishery, can from June and July hold a huge stock of fish. You would be unlucky if you did not come off with a fish or two if you spent a few days on the river during the summer in the right conditions. But during the early part of the year I would concentrate more on the lough.

A boatman can shorten your learning curve, and show you the productive drifts

The Sign of the Gorse

The gorse is well in bloom and the shores of Carrowmore a sea of yellow when I take a boat for the first time from the moorings at Bog Bay or Gortmore. Gorse is for me the flower of spring fishing, for both salmon and brown trout. Primroses, cowslips, the bluebell will all play their part in spring's tapestry of colour but so long as the striking yellow of the gorse flower litters the shores of the Irish loughs, we will have good fishing. As the flowers fade towards the end of May, so too does the best of the brown trout fishing and although there are the summer runs of salmon to look forward to, along with the summer and the back-end for the brown trout, I cannot help feeling that the best fishing season of the year is behind me.

TACKLE FOR LOUGH SALMON IN THE SPRING

The rods and lines used for traditional wet fly fishing for trout are perfectly suitable for lough salmon. We are not expecting really large fish although there may be the occasional exception! Flies are similar to those used for brown trout, but a little larger and heavier.

Rods & Lines

Fishing traditional wet fly methods are best: short lining and working the bob fly, and I prefer the longer 11ft or 10ft 6ins rods. I find the slower through-actions of these longer rods lend themselves to this style of fishing better than the faster, shorter rods. For trout and summer salmon I prefer a #6 weight outfit and although this will cope adequately with the spring fishing, a #7 weight outfit is preferable. Although only one weight heavier, the fly line, even in a strong wind, will turn over the size range of flies in use even when fishing a heavy double on the point to hold the flies down. The heavier #7 weight provides a better balance too when fishing the larger flies and stronger leaders.

As to fly lines, a floating, sink-tip and an intermediate line are the flylines I prefer for lough salmon fishing and more often than not I will fish the floater. The only time that I feel the intermediate offers an advantage are on days of light wind when it is advisable to keep line wake to a minimum; or in very windy conditions where the denser line gives greater control.

On the few occasions when I want to fish my flies deeper, I will give the sink-tip an airing. For leaders I prefer a standard nylon to fluorocarbon or copolymer. There was a time when I thought that finer leaders offered an advantage when after salmon, just as I do when fishing for trout, but now I do not feel that they are essential, particularly with spring fish which are very free-taking. We should remember that we are not fishing for stale or potted salmon in low

The author and Stuart McTeare take a lunch break on Carrowmore with the hill of Derreen in the background.

river conditions and the higher water temperatures of summer. The fish we are seeking are fresh salmon in low water temperatures. If the fly is presented right and a fish sees it, then there is a very good chance that the salmon will take it.

Finding the fish is the hardest bit. I don't feel at all disadvantaged fishing with 8-12lb .285-.320mm diameter standard nylon and now very often fish with 12lb nylon from preference which many might consider too coarse but I think the thicker nylon balances the flies better, takes the knocks which no matter how careful we are will happen when salmon fishing with the heavier flies and gives a comfortable feeling if we do hook a strong wild fish.

For Carrowmore I either fish two droppers about 4 to 5 feet apart or just a single dropper about 6 feet from the point on a leader approximately 16 feet in length. When fishing the larger fly patterns, particularly in a fresh wind with a good wave, I prefer the simpler two-fly leader and a double on the point, combined with a hackled pattern that possesses plenty of movement on the dropper – a good combination. When fishing over known lies in a good wind, I have taken many salmon working the bob fly on the two-fly set-up. A bob fly with a straggly shoulder hackle can work wonders if the fish are in the mood and I find control of the bob is much easier with just the two flies, particularly if the point fly has some weight to it, such as a double.

For much of my spring fishing, whether using a floater, sink-tip or an intermediate line, I fish a double on the point but if the day were soft with some warmth to it, I would use single-hook flies on a floating line.

As the season progresses and the water temperatures increase, I reduce the size of the flies but still fish a double on the point. As with all wet fly fishing, the presentation and the colour of the fly are the key factors to success and for lake salmon it is important that the fly has a good entry followed by a smooth draw through the curve, ending with a steady lift. These are the factors which will entice a fish to take. From the moment the cast is made, the fly should be fishing at all times. Depending on the mood of the fish and the depth at which they are lying, a take can come from any point in the retrieve. Active fish that are lying well up in the water or are on the fin will take just after the fly has hit the water or early in the retrieve, often appearing to take the moment the fly has landed. 'Contrary' salmon, that are in the mood to follow, occasionally take as the fly is fished through the curve, but in general they are poor takers, and prefer to follow and then turn away at the last moment. They seem interested but not enough to commit themselves.

The deeper-lying fish are the most difficult to tempt as they have taken up a lie, indicative that they have been in the lough longer and are thus less inclined to move – but a well-worked bob fly can entice them up. It is therefore important when fishing drifts over known lies that every part of the cast is fished out. You can bet money that if after several hours of diligent fishing you fail to maintain your concentration and, without thinking, lift off the flies to make another cast, that you will leave a hefty whorl in the area your flies had just left. I have seen this happen many times now, not only to myself but to companions who have been fishing with me. Fate can be unkind if you let your concentration drop.

Which Fly to Use

Choice of fly pattern is controversial but I do feel that many anglers put too much emphasis on this. It can start when an angler catches a fish on a certain fly. That fly then becomes sacrosanct. The angler firmly believes that the fish would only have taken this particular fly and he will fish with this pattern to the exclusion of all others – when in truth the salmon would have taken any number of flies.

Colour, followed by size is, I feel, important but the actual pattern isn't critical. For spring lough fishing I would be more than happy with a range of flies in four colours: yellow, black, claret and orange. Light green is another good colour for spring fish. On Carrowmore I would never be without a yellow fly on the middle dropper, a claret or black fly on the top dropper and an orange or a black fly on the point. At the start of the day it makes good sense to avoid duplication of colour. However, if a particular colour is pulling fish or one of the flies has already taken a salmon, then it may be worth dropping one of the flies that hasn't been successful and to fish two flies of the colour that is attracting the fish. Flies which I find successful for spring fish on lakes are Kate McClaren, Claret Bumble, Golden Olive, Beltra Badger, Black & Orange, Stoat's Tail and an orange shrimp pattern.

DRIFTS ON CARROWMORE

A day in early April, or even late March if conditions allow, is a good time to make a start for a spring fish. An ideal day would have a steady wind with light cloud cover and just a hint of warmth, sufficient to lift the coconut scent off the gorse bloom. Filled with anticipation, we tackle up with a floating line and a team of three flies: Claret Bumble on the top dropper, Golden Olive for middle position (both size 8) and a size 10 double shrimp pattern on the point.

If I go out from Bog Bay at the southern end of the lough I would always give this bay a drift before motoring up the lough to the more distant fishing grounds. But as local man John Cosgrove, a mine of information when it comes to fishing Carrowmore once said, he 'would never leave Bog Bay without at least giving it a try,' and I have found that to be very good advice. Once out of Bog Bay, my next drift would be off the Black Banks. Ideally to cover this drift properly, a wind with a lot of south or north in it is best, but no matter what direction the wind is blowing, this is another area well worth a cast. Paradise Bay is the next port of call. Following the Black Banks I would drift across the first southerly point leading into the bay and then on across the bay itself. This bay is a very productive piece of water and if you have never caught a salmon in paradise then there is a good chance that you may achieve just that on Carrowmore. A salmon could come from just about anywhere in this bay.

So try several drifts with in the bay and even across the back of the bay from just inside the weedbeds on the southerly shore and along the eastern shore. Even though the water in places may be no more than two feet deep, produces fish. Pass it up at your peril. My only advice for Paradise Bay would be to avoid the very shallow inshore water from about a third of the way in along the northern shoreline. The maxim here is to fish studiously and cover the water. I would be amazed if there isn't a taking salmon or two holding in Paradise most months of the year and by early April there will certainly be fresh salmon about and willing takers if you can find them.

Coming out of the bay, try a drift across the northern point of Paradise. This is good holding ground of submerged boulders interspersed with sand.

Stuart McTeare takes the bow as we drift across Carrowmore in search of salmon, with Clontakilla and Carrafull in the background.

Fish will hold either side of this point, depending on the wind direction. Try and cover both sides if you can and then push on northwards up the lake until you round a point, after which the lake cuts back towards Glencullin. This length of shoreline up to where the shoreline cuts in again towards the mouth of the Glencullin is an excellent drift, as is the sandy delta across the mouth of the Glencullin river up to the point where the shoreline cuts back to the Glenturk river. Try several drift lines from the point up to and across the mouth of the Glencullin river. The fish can lie well off shore from the river mouth.

From the point where the shore cuts back to the Glenturk river, there is a huge shallow bay stretching across to the Bellanaboy river. You would not be out of your depth in chest waders in this bay, even though you could be hundreds of yards off shore and again this can all be productive water.

A springer is the greatest prize in salmon fishing

The final area I would recommend is the northern shore from the pump house down to the Bellanaboy river, but I would be surprised, if you fish the water thoroughly, whether you have enough time in a fishing day to cover all this water. If this isn't enough, there are good drifts around the Derreen Islands and along the western shore from Gortmore. The eastern shore is more productive for salmon and this is where the bulk of the fish are taken. For consistency in good conditions, it pays to stick with the known lies, but if all else fails, one of the less popular areas could be worth a drift.

On a stormy April day of blustery south-west winds I once hooked a salmon off the western shore that runs from the outflowing Munchin river up to Gortmore, but the fish shed the hook. Now this is an area of the lough I wouldn't normally recommend, but on that day, restricted by the weather conditions, I gave it a try and lost a salmon. The reason I fished this shore was to gain some shelter from a very strong south-westerly wind and the water hadn't coloured up in this area. Although I have tried that drift several times since, I have never moved another salmon along that particular length of shore line.

I have had good catches from Carrowmore in both spring and summer and although there may be more fish around during the summer months, the days that stand out, days which I remember most are those of spring. A springer is the greatest prize in salmon fishing, a superb-looking fish in the very peak of condition and it comes at a lovely time of the year. What better way could there be than to start a wild fishing season with one of these elusive fish?

A MEMORABLE SPRING SALMON FISHING BREAK

On Carrowmore the holiday I remember most was in the year of the comet Hal Bop. We arrived at Bangor at the beginning of April and experienced wonderful spring weather. Not only did our holiday coincide with a settled spell of fine weather but there was also a good run of fresh fish into the lough. Anglers are sometimes too proud to admit that luck plays a major part in success or failure when salmon fishing. Providing you get the basics right and fish hard then there is no accounting for the way the spoils of fishing are sometimes divided and this particularly applies to salmon. On this holiday I had more than my fair share of luck with no accounting for it; one of those runs where you throw a six every time you pick up the dice.

We went out for a few hours on the first evening from Gortmore and as it was a short session with a light south westerly blowing, I motored straight down to Glencullin to try a drift across the subsidiary points before the bay and then into and across the river mouth. I was fishing with floating line, a Claret Bumble on the top dropper, Golden Olive on the middle dropper and a Stoat's Tail double on the point.

The drift along the first part of the shoreline across the points didn't produce an offer but as we rounded the last point, which is shallow and well off-shore, I pulled the boat into a drift across the river mouth. In a south-west wind this is a lovely drift as you fish across the bay with the sandy delta of the river mouth on your right-hand side.

Half way down I rose a fish to the Golden Olive, a nice slow leisurely roll but he missed the fly. I covered the water again but he didn't return. However no more than five or six casts later I pulled another salmon, this time to the Claret Bumble and there was no mistake as the fish went down with the fly and all went solid. I landed a typical Carrowmore springer, a fresh fish of

The ultimate prize from a day's hard fishing and hard sitting – a beautiful spring salmon from Carrowmore.

about 7½lbs covered with the veining marks of sea lice. Now whether this was the same salmon that had come to me a few casts earlier and had dropped further back than I thought, is difficult to say but I believe it was a different fish. Either way it was a fresh fish in the boat and it was nice to land a Spring salmon so early in the holiday after no more than a few hours' fishing.

Day Two

The following day we were out by mid-morning, the only time we tried to fish a full day during our stay and this was curtailed by the wind failing totally in the afternoon. I was fishing with two friends and as I had already taken a fish the previous evening, I took the middle seat. As Glencullin had already produced a salmon, we headed for the same area again, but drew a blank first time down.

Before starting the next drift I felt a change of point fly (a key position) was required. So I took off the Stoat's Tail on the point, as it hadn't moved a fish, and replaced it with a Black and Orange double. This time fishing across the points above the bay, a salmon came to the Black and Orange and took with a solid thump.

I had another fish similar to the one the previous evening, silver flanks reflecting subtle hints of lilac and blue and covered in sea lice. We drifted the same line again and another fish moved to the Golden Olive, coming up with a slow head and tail rise but didn't take. After further fishing of the lie, no offers were forthcoming so we continued on towards the Bellanaboy river mouth.

This is a long drift and in the light south-westerly wind took some time to cover, over water no more than 4 to 5 feet deep. A fish could hold anywhere here but we didn't move a salmon. As the wind was already failing we decided to go in for lunch to wait and see if conditions improved. The wind over lunch became even more flukey, so in the hope of finding a breeze, we decided to move back down the lake to give Paradise Bay a try. As this move would bring us closer to base, if the wind failed, we decided it would make sense to call it a day, as there is no point in flogging on in hopeless conditions. Paradise was flat, but there was a bit of a breeze on to the Black Banks.

So more in hope than from calculated reasoning, we decided to give the banks a drift, in the lightest of wind ripple. We covered the water as the boat slowly drifted towards the shore. Allowing for the conditions I let my flies sink deeper.

It really felt as if the fishing was over, as the light wind had died, but a salmon had other ideas. Just as I was lifting off, a salmon took the Golden Olive on my middle dropper and powered off out into the lough. This fish was an athlete and put up one hell of a fight, taking me at least 80 yards on two blistering runs.

It was one of the best fights I have ever had from a salmon. I have had fish fight for longer than this one but they have been fights of stubborn resistance on a much shorter line whereas this salmon ran and didn't stop running until we had him in the net.

It was a truly wild fish in every sense, around 10lbs, looking as only a fresh spring salmon can - a picture. A timely end to a productive but short day's fishing.

Day Three

The next day was another day of glorious spring weather, and we spent of our time on the Bellmullet Peninsula, an area still unspoilt by tourism today. On one of the storm beaches we found a dead seal and had the greatest shock of our lives when it began to move! Imagine our surprise, when from inside the carcass emerged an extremely rotund cat. The children thought this was hilarious, as it was the fattest cat we had ever seen. Obviously a feral cat, the animal had gorged on the rotten meat. You could hardly see its legs as the barrel of fur wobbled away into some nearby rocks.

On our return to Gortmore in the evening, a light blanket of cloud began to build over the lake and the sun was already low in the sky as a breeze picked up from the west. We probably had no more than an hour's fishing left in the day, but decided to chance it. As the Black Banks were no more than 10 minutes away we decided to give the banks what little time we had. We motored straight over and lined the boat up about 150 yards off shore to drift onto the banks in the west wind.

Half way down this drift came the most beautiful head and tail rise to the Golden Olive and all went solid as the tail of the fish disappeared. After a hard but more typical fight, with none of the long runs of the salmon the day before, I landed another fish of around 10lbs. We had been out no more than 25 to 30 minutes and I had another fish to the boat – what wonderful fishing.

Day Four

The following day was cloudless with a total lack of wind so we gave the fishing a miss. After this, fishing conditions improved a little, but the weather for the time of year remained warm and dry with light winds.

I caught another two salmon both from Paradise Bay, one a fish of 8½lbs on a Beltra Badger which, because the Golden Olive was working so well, I fished as a second yellow fly; and the other a salmon of 7lbs which took an orange shrimp pattern on the point. With the improving conditions Vaughan too got in on the act and took two fish of around 7½lbs and was unfortunate to lose two other salmon in play that

My friend Vaughan Lewis drifting the Carrowmore across the mouth of the Glenkullin River.

This 11 lb springer was caught at Black Banks on Lough Carrowmore.

appeared to be well hooked but which for no account-able reason slipped the hook. Vaughan's luck was out on this trip as the fish didn't come to him until late in the holiday, but then he did have his run of luck the year before on a spate river off the west coast of Scotland when he landed 10% of the season's total run in a few days. It was the year the runs crashed on this particular river as they did on migratory systems all over the west coast of Scotland. What I found so disappointing was that the river was in perfect trim for most of our stay, running full with good flows, ideal spate river condi-tions and yet the river felt empty: the salmon were just not there. A spate river without life.

Back on Carrowmore we had family to consider, so we fished short sessions, mornings or evenings only and apart from the second day, made no attempt to put in a full day. Considering the short amount of time we spent fishing, this was wonderful sport, with all salmon taken on a floating line and a trout rod. We were short-line fishing – no more than five or six steady pulls before the lift.

This was traditional lough fishing for salmon in the true sense, as those beautiful spring fish came up, rolled over, and sailed away with the flies.

If we had been fishing full-time, how many springers would we have caught? For the number of fish-to-rod effort, it was the best spring fishing I have ever experienced. There is the little question of luck. I caught two salmon, fishing between two good anglers who didn't move a fin.

Later I had five salmon in the boat before Vaughan hooked a fish and yet we were fishing similar flies and method. These runs of luck with salmon I have seen before and will probably do so again and there is no accounting for it. Perhaps it had something to do with Hal Bop.

Late in the evenings, under a clear night sky whilst taking my dog for a walk along the shores of the lough, I could see the comet over the summit of Knocknascallop. Under the clear unpolluted skies of north-west Mayo, the comet made a stirring sight, the tail stretching out against the night sky appeared to be much longer than it did in my native Oxfordshire – in fact it seemed to be pointing downwards towards the lough – a sign perhaps?

SUMMER SALMON & SEATROUT IN SCOTLAND

Fishing for summer salmon and seatrout has taken me to beautiful and remote areas where I have enjoyed superlative lake fishing for these migratory species. Sadly, systems where one can now expect to catch seatrout in any quantity are a scarce resource. The demise of the seatrout has deprived so many of today's anglers of one of the best sporting game fish in our spate rivers and migratory lake systems.

The great fisheries off the west and north-west coasts of both Scotland and Ireland are but a shadow of what they once were. There are a few signs that they may one day be given the opportunity to recover, but remedial measures will prove costly and will require governments to take corrective action.

There are still a few migratory lake systems where it is possible to fish for both seatrout and salmon, and some of the best systems are in the Outer Hebrides. South and North Uist, Harris and Lewis offer an excellent opportunity to fish for both salmon and seatrout in lochs which still enjoy good runs of fish. The isolated fisheries of the Outer Hebrides have held up well. I have enjoyed some wonderful fishing for both seatrout and salmon, but especially seatrout from fisheries in the Outer Hebrides.

On North Uist both loch and sea pool provide superb late fishing for seatrout, across the Sound of Harris to South Harris the Obbe at Leverburgh, the Borve Lodge Estate (if a day is available to fish the lochs) and, on North Harris, Amhuinnsuidhe Castle – these offer some of the finest traditional loch fishing for seatrout and summer salmon in the UK. Lewis has some well-known migratory loch systems and the most notable are on the west coast of the island, systems such as the River Blackwater, Grimersta, Uig Lodge and Uig and Hamanavay – all first rate fisheries.

FIRST SALMON ON A FLY

I caught my first salmon on a fly from a small loch system on South Harris, from little Loch Laxdale on the Borve Lodge Estate fishings. For this feat, I am indebted to Tony Scherr for his help and encouragement. Not only did he give good advice to my endless

Playing a summer salmon at Fincastle on the Hebridean island of Harris.

The scene at the start of the memorable day on Fincastle in which we caught eight salmon.

queries concerning migratory fish but through his generosity I went on to catch a second salmon on the fly in the space of a few days. With the first salmon under my belt I was keen to try for another.

On the final day of that eventful holiday, I remember calling into the office at Borve to enquire about rod availability, as the lochs were not let and the fishing was obtained for a small fee at Tony's discretion if the owner or friends of the owner were not themselves fishing. Conditions that day were ideal for loch salmon, with a strong westerly wind and occasional showers. Two other anglers who had obviously been waiting for the change in weather were also in the office making enquiries similar to my own.

It transpired that Loch Laxdale was available and when they enquired my heart sank, but Tony turned to me and said, "But I believe this gentleman has first option." It was an act of kindness that I will never forget. In the evenings, I had fished the smaller lochs on the estate for seatrout under difficult conditions and caught some good fish to, up to 3½lbs. As a keen angler on holiday, I was willing to take any opportunity to fish and did not just turn up out of the blue when conditions were good to see if there was any

fishing available. I believe Tony recognised this and that is why he made the gesture he did.

Through the kindness of Tony and the goodwill of the owners of the Borve Estate, we enjoyed some good sport on South Harris. The most notable was in July, one of bright cloudless skies, high temperature and a south-east wind: appalling conditions for migratory fish on a loch. The owners had decided, because of the conditions, to sail out to Iona, so we were offered fishing on Fincastle, the principal loch on the estate. Vaughan Lewis and I ventured out that day assured that the loch held a good stock of fish although nothing of note had been taken that week.

Damaged salmon are often the free takers

Under an azure sky with a warm dry wind we made a series of short drifts across the loch and first drift down, a salmon took a fancy to a Kate McLaren fished on the middle dropper. The fish had a large seal bite down one side and, as damaged salmon are often free takers, I wrote this capture off as a fluke. And so it seemed to be, as we didn't move a fin for another two hours until just before coming in for lunch when

Vaughan took a nice fish to his point fly which was I believe a Dark Mackerel. We were happy in such conditions to come in with a fish apiece.

Fincastle is separated from the sea by a man-made dam. This dam, built in the late 1800s for the cost of £200, formed the artificial loch which now looks as natural as any loch on the island. In a high spring tide, sea water floods over the outflow in to the loch, and the bay of Seilebost looking out towards Luskentyre could be seen beyond.

As the tide was falling the bay was now emptying at a rapid rate leaving a nice sea pool below the loch. This sea pool, which has been scoured by the outflowing waters from the loch, is always worth a cast (especially on a falling tide) for a few seatrout if they are in the mood.

Following lunch, Vaughan couldn't resist it, and as the day was now becoming hot, I just lay back and watched. I was observing my piscator pal being foiled by the quick-fire reactions of the seatrout in the pool, when a salmon leapt just out from the dam wall. I noted its position but didn't pay the fish too much attention. Vaughan was obviously having fun.

Then my attention was drawn again to the loch, as another salmon leapt in a similar position to the first fish. It was hot and the sun was beating down but I couldn't just ignore it. Picking up my rod and working down to where the fish moved I had a solid take from a salmon which had to be looking for a Kate as it hit the fly so hard. I called to Vaughan, but he was too interested in the sea pool which had fallen to a nice height and was seething with seatrout, fiesty fish that refused to stay on the hook.

However, when a another salmon took a liking to my fly on the second cast into the same area where that last fish took me, I was quickly joined by my friend. Inside an hour we caught four salmon apiece by taking turns to fish the hot spot, one at a time.

For a short spell the salmon for some reason had gone mad on the take but the last fish which fell to Vaughan kicked up quite a commotion and disturbed the area, putting the fish down, and that was our lot for the rest of the day. But what a wonderful day, with the spoils equally shared. You never know with fishing. Those salmon defied all logic.

ARDTORNISH, LATE AUTUMN

A memorable holiday on the Morvern Penninsula, north-west Scotland which I remember with fond affection was a week at the end of the season in the early 1990s. Frosty nights gave way to lovely autumn days. With no rain, the Aline was running low, and there was little prospect of a late autumn salmon from the river, so we concentrated on the lochs Dior Na Mart and Areanas. Fishing with Vaughan Lewis, I spent some heavenly days, particularly the evenings, drifting on the lochs.

As the light faded, stags came down off the hill, making their rutting calls, and a few seatrout would take with a free spirit to suit the occasion. Drifting across a small bay one evening I took a cracking brace of seatrout on a Claret Bumble top dropper.

The fish came with a vengeance, savagely hitting as I lifted the bob fly into the skin of the surface film. The biggest fish of the brace was the fattest seatrout that I have ever caught; it looked like a very well-fed Sheelin trout – almost obese. I believe we caught seven fish that evening: it was one of the better sessions in terms of numbers. The back-end salmon, rusty fish the colour of autumn, eluded us. I do not think, however, that we were too disappointed, as the conditions simply didn't suit them. Our best flies were the well-known classics: Claret Bumble, Kate McLaren, and Vaughan's favourite – a Dark Mackerel.

On the last evening we struggled for a few brownies and seatrout, but just as our hopes were rising with the fading light, the optimum time for a fish, the wind fell and the loch went flat. Consequently the fish went quiet also, so we called it a day; the end to our sojourn in Scotland for another year.

We pulled the boat up, sat on a rock and drank whisky. As the air temperature dropped, a light mist rose from the mirrored surface of the loch. Looking across the loch to the far shore, the bracken (russet brown at this time of the year) on the upper slopes of the hills merged with the different-coloured foliage of the trees lower down. Ash, birch, oak, beech, sallow and hazel were dressed in all their autumn glory. With high octane stags, hormones racing all around us, we listened to the great beasts warning any male neighbours with amorous intentions to stay off their patch. The rut was in full swing. I remember saying to Vaughan as we

Pondering the fishing prospects for the afternoon on the edge of Loch Arienas. Is that a storm coming or will it remain flat calm?

sat there drinking (the alcohol was obviously helping the mood!): "Fishing takes us to these wonderful places but it isn't just the fishing that you remember. I will take this with me and cherish it."

OTTERS

Fishing takes us to areas where we experience new sights, hear different sounds, see unfamiliar species of birds, animals and flora, all of which add another dimension to the fishing day. Otters are a favourite with most anglers and I have seen them in just about every conceivable habitat – moorland, open ditches and drains, the sea, lakes and rivers – but one of the most amusing incidents that I recall is that of a large dog otter playing with some tethered buoys in Loch Laxdale on South Harris.

I had set out for seatrout one evening just before sunset and intended to fish from a boat for a few hours into the dark. As the loch was small I wanted to avoid disturbing the areas I intended to fish, so I quietly rowed the boat to the top of the wind and held position

waiting for a movement of seatrout which usually occurred around dusk. On this particular evening the seatrout were slow to materialise. But in the knowledge that, if a trout rose and you were quick to cover the rise, the fish would invariably take you with a wallop, I patiently waited.

The light faded into that twilight world of indefinable distance and moving shadow. Noises sound different too and as I waited I became aware of a sound which sounded very much like a dog snorting whilst swimming with something in its mouth.

I had heard this before and knew it to be an otter but in the darkness I did wonder, particularly as the sound was growing louder. The animal responsible was coming closer, and then very close to the boat. Down the middle of the loch was a series of buoys and from them was suspended a tangle of barbed wire. This nightmare was put in to deter poachers from netting the loch and I was holding the boat near to the upper-most buoy in the line, no more than an oar's distance away. As the sound grew louder and louder the buoy began to shake and move. It was like a scene from

Jaws! But instead of the buoy submerging, it dipped and bobbed, and a tail began to rise serpent-like from one end, then the head of an otter appeared from the other end as the animal curled itself around the buoy and began to play. The otter lay on its back with the buoy on its stomach.

For several minutes it played with its new toy, totally oblivious to my presence. Sitting in the boat keeping perfectly still, I was so close to the animal that I could almost touch it.

Then, for no apparent reason, the otter just lost interest in the toy and casually swam past me towards the outlet from the loch. I could hear his snorting fading away as he made off into the distance, heading for the sea, and he was a good way off before I lost track of him. As for the fishing, it was a failure. I came off blank – perhaps the otter had disturbed the loch and put the fish down? An evening I shall never forget, but for reasons other than the fishing.

LOCH FISHING IN THE HEBRIDES

In early July one year, as I looked for signs of recent rain whilst driving northwards through Scotland, I was greeted by the depressing sight of rivers in drought. Warm water languidly flowing between parched boulders, bleached by exposure to the summer sun, made a sorry sight and spelt disaster for an angler pursuing migratory fish with a fly.

Prospects looked bleak, but they looked even more depressing when we arrived on Lewis, as the rivers here did not even appear to be flowing; they just consisted of a series of unconnected stagnant pools. Sunday, the day after our arrival and a non-fishing day, was a one of unbroken sunshine, with no sign of a break in the weather. The machair in the evening was stunning.

As the wind fell, the air became heavy with the scent from the floral carpet all around us. Two corncrakes were calling, hidden away amongst the iris and meadow sweet which grew thickly along the edges of the land drains. It was the perfect evening. I really couldn't see the weather breaking and in many areas it didn't.

Monday, the first day of our fishing week, appeared no different. I was preparing myself for a week of sea fishing, sightseeing and beaches. So imagine my total surprise when I was greeted by a beaming Richard Davies, my boatman for the week.

Releasing a mature seatrout.

The wild setting of Loch Ronasgail on the island of Lewis where careful oarsmanship and a stealthy approach are the order of the day.

I couldn't understand why he was looking so cheerful. He studied the bemused look on my face and said in a slow drool, "Didn't you hear it?" "Hear what?" I asked. "The thunder last night!" he exclaimed with huge grin.

I thought Richard had been out partying all night but he was serious.

> **The pools were alive with running fish**

And he was right. For two incredible hours, an isolated storm had hit our catchment with a deluge. As we drove up the pass beside Loch Raonasgail and over into Glen Tamanisdale, the truth was beginning dawn. Cascades of white water were streaming off the mountain sides. By the time we reached the lodge, the lower part of the Hamanavay river was already coming into spate. While the rest of the island and probably most of north-west Scotland was suffering from a severe lack of rain, we in this isolated area off the north-western seaboard had been blessed by this storm.

It was the only rain for the week, but it was all that was required to get the fish in. The pools were alive with running fish as we walked up the river to Loch na Craobhaig, and as I had never witnessed a run of migratory fish before on this scale, I spent a good part of the day observing the run moving up river. The pools with a more difficult obstacle at their head would quickly fill with salmon and seatrout, their tails, dorsal fins and backs continually showing in the white water below these small falls.

Then slowly, one after another, fish would throw themselves into the foaming white water to ascend the obstacle, and push on upstream. It was a magnificent sight. I think what made it so amazing was the size of the river – a white water torrent in miniature. One could observe at close quarters, if you kept well down and out of sight, literally hundreds of fish progressing upstream.

The walk from the lodge to the loch would normally take about 45 minutes, but it was around two o'clock when we made the shores of Loch na Craobhaig. And instead of heading straight for the boat, we decided to have lunch by the outflow from the loch. This was the sort of fishing lunch I could learn to enjoy, as we bathed in warm sunshine on a patch of well-cropped turf, watching fish, one after another stream through the outflow and into the loch. It was a heartening sight.

It was well after three o'clock, before we pushed the boat out from the shore by the bothy. As we were to be off around six, this was going to be a short session. With so many fresh fish running into the loch, I put up a Kate McClaren on top dropper, Blue Teal & Silver on middle dropper (both size 10) and a Silver Stoat (size 12 double) on the point. I felt no urgency to begin fishing, as I had previously read several accounts of how salmon and seatrout need time to settle before they will take.

In truth, I was unsure how we would fare, but wasn't unduly worried, for I now knew that the lochs had a good stock of fish for the rest of the week. In bright sunshine and light wind, the next three hours disproved the theory about fish requiring time to settle, as seatrout, one after another, slammed into the flies. There was no coming short, they really wanted the flies and by the time we came off the loch I had taken about 17 good fish up to 3lbs.

Sidney Spencer loved Loch na Craobhaig for summer salmon and seatrout

I have had many good weeks at Hamanavay but this was to be my best. On the Wednesday, sharing the boat on Loch na Craobhaig with a guest Simon Hook, we caught 53 seatrout, a record for the loch and the best bag of seatrout I have ever taken in a single day. And remember, this is a short fishing day, for this is remote fishing that requires nearly an hour's off-road driving and 45 minutes walking before you reach the loch.

I cannot recall the total number of fish that I caught that week, but all were returned, except for one salmon and one seatrout taken on the last day. The seatrout, caught just before lunch, provided a wonderful meal, cooked in the embers of an open fire on the shores of the loch. A fitting finale to a superb week's fishing.

Loch na Craobhaig is one of the finest lochs for summer salmon and seatrout that I have ever fished, connected to the tide by a short river, remote, surrounded by open moorland with its many rocky points and clean gravel bottom. Sidney Spencer once described the loch as a "fishing El Dorado" and I would not contradict him.

I have always said that luck, particularly where salmon are concerned, can make such a difference when it comes to success or failure. So many factors have to come together to provide good fishing for the migratory species, and without a strong presence of fish, all time and effort will be in vain. A week which was looking like a disaster as far as fishing was concerned, was turned on its head by a fluke of the weather – that luck thing again. I was certainly up with the clouds as we drove south through a parched and very dry looking English landscape, on the return home journey.

Readers of angling literature who enjoy the works of Sidney Spencer will have read unknowingly of Loch na Craobhaig. It is the loch featured in *Salmon and Seatrout in Wild Places*. It is one of the most evocative essays on traditional lake fishing for migratory fish that I have ever read.

The original clinker-built boat he describes, which is still used today on the loch, is said to be now well over eighty years old. Looking out across the loch from the boat mooring to the point, I could always visualise that very same boat drifting, head to the wind, against the thirty foot bluff, a boatman holding the boat in position with an angler, cigarette in his mouth, wearing a wide-brimmed hat and sitting in the stern, plying his craft.

BIRDS OF PREY

As well as the fishing at Uig & Hamanavay, there is always the opportunity to see interesting wildlife. The estate is set in wild and remote country, and on most visits to the island we saw something unusual. While out on a fishing trip with Vaughan, we once saw seven different raptors in one day, including rare raptors, such as white-tailed eagle, peregrine and merlin.

We were travelling along the rather tortuous rough track over to the lodge when we saw white-tailed eagle, buzzard and a kestrel. Walking from the lodge to the loch, we added a merlin to our list and while out fishing we saw a golden eagle and a pair of peregrines against the backdrop of North Harris.

It was a good day's fishing on the loch too, with a salmon apiece and a nice catch of seatrout! And to round the day off, on the walk back we witnessed a female sparrow hawk ambushing some pipits near a rocky bluff close to the lodge.

A typical Lewis seatrout – this one from Loch na Croabhaig, a place much favoured by Sidney Spencer.

CORNCRAKES

Corncrakes were another favourite. Now a rare sight, this migrant bird was once considered a nuisance in some areas, with its persistent repetitive call all hours of the night. I have seen and heard corncrakes in both Scotland and Ireland. The majority of sightings have been on the Western Isles, but one bird I remember in Ireland in particular, was a calling male one lovely late May evening whilst fishing the spent gnat on Lough Derg.

This bird called incessantly from some thick cover, while we waited patiently in a boat moored close to the shore, for a trout to rise. The fishing was slow, but that calling male meant a lot to me, as it was one of the few corncrakes I have heard or seen in Ireland. But the corncrake which I remember most was on the Western Isles.

We were returning from a successful evening's fishing for salmon in the sea at Uig Bay. The sculking male was calling from a bed of nettles, close to where the car was parked. We discussed how it was possible to mimic the call by running your thumb nail over the teeth of a plastic comb. This inspired Richard Davies, one of our party, to come up with the novel idea of using the ratchet on his reel to mimic the call. A quick forward and backward movement of the reel drum produced a realistic sound which was good enough to fool our friend in the nettles, for he immediately replied to Richard's efforts. That calling male had us in fits of laughter, as the bird repeatedly replied to Richard's prompting with the reel.

Most fishermen have an interest in nature, but good anglers tend to be particularly observant about what is going on around them: it broadens your outlook and provides another form of interest when the fishing is tough.

BOAT METHODS FOR SALMON & SEATROUT

For summer salmon and seatrout on lakes, I use lighter lines and rods than I do for the spring salmon. A 6-weight rod, of 11ft to 10ft 6ins, balanced with a floating or an intermediate flyline and leaders of 5 to 8lb breaking strain, would be fine. If I were fishing especially for salmon, I would use 8lb nylon. But many of the systems that I fish are mixed fisheries, with seatrout providing the bulk of the sport, so I tend to go a little lighter and 6lb standard nylon is a good all-round leader strength to fish.

I have landed a good many loch salmon, on 5lb or 6lb leaders when seatrout have been the primary species. Providing there are no obvious snags around, playing summer salmon between 4 and 7lbs should present no problems. If you are unsure, always err on the stronger side to help your confidence.

Flies would be similar to those we fished for spring salmon in lakes, but in smaller sizes, down to size 14. To the colours of the spring fishing: black, claret, yellow and orange, I would add blue, particularly for fresh summer fish.

Flies which I have had great success with are: Kate McClaren, Claret Bumble, Blue Zulu, Pheasant & Yellow, Mallard & Claret, Teal Blue & Silver, Invicta, Silver Invicta, Mini Muddler and a Silver Stoat or Silver Thunder Stoat.

I dress the fly patterns which are fished on the point, on both single and double hooks. This allows me to fish the same pattern, of a similar size, on different

Waiting for the breeze to gather on Loch na Croabhaig.

weight hooks and I quite often use a heavier double on the point.

With the heavier fly, I find the leader digs in better and the fly acts as a good anchor when I make the lift to bring the top dropper to the surface. In windy conditions, this drag gives better control of working the top dropper, in an attractive way, through the surface wave. Also, the heavier weight of the double fishes the point fly deeper than a single iron. So my team of flies are covering different depths, which again can be a useful way of determining the taking mood of the fish.

If you find that one fly in particular is attracting a lot of attention from the fish, note its position on the leader and then try to work out if it is a colour preference or one of depth.

On the days when the dropper flies are taking fish to the exclusion of the point, change the double on the point to a single, to bring the point fly up in the water. This subtle change of weight to the point fly very often brings the tail fly into play, especially if the seatrout are showing a preference for a fly well up in the water.

Soft days with no hint of sun are normally the best days to fish a single on the point, as seatrout seem to prefer the flies much higher in the water in these weather conditions.

LIFTING THE BOB FLY EARLY

Seatrout in lakes, particularly if the lake contains a good stock of fish augmented by small injections of fresh-run fish, can respond positively to a well-presented top dropper. If the seatrout are in the mood, and can be worked up to a dibbled fly, it is advisable to make the lift early. One can then hold the top dropper in the skin of the surface for much longer.

This presentation can entice the fish up to wildly slash at the fly, or better still, just roll over and take on their way down (*see* Diagrams 12 & 13).

When the dropper flies are taking fish to the exclusion of the point, change the double on the point to a single, to bring the point fly up in the water

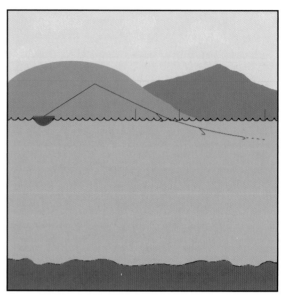

Diagram 12: If the lift is made early, the distance over which the top dropper can be worked is increased.

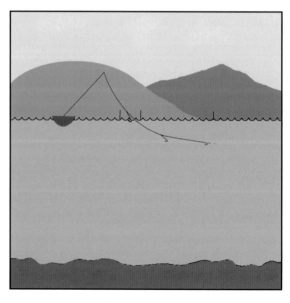

Diagram 13: If the lift is made late, the distance over which the top dropper can be worked is very much restricted.

Vaughan Lewis fishing the top dropper in good conditions on Lough Currane, Co. Kerry.

But if the seatrout miss the fly, they very often take the middle dropper or the point pattern following behind, with some gusto. This type of fishing isn't for the faint-hearted, but it is great fun when the fish chase and slash at the flies.

Mid-day Seatrout

In lakes during the middle of the day, fresh seatrout seem to throw off the shackles and take freely, unlike their river counterparts, who skulk away for most the day, only coming out to play in the falling light levels of dusk.

Seatrout at Dusk

Dusk is always a good period for boat fishing, no matter what species of fish you are after, including loch seatrout. But falling light levels are not vital for success; certainly not to the same degree it is with seatrout in rivers. When seatrout have been in a lough for a while, the aggressive sea-feeding characteristic diminishes. By this time, some members of the shoal will have been caught or hooked and lost, so the remainder will be shyer and much harder to tempt. Dusk then will become a key taking period.

Tinsel Flies versus Sombre-coloured Ones

For fresh seatrout, I would always favour flies with tinsel bodies, or broad flat tinsel ribs. These, I feel, appeal to the seatrout's sea-feeding instincts. But once the fish have been in the system for some time, then fresh water feeding behaviour takes over, and I tend to fish more sombre-coloured flies, particularly claret and fiery brown.

Dry fly is an alternative method for the more difficult fish, and I have certainly caught a good few seatrout on dries. But the method does not appear to be as effective with the sea-run brown trout as it is with the non-migratory fish.

Wet-fly Seatrout

The most successful method, without doubt, for lake seatrout, is a well-presented wet fly. Some anglers would suggest, because we are supposedly dealing with an ultra-shy fish, that long casting is a must. Unless the day is one of light wind and bright conditions, I do not find it essential to cast a long line when fishing from a drifting boat. In good conditions, with cloud cover and a wave, I would feel confident of catching seatrout fishing traditional wet fly, just as I would for brown trout. In fact, if it is essential for an angler to cast twenty five to thirty yards in such conditions, I would venture to suggest that they are doing something wrong. When I fish traditional flies, I cast a slightly longer line, but it certainly isn't over twenty five yards. And I would pull no more than the distance of the length of my leader, before making the lift. There is no point in casting a long line and then pulling for ten or fifteen yards, much of which will be over water already covered by your fish-scaring fly line, no matter what colour it is.

There is no point in casting a long line and then pulling for ten or fifteen yards, much of which will be over water already covered by your fish-scaring fly line

What is required is for the seatrout to see the flies and the flies only, without detecting your presence. One should be able to achieve this without casting a long line. By casting a long line, particularly a floater, all you are doing is pushing the fish out further and if both anglers are doing the same, that exclusion zone will become a broad arc in front of the boat. Lake seatrout are no more difficult than educated wild brown trout: in fact fresh seatrout are much freer takers.

Wild brown trout can, if they are released, be caught again, and likewise so can seatrout. On the Hebrides we practised catch-and-release with loch seatrout, and recognisable fish were caught again. One fish was caught three times on traditional wet fly – a seatrout, which does little fresh water feeding and is very shy.

When they are in the mood, seatrout can provide superlative sport on light, balanced tackle. Fresh seatrout can be very free taking, hitting the fly like a fish treble their weight and are the gamest of fighters.

It is a great pity that the demise of the seatrout is depriving so many of today's anglers of a unique experience where traditional flyfishing is concerned.

A fresh Carrowmore springer, showing the sores from the recently-detached sea lice.

WHERE TO GO

Although I have experienced good sport on fisheries off the west coast of Ireland, north-west Mayo and Donegal, many of these systems have been affected by the decline of seatrout stocks. Glen Lough in Donegal, Carrowmore in Mayo and Currane in Kerry are fisheries where I have enjoyed good seatrout fishing and Carrowmore would be also an outstanding lough for summer salmon. But the most consistent fisheries for lake seatrout are the systems on the Outer Hebrides. From ten or more visits to the Western Isles, I can recall only two poor years due to lack of rain and even then, we managed to put reasonable bags of fish together.

Seatrout Preference for Shallow Water

Lake seatrout tend to hold over relatively shallow water, in bays, around river mouths, and over features close to deep water such as off-shore reefs or islands. Water close to the marginal drop-offs, particularly off rocky shorelines, promontaries or the points of bays are all good areas to find fish. Very rarely would you find them over deep water well off-shore. The exception to this is Lough Currane in Co. Kerry, where I have taken seatrout well out in open, featureless water. Water greater than 15 feet deep would, in most situations, be a waste of time, rarely producing fish. Occasionally, if terrestrial flies are blown onto the water in sufficient numbers to interest the fish, a rise will occur over deep open water, but this is infrequent.

Anglers tend to be observant about the natural world. When I see certain plants coming into bloom,

This summer salmon was taken on Lough Corrib on the dry fly.

or trees breaking bud, I tend to connect the event with a particular phase of my fishing year. The gorse, for instance, is my spring fishing flower, a season of early salmon, duck fly and lake olive fishing for brown trout. The last of the gorse overlaps with the hawthorn and the mayfly, the end of the true spring fishing. With the mayfly, as the hawthorn and the gorse flowers wither and die, some of the best imitative fishing for wild brown trout comes to an end. It leaves a certain hollow feeling as I see the banks of yellow fade from the shores of favourite loughs. However, on certain lakes we can look forward to the sedges, the summer mayflies, and at the back-end, the daphnia-feeding trout over open water. And of course there are the summer runs of migratory fish to look forward to.

For the summer fisher, salmon and seatrout fishing in beautiful remote areas is a season of pink and magenta, with rosebay willowherb and purple loosestrife. My fishing has taken me from the chalk streams of southern England, to the remote hill lochs of the far north and to the islands. For the migratory species, it is to the north and west coasts that I travel, to catch these fish in lake systems. And it is to the Hebrides the Western Isles in particular, that hold the fondest memories of fishing for summer salmon and seatrout. The trip northwards, up the M6, M74 and the A9 with great swathes of willow herb filling the roadside verges with colour, used to fill me with anticipation.

CHAPTER 7

Brown Trout Boat Fishing

The large limestone loughs in the west of Ireland produce big trout. These loughs are food-rich environments, ideal habitat for *Salmo trutta* to grow to a large size. The trout of Lough Melvin have been the subject of detailed research. On Melvin, three distinct strains have been identified: Gillaroo, Sonaghen and Ferox. The Gillaroo is reputedly a bottom-feeding fish with an adapted stomach (the subject of much debate); the Sonaghen is an open water plankton feeder; and the Ferox is a cannibal, a fish feeder which has to go wherever the prey fish are.

It is perfectly credible that these strains have evolved so that they do not compete for the same food; and because they inhabit different areas of the same lough, they display different liveries.

Some anglers claim to be able to distinguish the different strains of trout, on the basis of their shape, colouration and spotting appearance, in association with their feeding pattern. Whilst I accept that identification of the three types may be possible on Lough

Melvin, I do not believe this to be true for all systems.

All strains of brown trout feed on plankton, wherever it is present in sufficient quantity. This type of specialist feeding isn't just limited to the Sonaghen. Certainly the young of many fish species, feed on plankton until they reach a certain size. They cease to feed on plankton when it is no longer energy efficient to continue cropping such a small food organism.

These fish will then switch to a different food resource. Brown trout in a river, pond, reservoir or a large lake are all capable of foraging on the bottom, and if a certain food such as snail is there in abundance, they will crop it. If they continue feeding on hard-shelled molluscs for some time, their stomach walls may become hardened and extended.

I have taken brown trout which have been feeding exclusively on snails from reservoirs. The shells of the molluscs could be felt in the stomach, and undigested fragments of the shell were being passed through the digestive tract to the vent. Is this any different to the adapted stomach of the Gillaroo trout of Lough Melvin?

Brown trout are predatory and they eat fish, no matter which environment they live in. I have taken browns which have gorged on minnows from rivers, particularly when the minnows mass together pre or post spawning. So aggressive is the trout's behaviour when they are gorging like this, it is possible to hook them several times if they slip the hook. Some of those river trout, may have been of true wild strain but it is more than likely that they were first, second or more distant progeny of stocked trout or acclimatised stock fish. Brown trout which turn predatory and possess the longevity trait, may grow to a prodigious size – but does that make them a Ferox?

Mixing the Gene Pool

Gene mixing may occur. It was considered impossible for coarse fish species such as roach and bream to hybridise and breed, and yet this has happened in many parts of Ireland and is now happening on the Corrib. I find it difficult to believe that even on a large lough such as Corrib, some mixing of the brown trout gene pool has not occurred.

Since Victorian times there has been at least one hatchery on the Lough, and in the early days fish were trapped in a number of locations around the lough for the hatchery at Oughterard. In the book *Reflections on Lough Corrib* by Maurice Semple, it states, that in 1913/1914, over one million fry were distributed around the lough, into the bays, around islands and in the feeder streams. Is it possible for a strain such as Ferox to remain genetically pure in the presence of such large scale intervention by man?

It's Big, but is it a Ferox?

If I were to catch a big trout on, say, the Corrib, do I automatically assume that it is a Ferox because of its size? That would suggest that no other strain of brown is capable of growing to a large size, and this I feel just isn't true. The gene pool of the brown trout stocked in English reservoirs is probably so mixed it would be impossible to classify them, and yet these fish grow to over 16lbs. A brown trout of over 24lbs was netted from Bewl Reservoir. These brown trout may possess the Ferox gene, but they are undoubtedly of mixed race. Stew bred, with no genetic purity, stocked at twelve to thirteen inches, they are fish that have simply taken advantage of rich reservoir environments.

If I were to catch a fish of between 14 and 16 inches on a fly in a specific area, could I say with any certainty what strain of brown trout that fish was? Would the fly pattern the fish took help me identify the strain of brown trout? Would the area where I caught the fish be a good indicator of which strain? The colour and spotting livery can be very distinctive, but could I tell with absolute certainty the species from the appearance of the fish? Are these characteristics dependent on the genotype alone or the environment in which the trout has lived in its recent past? Without the help of science it is impossible to say with any certainty what strain of brown trout the fish is.

Sonaghen, Gillaroo or Ferox: different species?

The Assynt area of north-west Scotland resembles a lunar landscape of moorland and mountain indented with numerous basins of water that vary in size, and shape as much as the trout they contain. The trout from those lochs vary considerably in size, colour and spotting configuration. One small hill loch of six or seven acres, has a broad sandy delta at the foot of a small incoming burn which comes straight off the mountain, and in a flash flood brings down a deposit of fine clean sand and gravel. Trout from this small loch are all uniform in size, dark brown in colour; typical hill loch fish.

However, those taken from off the delta, although similar in size to the rest of the stock, are a lovely light golden brown with fewer but more pronounced spots. Two different species? I doubt it. The same argument would apply to a trout with the Sonaghen gene. If the fish switched from plankton feeding, to bottom feeding (possibly forced by a shortage of food or just an instinctive response, going where the food is more abundant or easier to find) the colouration of the trout would change. Are Sonaghen, Gillaroo or Ferox so distinc that we could classify them with absolute certainty, as separate species?

Wild fisheries are a precious resource, and need some form of protection from angler abuse. This is especially so on popular waters such as the large Irish limestone fisheries, where the catch regulations applying to the number of fish an angler may take are a little vague to say the least. Size limits are not a strong

Playing a lively Irish trout on Lough Sheelin with Mount Ross bay in the background.

enough measure to protect fisheries from the impact of uncontrolled angling pressure. Some sizeable fish are now returned, but it is still a rare event, and we cannot depend on the goodwill of anglers to put self-imposed catch limits on the number of trout they take.

Overfishing or Pollution

Overfishing is a sensitive issue as we all by nature want a slice of the cake, but overfishing an unsustainable wild stock of fish is a road to ruin. Unlike a catastrophic event such as pollution, angling pressure on a large lough system will not totally eradicate the stock but it will reduce the stock density to a level where it will no longer provide good sport to fly anglers, and could well damage the line of long-lived fish.

We all talk of the effect of pollution, habitat degradation, the weather and lack of fly. However, I find it interesting that a lot of anglers, fishery scientists included, avoid the touchy subject of rod pressure on wild stocks, or that – God forbid – overfishing may be responsible for a fall off in catches. As much as I loathe rules or regulations when it comes to fishing matters, I feel that some measures are now necessary to preserve the status of some wild brown trout fisheries in Ireland. Visiting anglers, and sport fisherman within Ireland, are now becoming increasingly aware of the need to

conserve stock. There is a growing interest in issues such as catch-and-release, water protection, preservation and improvement of habitat, issues that affect the long-term preservation of our sport, and issues where angler awareness has improved considerably. These same anglers would willingly comply I feel with any measure to preserve wild fisheries, if sensible regulations were imposed.

Catch Limit to One or Two Trout

If anglers are actively encouraged to release fish, retaining one or two trout if they so desire, then in time a mandatory catch limit will become less important. I believe that most anglers will accept that it is in their best long-term interest to return trout, although they may find it difficult to make the adjustment initially. However, until anglers become enlightened to catch-and-release, a catch limit would be of particular benefit to the popular, free, state fisheries, which are coming under increasing rod pressure, and are open to abuse by all and sundry.

No matter how large the lake, no wild fishery can sustain the impact of modern angling pressure without ill-effect, if no measures are imposed to restrict the numbers of fish taken. The Corrib has over the past two seasons been subjected to intense rod pressure, and yet has held up incredibly well. But for how long can

Dogs are great companions but the shared excitement when a fish is being played can become tiresome.

it sustain such rod effort, without ill effect? At 44,000 acres, some anglers believe that the lough can more than cope with this increase in angler effort, but I have my doubts, and there were distinct signs that the lough was suffering from over-fishing following the mayfly of 2003. The summer and autumn fishing was nothing like as consistent as previous seasons, and 2004 fared no better.

Sport was there to be had, it is true, but it was patchy, with short rising or abortive takes a common problem, behaviour indicative of angler rod pressure. The spring fishing of 2005 was also poor, with one of the worst mayfly seasons that many anglers can remember. After three years of very intense rod pressure on the 5+ to 3+ age group of fish, the main spawning stock, are we now seeing the effect of over-fishing?

Intense Pressure at Rutland & Grafham

Fish in both Rutland and Grafham, behaved in a similar fashion once they had been heavily fished, following the opening of the two fisheries. In his book *Stillwater Flyfishing*, T.C. Ivens wrote of fish coming short, and he mentions that abortive rises were a common problem in 1967. This was the season following the opening of Grafham, a reservoir that changed our approach to stillwater angling, and a water that was subjected to some intense pressure following its opening.

The Corrib is a big lough but anglers are misguided if they believe the lough is too big to be over-fished.

Anglers are faced with a huge area of water, and automatically assume that the lough contains a large head of fish. But stock numbers will be governed by factors that bear no relation to the size of the lough, such as productivity of the nursery areas, and the survival of the progeny to make 3+ years. Nor are those fish which survive to a takeable size, evenly distributed throughout the system.

There are large areas of barren water, or water holding a relatively low stock of fish. The productive areas are now becoming well known, and it is these areas that are obviously seeing the greatest rod pressure, particularly during the first half of the season when the fish are inshore, over the shallows, and in the bays. Even though good numbers of trout may move out of the bays and into open water from June onwards, the greatest density of fish, particular trout from the 3+ to 5+ year age group, will have been very vulnerable to angler rod pressure from the middle of February.

LONGEVITY OF BROWN TROUT

It takes three years for a Corrib trout to make 12 inches. So in the spring following its third year, a wild brown from the Corrib will have reached a takeable size, and it is these fish, along with the 4 and 5+ year age group – fish up 20 inches long – that form the backbone of our fly-caught sport.

Those fish that survive to the 5+ age group, will either cease to grow, possibly because of limited feeding, or because of a factor that is gene related. Thereafter they will maintain or lose weight, depending on food availability. These large browns will live on for a good number of years, and provide sport for the fly angler. This is why we can catch trout between 3 and 5lbs, that look old.

Not all of the survivors will make specimen size, and these fish, I feel, live for much longer than we are led to believe. A year class of brown trout from Farmoor regained condition following a lean spell of poor feeding. The bigger fish in this year class grew to around 23 inches in length, and weighed up to 5¾lbs.

The following season, through a lack of good feeding, these same fish had not only lost condition, they had also lost weight, and I didn't think they would survive the winter.

How wrong I was, when in the season following the year they had lost condition, these same fish had recovered and looked tremendous. A brown which I took in May of that year, measuring just over 23 inches, weighed well over 7lbs. In its eighth year, that fish stocked as a three-year-old provided sport for at least 5 seasons, and in that time it had gained, lost and regained condition.

The previous year when the trout had lost condition, it would probably have looked an old fish, but when I caught it, that trout looked a picture. It had probably ceased growing in its sixth year, therefore a scale reading could not have predicted its age but it was at least eight years old. Scale readings are not definitive for ageing a fish, once that fish has stopped growing.

In large limestone loughs like the Corrib or Mask, the fish that continue to grow will become highly predatory to sustain their growth, and we know

A fabulous, fat fish taken from an area of shallow water on the lower Corrib.

111

from scale readings that they may continue growing until their 10th or 12th year. But are they consecutive years of growth, or do they grow for a number of years, and then plateau at a certain size for a number of years before putting on another spurt of growth? How would we know? All we are measuring are periods of growth, not an ageing process.

I am not arguing a case that all trout may live longer than is generally thought, as I am well aware that the faster growing trout (such as the fish in Sheelin for example) which make rapid growth, and which by their 7th or 8th year can be very large fish indeed, may not live as long as the slower growing trout of the west.

Longevity is obviously gene-related. Ferox trout are known to be long-lived, and in the western loughs through genetic diversity, it may be possible that the trout that are not ferox may have this trait.

It may take longer than we care to accept, for a balanced stock of fish to build up

Genetic diversity in these lough systems has evolved since the last ice age, and it is possible that a good many of the trout in the western loughs have the longevity trait.

If this is the case, stock in loughs such as Corrib and Mask will have a larger spread of age groups, particularly older fish, than say loughs such as Sheelin. It may take longer than we care to accept, for a balanced stock of fish to build up.

A similar scenario applies to the pike in the reservoirs. These fish grow to prodigious sizes very quickly, on a diet of protein-rich stocked trout but it appears that these faster growing pike, although fit and healthy, do not live as long as fish from unstocked lakes, gravel pits and rivers. I believe trout in a wild natural environment survive longer than fishery data suggests, or fishery scientists would have us believe. In the western loughs, I believe brown trout can live possibly well into their teens.

I have no scientific data to support this theory but if it was not for carp anglers recognising identifiable carp, we would have no idea how long-lived carp can be. Perhaps a tagging scheme, with a long follow up programme of monitoring the fish, would produce meaningful figures for the longevity of wild brown trout?

IMPACT OF ANGLING PRESSURE

It is important to understand how long it could take for a natural balance of sustainable trout stock to build up. In the rich limestone loughs, if the trout that avoid predation survive until they are well in to their teens, it could take longer than many of us would care to imagine. In any year the 3+ to 5+ year fish are our target stock, and these are the fish which provide the best flyfishing. Anything smaller should be returned, and anything bigger is, for the fly angler, a bonus.

These fish are not augmented by a regular stocking of trout. Unlike the English reservoirs, there are no regular injections of fish in Ireland to liven things up and get the resident fish moving again. We start the season with our target fish, and thereafter, due to angler pressure, our stock is a reducing number.

Competition Angling

One only has to fish a water such as Rutland, after it has hosted a major competition, to witness the impact of angling pressure, and this is on a water that receives a regular injection of stocked trout. Imagine the impact on the target stock of trout on the Corrib after the duck fly, the olive and the mayfly seasons. Anglers are well-equipped, boats have bigger and faster engines, there are no areas on the lough that hold pockets of unmolested fish, no distance it would appear is too far, all the fish are vulnerable. As more of the 3+ to 5+ year age group are caught, so will the impact on the main spawning class increase.

Ireland has some of the finest wild brown trout fishing in Europe, and yet we are still witnessing a degradation of the superb wild fisheries of Ennel, Sheelin, Arrow, Derg, Cullin and Conn. Even Carra is now a fishery of concern. This only leaves Mask and Corrib, the two great limestone loughs of the west where the fishing has held up largely because of the input by the fishery boards, local angling clubs, and local anglers who are concerned about the welfare of these great fisheries.

A lot of money has been spent, and a great deal of effort has been put in by the dedicated few, for the benefit of all those who fish these two fine loughs. Regrettably as the fishing is falling off elsewhere, so more and more pressure is now coming on to the Corrib and Mask. This increased pressure is not, as

This brown trout from the middle Corrib was an early-season capture, on the buzzer.

many would believe, coming from tourists: it is indigenous. As leisure time and employment have improved, so anglers from within Ireland have taken advantage of the change in fortune, and why not? It would be a great pity, however, to see the success from all the effort and hard work put in by those who do care about the loughs, offset by the effect of increased rod pressure.

Because of intensive farming practices, sewage discharges and poor quality septic tank waste discharges, water quality on the wild lough systems of Ireland is deteriorating, and this is having a grave impact on many of the classic fisheries, as we are all well aware.

Collective Action

Anglers should do all they can to support any body or active group tackling this problem and we can also help beleaguered fisheries by changing our attitude to the taking of wild brown trout.

In America, they realised back in the 1970s, even in wilderness areas with low populations of people, that many of their wild fisheries could no longer sustain the angler pressure they were subjected to. Stocking with trout of a takeable size was not working, so they took a radical step, and imposed protective measures to conserve stock. They made catch-and-release mandatory on selected wild systems. We now know the benefit of this radical move, with the consequence that many sport fishermen now travel from Europe to fish American waters.

Wild fisheries within Ireland now need a package of protective measures and this should include a new attitude from fishermen. Anglers should be actively encouraged to release fish but until this becomes common practice, a sensible mandatory catch limit would, I feel, be accepted by the majority of sport fisherman as a positive move to conserving stock. A mandatory catch limit would remove the issue of self-regulation, which is always open to abuse.

Catch limits are not the only protective measure the fishery boards should be considering to protect wild brown trout stock. They should also tackle the thorny issue of the sale of wild brown trout to local shops, restaurants and hotels. A number of commercial outlets local to the Corrib have stopped taking and selling wild brown trout, and the proprietors of these establishments must be commended for their actions, but a ban on the sale of wild brown trout would prevent any form of over-exploitation of wild brown trout fisheries. The taking of wild fish for commercial gain, on a rod and line fishery, is a practice which in this day and age should be condemned. Take away the financial incentive, and you attack the problem at source.

Measures have been introduced to protect salmon stocks and now the protective measures should be extended to give wild brown trout the level of protection they also deserve.

I find it interesting that the fishery boards go to great lengths to improve fisheries, and yet on designated western wild brown trout fisheries, where pike are culled to protect salmonid stocks, there is a fishery byelaw on the removal of pike by rod and line anglers. It is illegal for rod and line fishermen to remove more than one pike per day, and that fish is not to exceed 3kg in weight. If this isn't a mixed message, I do not know what is.

A sensible catch limit, and a ban on the sale of wild brown trout, would be two protective measures that I feel the majority of sport fishermen would now approve. And an active campaign to encourage the release of trout would be a constructive step in the right direction. The younger generation of anglers will grow to accept these measures. In time, catch-and-release will become the norm, but time isn't on our side. Do we not owe it to the future of these wonderful wild limestone lough fisheries to act now?

Above: Drifting across Inny Bay, Lough Sheelin.
Facing page: playing a brown trout on Lough Mask.

CHAPTER 8

Irish Lough Fishing

Angling for wild brown trout, and in particular the brown trout fishing on the large limestone loughs of Ireland, holds a deep fascination for me. It is without question my favourite piscatorial pursuit. The capture of a wild brown trout provides a joy which will draw me back again and again. Boat fishing on the Irish limestone loughs gives me the most pleasure of all.

Wherever I cast a fly to wild brown trout, my approach is to keep things simple. Anglers can become obsessed with method, tactics, and the accumulation of angling impedimenta. But once we become aware of

the methods and tactics to employ in different feeding situations, catching fish should be relatively easy. Finding feeding trout, however, is the tougher goal, and one which many anglers fail to come to terms with. Unless we can locate feeding fish, we are wasting our time, no matter what tackle we use.

You have to be prepared to hunt over a wide area to locate trout which are feeding confidently, or undisturbed trout that are more willing to rise. Apart from blaming the weather, the wrong method, or the wrong fly are amongst the most common excuses for failing to catch fish. With stillwater fishing, where we cannot see our quarry, or where no obvious pools or lies exist, we can spend much of our time fishing over water which holds few, or no trout. The right fly and method are no good to us here. If we persist in fishing over such water, then the result will be obvious. It is essential to seek out and cover water which holds a good stock of fish. This intuitive seeking of the catchable fish, and an awareness of the trout's seasonal movements under given conditions, can only come with experience.

Most of the well known classic waters have now been well covered in journals, books and magazines, and one can at least approach a new water with some idea of where to go. Vacation time is precious, however, and I would suggest that for any visitor to a new fishery, the services of a good boatman for a few days will be money well spent. Not only will this save much frustration, and wasted valuable time locating fish, it will also be a much safer way of exploring unfamiliar ground. Local knowledge is hard won. A boatman will accelerate your understanding of a strange water, particularly the larger lakes. If you are put over trout, confidence soars.

HOW TO FIND FEEDING TROUT

Location is the key to success, and given time one can acquire a much deeper understanding of the fishes movements within a fishery in response to the seasons, and prevailing weather conditions. On a new water, with no obvious signs of moving fish, we are faced with a dilemma: where do we go; how do we locate wild brown trout? If we approach the unknown in a logical way, it should not take too long to build an understanding of the fishes' movements within a fishery.

There are always surprises. You produce a theory, and the fish will do their best to prove you wrong. Even on the smaller lake fisheries, the fish can be most contrary, and turn up in the most unlikely places. This could be a small bay, a lagoon or in the lee of an island with the wind blowing from a particular quarter.

Even if an area contains a low stock density and therefore does not warrant much attention, it always pays to be open-minded. However unlikely the less popular areas may at first appear, I would never completely rule them out for a fish, until experience has told me otherwise.

This hefty character – my biggest Corrib trout to date – weighed in at 10lbs 6oz.

WILD BROWN TROUT: THEIR SEASONAL PATTERNS

No matter what lake system we fish, certain factors will govern the trout movements within a fishery, and on a large, stillwater fishery, the most important factors will be the season, the food on which the trout are feeding, and the weather. The season and the food will determine the areas to which trout will migrate at particular times of the year, and the weather to a lesser extent will determine where within that area the trout are most likely to be. Although the least important of the three factors, weather is still a key factor.

Early Season in the Shallows

T.C. Ivens, in his book on stillwater flyfishing, wrote of the early season inshore migration of brown trout on the English reservoirs, and this inshore movement still applies today. To gain condition following the rigours of spawning, the fish move inshore to the productive food-rich shallows to feed. This is a natural post-spawning movement that is repeated every year. The need to gain condition quickly will drive the fish in search of food.

Shallow water warms quicker, and this is where the trout will find the greatest abundance of food. Extensive areas of shallow water, offshore reefs and the margins around islands are the areas trout will naturally move to in search of food, typically shrimp or asellus, (hog louse). However, other bottom-feeding organisms such as chironomid larvae, snail and caddis will also figure in the diet. Many of the larger trout, those fish in the six year plus age group, will be eating fry to build up and maintain body weight. Brown trout, once locked into a fish diet, are lost to fly anglers, and will not figure in our catches. Very rarely will one move to the surface, and take a fly.

Lifting from the Bottom

As the weather warms and the days lengthen, chironomid activity will increase. The available food density builds and from mid to late March, the trout will switch from bottom feeding to the much easier, and freely available zone feeding on chironomid pupae. Again, this will be over relatively shallow water, no more than 10 to 15 feet deep, and the shallower the water, the earlier in the season the fly will hatch.

The midge feeding will continue until another food resource becomes more freely available, to pull the trout off a diet of chironomids. On some waters, midge feeding can last well in to the summer months but on the limestone loughs which enjoy good hatches of ephemerids, the olives will be the next abundant food item to figure in the trout's diet. This does not mean that the trout cease feeding on midges once the olive hatches begin in earnest.

On the contrary, many of the fish will remain feeding on midge pupa if it is still abundant. Trout are opportunists and will always take the most freely available food resource. So providing the density of midge pupae remains abundant in the zooplankton, the fish will continue cropping them. Unlike the more active ephemerid nymphs, midge pupae are an easy target as they lie suspended somewhere between the bottom and the surface, waiting to make the slow ascent to hatch.

Sheltered bays provide ideal habitat for the olives. Look for water of shallow-to-medium depth, certainly no deeper than 15 feet, with a marl or silty bottom. Unlike the midge pupae, once the active, free-swimming olive nymph decides to hatch, it will waste no time in its ascent, and if the hatch is a good one they can cause some very frenzied rises.

The Switch to Olives

From mid-to-late April, as the olive hatches increase, a greater percentage of the trout stock will switch from midge to olive feeding. The fish follow the more agile nymphs to the surface, where they hang momentarily in the surface film, before emerging as a winged fly, the dun. This pause in the surface film, before the fly breaks through, is a very vulnerable period for the olive, and the trout are drawn to the surface to feed heavily on the emerging fly, and duns.

Mid-day Surface Feeding

Surface feeding will reach optimum levels at the peak of the hatch, sometime between 12 noon and early evening. The olives are an important fly for the imitative fly fisherman who enjoys surface sport, and along with the midges provide, I feel, the pinnacle of our imitative fishing. A rise to emerging or adult midge is exciting, and they can produce fish of a high average weight but the weather conditions are far more exacting for the midges than they are for the olives. Therefore a good rise to the midge is less predictable and very weather dependent, whereas with the olives, no matter what weather conditions prevail, surface sport at some time during the day can be expected with some degree of confidence. Even in the foulest of weather, they will emerge in sufficient numbers to induce the trout to the surface. Not only is the rise more reliable, it is also a good sized fly, which we can easily imitate with our artificials in both the nymph, emerging and adult form.

The Mayfly

The crowning of the olive season comes with the mayfly, and although the mayfly prefers a similar bottom to the olives, the flies emerge in greater numbers from the more open water shallows.

Once the mayfly hatch begins in earnest, the fly will draw fish from a wide area, and on lakes that enjoy a good mayfly hatch, some of the biggest trout of the season will come to the surface. It is a big fly, easy to imitate, and one which, along with the sedge, provides the fly angler with his best opportunity of the season for a big brown.

Like the olives, the mayfly nymph is an agile swimmer, and once the nymph leaves the sanctuary of the bottom it will waste very little time in its ascent to the surface. Upon hitting the surface, the nymph will hang suspended to the film while emergence takes place. Emergence can take up to 30 seconds or more before the dun finally pushes through, casting off its skin. In cold weather they may never get off the water at all, and are then dependent on the wind and waves to push them on to the shore. If such conditions prevail while a hatch is on, the duns are very vulnerable to predation by fish.

Close of the First Half of the Season

A good mayfly hatch can lead to some pretty frenzied feeding. Cover a rise at this time of year with a good imitation, and you have every chance of catching the fish but do not be blasé in your approach, as they do not always give themselves up as easily as we are sometimes led to believe. With the end of the mayfly, so the first half of the flyfisher's season comes to an end.

WILD BROWNS: MARCH TO JUNE

• At the beginning of the season, we started fishing close in-shore, over shallow water for bottom-feeding fish.

• The next phase is the zone feeding over shallow-to-medium depth water for trout feeding on midge.

• This is followed by the more active olive feeding, again over water of shallow-to-medium depth, particularly in the bays.

• The final phase is the progression to more open water of medium depth, interspersed with stony shallows for the mayfly feeding trout.

Second Half of the Angling Year

On the large loughs, the second half of the angling year is far less predictable. Most fishing activity will take place over open water, particularly from late summer to the back-end for daphnia-feeding fish.

Following the mayfly, there is a fallow period for surface activity, and I was led to believe from all that I have read and heard that this was due to the trout recovering from a feeding glut on the big fly. Many anglers held the belief that the trout were satiated with mayfly, or turned to feed exclusively on perch fry, or simply did not need to feed for several weeks following the hatch.

Myth of Mayfly-sated Trout

That was the theory, and one which we now have to question. To hold or improve condition, brown trout require food, particularly as their metabolic rate will increase in the higher water temperatures of summer. Brown trout can cease feeding for lengthy periods, but there would have to be a very good reason for a cessation of feeding, such as high water temperatures, algal blooms or preoccupation with spawning.

Healthy fish will not just cease feeding for several weeks or more because of previous over-feeding. If an

Two of the robust clinker-built boats typically used on Lough Mask. They are heavy to manoevre out of water but have the necessary sturdiness and 'ballast' to ride the squalls and hidden rocks on this huge lake.

abundant food supply becomes available, they will take advantage of it.

The water temperature by the end of May is still rising, but hasn't reached the summer highs which, in prolonged hot weather, would slow feeding down and send the trout seeking the comfort of deeper water. If this end of May fall-off in trout activity is not due to hot weather, or high water temperatures, or over-feeding on mayfly, then why do the fish appear to go off the feed? Trout stop moving at the surface, if there isn't any surface food to entice them there. This may be stating the obvious but a lot of anglers appear to overlook this simple fact. Daytime hatches of fly radically fall off at this time of year, and on the Corrib it is noticeable that there is no abundant surface fly for some time following the mayfly.

The fish haven't ceased feeding; they have ceased *rising* during the daytime. This is understandable, when there is a distinct lack of food at the surface. With a lack of surface food, the trout either turn to bottom feeding, daphnia or if there are plenty of fry, they will prey upon this rich food item. If fry are abundant, the fish can be very difficult to tempt with a fly, as they become locked into the translucent centimetre lengths of jelly protein.

Summer mayflies and, towards the end of August or early September, the lake olives will again put in an appearance. These flies can stimulate a rise of fish if the hatch is sufficient, but in the summer, daytime hatches tend to be less predictable than the spring hatches of fly. Early morning and late evening are the key times for summer hatches of fly, and midges, caenis and sedges are the flies that can produce some prolific rises if the conditions are right.

LOCATING THE RIGHT SPOT

It is very difficult to predict fish movements within large lough systems, but the trout do tend to follow specific behavioural patterns, which are repeated annually, with regard to their migration from one area to another. Food will always be a deciding factor deter-mining their movements but comfort, and spawning, are also factors we need to take in to account when attempting to locate trout. In warm weather, the fish prefer open water deeps, possibly for the cooler, well-oxygenated water rather than food. Certainly the shallow bays can appear to be devoid of stock during the summer months, but higher water temperature may not be the only reason for the apparent scarcity of fish within the bays at certain times.

Warm settled weather with periods of prolonged sunshine, and shallow water, are a combination that in most situations I would wish to avoid. Trout do not rise well in bright sunshine. This is supposedly because the fish do not like bright light, yet I have witnessed good rises in hot bright conditions on a number of occasions. Two instances spring to mind. One was a rise to bloodworm on Lough Sheelin, and the other was a surface movement to asellus on Farmoor, when a proliferation of this small crustacean became suspended in the upper layers in bright very hot weather.

Trout do not rise well in bright sunshine

In both these instances, the fish moved well for several days in conditions which would normally have been considered hopeless for surface sport, and they rose because food was present in large quantities, even though it was warm and bright.

Another example were the early mornings in the settled hot weather of the summer of 2003, when we found Corrib brown trout would consistently rise to a hatch of caenis. The fish moved well for several weeks, not because of the time of day – early morning around or just after sunrise – but because food was present, masses of it suspended in the surface film. This was in shallow bay areas which during the day appeared devoid of fish. These trout hadn't just swum two miles from the open water deeps to feed: they were there all the time but during the day there was nothing to entice them to the surface.

Lack of Surface Food

Contrary to popular opinion, I now feel that it isn't just bright sun that puts the fish down. The fish go deep, and stay down because there is no food to keep them in the upper layers. Why is it that brown trout rise well in other countries under azure skies, high temperatures, and burning sunshine? Quite simply, because there is food for them to rise to, whereas in the UK and Ireland in bright weather, there is very little food, certainly not in sufficient quantity to hold the trout in the upper layers.

It is well known that in hot bright conditions, aquatic insect activity falls off. But a big fall of ant, or a surface migration of snail on a bright day in July or August, will bring the fish to the surface as does the blood worm on Sheelin, or the asellus on Farmoor.

So keep an open mind, and you will catch trout that those stuck in the mire of tradition fail to catch. Locating feeding trout is the key. Find feeding fish, and you have done the hard work. The rest is down to tactical application.

Facing page: Evening light in July on Lough Mask, a time when all the angler's instincts are telling him to expect some action.

120

CHAPTER 9

Wild Trout Boat Techniques

A common mistake anglers make when fishing from a drifting boat is that they overlook the obvious, which is that they are fishing from a moving platform. They treat it as though they were bank fishing, and fall into the trap of casting too long a line. Surface fishing with a floating line requires good presentation. With wet fly, a lot of fish will take, just as the flies hit the water, or on the first few pulls after the fly's entry.

Good presentation at distance requires timing and control, and not many anglers can do this consistently. Where wild trout are concerned, particularly those subjected to angler-pressure, presentation is important.

Another problem many anglers are oblivious to when fishing a floater, is that trout do not like passing under a line, especially a flyline, and it doesn't matter if the line is clear, white or any other colour. A floating line sitting in the surface distorts the surface film and causes a shadow. Even on a dull day, when the fish are confident, they will be wary of passing under the line. Just because we are fishing a big water, does not mean that mindless casting, and lining of the water, will not scare fish.

An angler fishing from a boat should treat the water in front of him just as he would when approaching a trout on a river. In a river we can see the trout or the lie, and we avoid lining the fish, as we know the consequence of committing such a folly. The same should apply to the arc of water in front of an angler fishing from a boat. Keep the cast short, and the trout sees only the fly. You should avoid lining the fish, and making him wary. All one achieves by casting a long line is a much wider no-go zone into which the trout will not enter, because they will not pass under the flyline.

EARLY SEASON TECHNIQUES

Apart from very early season fishing, I now rarely use sunk line methods on wild fisheries. This is purely personal preference, and it may limit my opportunities. But I feel confident that I can catch a few trout on a floating line in just about any condition of weather or season. So apart from the first few weeks of the season, to the third week of March, when it is necessary to get small wet flies down in the water quickly, on long casts, a floating and an intermediate line are the only lines I fish the rest of the year on wild fisheries.

FINDING THE RIGHT LEVELS

Once I feel that the fish are moving through the upper layers, or looking to the surface for food, I concentrate on dry fly, nymphs and short lining for the rest of the season.

The transition from bottom feeding to zone feeding occurs with the buzzer hatches sometime around the third week in March. Once the olives start hatching in April, top water methods come to the fore. The period from the third week in March to mid April can be the most unpredictable of the fishing year, a time in the season when there is great fishing to be had, but there is a need for flexibility in one's approach.

For the very early season, fishing a team of wet flies on a sinking line, and searching the shallows for feeding fish, would be my chosen fly method. In light winds, I have found a floating line with a weighted nymph on the point, an unweighted pattern on the first dropper, and a wet fly on the top dropper, to be a good combination.

The important considerations for this early season fishing, are:

- the areas we fish
- the depth at which we fish
- and the speed of the retrieve

With wild fish, the takes will come either on the first few pulls; through the curve; or on the lift. So it

Fishing with Denis O'Keefe at Salthouse on Lough Corrib.

is essential that the flies are fishing from the moment of entry, and that you maximise the curve of the line during the retrieve.

Sinking Line Fishing

With a sinking line, use the drifting bias of the boat to create as much curve in the line over the given casting length, and control the speed of your lift as you raise the flies through the water. This will improve the catch rate. Avoid making a casual sweep of the rod during the lift, as a lot of trout will follow the flies up, and take as they rise in the water.

But trout which have followed will also take if you can hold the flies in the water for as long as possible. The boat will be bearing down on the flies all the time, and this will restrict the amount of time you can hold the flies at the end of the retrieve. Do not be in too much of a hurry to lift the flies. I have had a good many fish take a fly in the shadows of the boat.

The sinking lines I prefer for the early season fishing are a Wet Cel II or a Cortland 444 fast sinker. I would avoid the ultra-fast sinkers. For medium depth (water up to 10 feet) I fish the Wet Cel, and for a faster sinking rate in a fresh wind, to compensate for the speed of the boat's drift, or for water between 10-15 feet, the Cortland is ideal.

In the early season, we are fishing for trout that are feeding hard inshore over shallow water on asellus, shrimp, snail, caddis and any other bottom-living organisms that are accessible to the fish. The main food items will be asellus and shrimp, and it is these small invertebrates that we should be suggesting with our artificials. Flies such as March Brown, Hare's Ear, Fiery Brown, Sooty Olive and patterns that incorporate some hare's fur, mixed with olive seal's fur or ginger seal's fur in their body dressing, work well. I certainly would not like to be without a Hare's Ear, or a March Brown on the point at this time of year, as these are excellent suggestive patterns of asellus.

A steady retrieve, and not a rip, is all that is required to tempt the fish. When fishing with a sinking line, the presentation of the cast is still important.

Even though the trout may be feeding well on the bottom, if they are in clear shallow water, they will still notice the entry of the fly.

An angler fishing from a boat should treat the water in front of him just as he would when approaching a trout on a river.

If the flies fall in a heap, or land heavily with line splash, the trout will ignore the flies, even when they have sunk to the required depth. Good entry is important even when fishing sunk line, and if the trout's attention is aroused without suspicion when the fly enters the fish's zone of vision, there is a good chance that it will take the fly in the first few pulls.

LONG-CASTING

With dry fly fishing especially, long casting is a handicap which should be avoided, unless one is casting to a rising fish – a seen target. The only other time I would recommend fishing a long line when drift fishing for wild fish, is for nymphs or sunk line methods. For these two methods it is essential to cast a longer line so that the line and the flies have time to sink to the fishing depth.

THE FIRST BUZZER HATCHES

Around the third week in March, the first real midge (or buzzer) hatches of the season occur, and this earmarks a change in my approach. This is what I call the transition period, when the trout leave the bottom, and begin zone feeding. Depending on the weather, the fish will rise and fall with the midge pupae that have risen from the bottom mud-dwelling larval stage (bloodworm).

Once the bloodworm have made the change to the pupal stage, they ascend and descend through the water layers, until conditions are right for them hatch. The pupae are not free swimmers like the ephemeroptera nymphs. Movement through the water is a rather haphazard rapid wriggling motion, so they are very vulnerable to predation by fish, particularly as the pupal stage can last for days, possibly even weeks before the right weather conditions occur for them to hatch. When the weather conditions are suitable, then the pupae ascend to the surface and hatch into the winged adult. Unlike the upwinged mayflies, ephemeroptera, members of the diptera family, do not emerge as duns. There is no dun stage, so once the midge emerges as a winged adult, it does not undergo a final moult before mating and egg laying.

Sub-surface Nymph Tactics

Until conditions are suitable for top water fishing, I concentrate on sub-surface nymph tactics during this transitional stage. In the three or four weeks, until the olives hatch in numbers, there may even be a handful of opportunities to fish dry fly to rising trout in good conditions.

The weather we are waiting for is that of light wind, and rising temperature. Ideally, we want both emerging and egg-laying adults on the water for good dry fly fishing. Sadly, if the last few seasons are any thing to go by, this happens all too infrequently. If the weather is right, early dry fly fishing can be superb. Wind isn't such a major factor with the olives and the mayfly, but for good surface sport with buzzer-feeding fish, the weather is an important considera-tion, and one which will have the greatest influence on whether the trout will rise or not. Spring and wind go together however, and much of the buzzer fishing will be using sub-surface with nymphs.

A slow presentation is the key to successful nymph fishing, so it's essential to slow down the rate of drift

I prefer to fish with a floating line, so I use a fluorocarbon leader at least 20ft in length, to take my flies to the required depth. Deep fishing with buzzer imitations is a method that has really caught on in Ireland recently but it is a method that many anglers do not exploit to its full potential.

For good nymph fishing, especially on the windy days, it is not enough to have the right tackle, flies and an understanding of how to fish them. All this is wasted, if you do not control the boat's speed of drift.

A slow presentation is key to successful nymph fishing, so it is essential to slow the rate of drift down. If the boat is drifting too quickly, a fast retrieve is necessary to maintain contact with the flies. The boat's drift, the line recovery, and the length of time the flies are fishing in the zone are all related.

With an uncontrolled boat, everything is happening too fast. In light winds, a drogue will not be necessary, but in any wind greater than 10 to 15 mph, the boat will require a drogue to allow the angler time to fish his imitations correctly.

Nymph Patterns

Nymphs that I favour for wild browns feeding on buzzer are patterns tied with grey goose herl, or peacock herl bodies, as well as Diawl Bach, Pheasant Tail and Hare's Ear, patterns similar to those I fish on the reservoirs. I favour flies with natural herl bodies, in preference to the current vogue of flies with epoxy or nymph body materials. Pheasant Tail, grey goose, heron or peacock herl are the natural materials I favour for the bodies of my nymph patterns.

A buzzer pattern tied with a Canada goose herl body, silver or copper rib, peacock herl for the thorax, and a few white fibres for breather filaments, is not only simple to tie but also takes some beating as a deceiver of trout. Keep the flies simple, particularly the deceiver patterns, and do not fall into the trap of accumulating endless different patterns of fly. All this will achieve is to deflect your train of thought from the important issue of finding feeding fish, and working on the presentation. I fish similar leader set-ups to those already described in the reservoir section for nymph fishing, and these are made up using 5 or 6lb 0.185 to 0.205mm fluorocarbon.

With fluorocarbon and slim nymph patterns, I achieve the taking depth on most days without diffi-culty. If, however, I require more depth, I fish a leaded fly on the point as opposed to the competition angler's solution of using heavy wire hooks. I find that fishing a weighted fly on the point is far more versatile than the epoxy buzzer tied onto a heavy wire hook. A mistake that a lot of anglers make fishing a weighted fly or epoxy buzzer over wild brown trout, is that they let the flies sink too deep. Bright sunny days are classic condi-tions for deep nymph fishing but do not automatically assume that the trout have retreated to twenty feet, or deeper. The fish will be where the food is, and for spring trout feeding heavily on buzzer or olive nymphs, that will be over water no deeper than 10-12 feet.

It is only in prolonged hot weather that the wild trout head for deep water, and leave the food-rich shallows. So even in bright conditions, the fish are going to stay with the food, and if that band of food is lying at a certain level (zone), they will remain at that level even if the bottom drops away to twice or three times the holding depth. The deep water methods that work well on the reservoirs work equally well with wild fish but it should be remembered that you are not going to get a lot of nips and pulls to help guide you in to the taking zone. The concentration of wild trout will be never as great as the stock densities on the reservoirs. Therefore the number of takes will be far fewer but that does not mean you are fishing at the wrong depth, or with the wrong imitations.

If in Doubt, Go Shallow
My recommendation to anglers who are unsure about which flies to use, and at what depth to fish, would be to use slim buzzer patterns, and to think shallow rather than deep.

At least if your imitations are above the fish, there is a good chance of the trout seeing them, and taking, whereas if they are below the fish, there is very little prospect of this happening. With the wild fisheries, if we guess wrong, there are no wayward rainbows to help guide us into the optimum taking depth or help with location. Guess wrong, and your flies will be fishing in a lot of empty water.

Keep it Slow and Keep in Contact
It cannot be over-stressed that, to be successful with nymphs, the speed of retrieve should be as slow as possible, and that contact with the flies should be maintained at all times. Once the cast has been made, ensure that flyline and leader are straight between fly and angler from the moment of delivery. Should the leader fall untidily, it may be necessary to give the line a steady draw immediately after the cast has alighted on the water, to straighten the line.

Once contact with the fly has been made, the angler should maintain contact by keeping the flyline straight. This is best achieved with a figure-of-eight retrieve, as it produces a continuous movement.

Maintaining contact with the flies as the boat drifts down onto them, ensures that the flies are fishing all the time, and should a trout take, it will be detected. Remember, we are fishing these flies dead slow, so for the first part of the drift they will be sinking through the water, as we are imparting very little lateral movement. We cannot see, or detect by feel, the level to which the flies have sunk. However, we can either time the sinking phase, or determine over a set distance when we need to slightly increase the rate of retrieve.

The Lift
Once the flies have sunk to the desired level, it is essential to slightly increase the speed of recovery, so that the flies fish on a level plane or through a shallow curve until we lift them in the water, prior to making the next cast. Be very watchful when making the lift. This can be a very productive part of the retrieve. Ensure that raising the rod, and hand manipulation of the line, work in unison to produce a continuous movement throughout the lift.

Watch the fly line and leader, as you raise the flies in the water, for any sign of movement, and strike at the slightest indication of a take, particularly when you hold the flies at the end of the lift.

In areas where, from previous experience, we know there is a concentration of fish, such as the corner of a bay or a channel between reefs, the use of an indicator can be worthwhile – especially in bright conditions and light winds.

A mistake that a lot of anglers make fishing a weighted fly or epoxy buzzer over wild brown trout, is that they let the flies sink too deep

Indicators
Indicators are floating visual aids from which a nymph or a team of nymphs are suspended. There are many commercially-produced indicators and they come with instructions for attaching them to the line.

As an alternative to the commercial product, one can use a piece of polyester floss or a buoyant dry fly such as a Deer Hair Sedge. The indicator floats on the surface, supporting the flies suspended beneath it, and provides a warning when a trout takes. It also holds the trailing nymphs at a constant depth, much like a coarse angler's fishing float.

The advantage of this method is that, once the holding depth of the trout has been established, the angler can fish the nymph imitations for longer at the productive level. By setting the indicator to the required depth, a very natural presentation can be achieved. The flies sink to the fish-holding zone and are then suspended in the productive layer.

It is essential to avoid any movement of the indicator, caused either by the effects of wind and current on the line, or through irregular retrieving, because this gives the nymphs an unnatural appearance.

> *Occasionally, a bit of movement can induce a take*

On occasions, however, I have found that fish can be induced to take a suspended nymph by slowly lifting the rod to ease the flies up in the water, and then letting them fall again. This is a *steady* movement of the fly, and very different to the unnatural movement imparted by too much line drift, or excessive hand-retrieve.

A good time to make this controlled lift, to induce a take, is after a fish has shown interest by just touching or 'knocking' the flies.

Exponents of the 'indicator method' will tell you that the best presentation is dead slow or completely still, but there are situations, such as the one just described, where a bit of movement can induce a take.

The Depth Range

Finding the taking-depth requires a little detective work. You have to imagine a 20-foot water column divided into 3-foot bands. I would never consider going deeper than 20 feet, and for most of my nymph fishing I would rarely go beyond 12 feet.

For depths greater than 9 feet I fish three nymphs below an indicator, and for 9 feet or less, I fish only one or two imitations. For depths shallower than 3 feet, I would opt for a different method such as the Washing Line, or fishing a nymph using the New Zealand style – both of which I shall describe.

Washing Line Style

This style demands a dry fly on the point and two nymphs on the droppers, about 5 feet apart, on a 20-foot leader. I keep the end of the flyline well greased to keep the tip of the line floating, and prevent it from being drawn under the water by the weight of the sinking droppers or water absorption through the tip of the fly-line. The floating flyline and the dry fly on the point of the leader will hold the droppers high in the water, even if you impart a little movement to the line.

New Zealand Style

For this style you tie about 2 feet of monofilament to the bend of a dry fly and then tie a trailing nymph to the end of the leader. The dry fly acts as both lure and indicator. Both these methods are ideal for light wind conditions and you want to fish the flies with as little movement as possible.

There are two tactics with nymphs which I have found successful for wild browns when the trout are up in the water. One involves fishing the water blind with a retrieve similar to wet fly fishing, only slower, to allow the flies to sink a little deeper. The second is for rising fish that are preoccupied with the ascending pupae, or pupae near the surface prior to hatching. These fish take a fly that is slowly falling. It is essential that no movement, other than a natural descent, is imparted to the fly.

Fishing the Water Blind

For fishing the water blind, I cast a short line no more than 15 yards, and retrieve with long slow deliberate pulls. These would be much slower pulls than I would fish with wet flies, and no more than half a dozen pulls, before lifting off with a long steady draw and a simultaneous raising of the rod hand, thus lifting the flies a good distance from the boat.

Because of the greater distance from the boat when making the lift, the flies follow a much narrower angle, and therefore the lift covers a much broader band of water.

With slim nymph patterns, a hackled nymph on the top dropper, and a fluorocarbon leader, the path of the flies follow a shallow curve with this type of retrieve, going down no more than 3-5ft.

On cloudy days when fish are not showing during the buzzer and olive hatches, I have taken good

Buzzers can come in all shapes and sizes. This is a selection of my own favourite patterns with varying amounts of hackle, body weight and thorax colour. When the duck fly or summer midge is hatching there is no better fly pattern than the sunk, or emerging, buzzer.

numbers of trout with this method.

This is a classic case of keeping your flies in, or just above, the holding depth of the trout, rather than letting your imitations sink through the productive zone. If a trout should rise, lift off and cover the fish immediately. Very often they will take during the first couple of pulls.

Be deliberate with your movement when raising your leader to the surface before lifting off, and covering a rising fish. Failure to raise the line, and the leader, prior to making the back cast, will put too much stress on the rod when you lift off. At best you will bungle the cast with a sloppy presentation: at worse you will shatter the butt section of the rod just above the handle.

Ascending Pupae

The second tactic is for trout feeding on ascending pupae in the late afternoon or evening, when they become locked into the sub-surface fly, and completely ignore dry flies. You can often see them feeding just below the surface. In situations such as these, I tend not to target individual trout but to cast my flies into the general area of activity, and then maintain contact with the flies as they sink.

Very often the trout will take the fly on the drop

– but they will completely ignore it if you impart any sort of lateral movement.

When they are in this sort of mood, the most productive presentation is the falling fly. If the fish do not take on the drop, and you feel that the nymphs have fallen below the trout, lift off with a smooth draw, and repeat the procedure. This, on the right evening can be a deadly method, and one that will take fish quickly.

For fishing on the drop, avoid slim heavy flies or flies with any sort of weight in the dressing, or a sinking leader material such as fluorocarbon. We are trying to hold up the flies' rate of descent as much as possible.

We are trying to hold up the flies' rate of descent as much as possible

Nymph patterns with some hackle or wing in the dressing, or standard nylon for the leader material, are ways of achieving this.

In fact, for fishing nymphs close to surface, I would always prefer standard nylon to fluorocarbon, even though the latter now appears to be an automatic choice with most anglers for sub-surface work.

THE FIRST OF THE DRY FLIES – THE 'TRANSITIONAL STAGE'

The season began with wet fly for trout feeding hard on the bottom, later moving on to nymph fishing as buzzer activity increases. This is what I call the 'transitional stage', as the fish leave the bottom and move up through the water to feed on the fauna.

A good indicator that this movement is taking place can be observed in the digestive tracts of any fish that are killed for eating. The lower end of the stomach can be crammed with asellus, snail or shrimp whereas nearer the throat, the stomach contains buzzer pupae. This would suggest that the density of buzzer pupae is now sufficient to entice the trout off the bottom.

At some time during the transitional stage, there will come a day when the wind will ease, producing a nice pin ripple. These are conditions beloved of the imitative flyfisher, and if there is a good fall of egg-laying adult fly, combined with the emerging midge pupae, we will have our first realistic chance of trout on the dry fly.

Even in March, if trout are rising to the pupae,

and they rise well in calm or light wind conditions, it is possible to take a fish on the dry fly but it does pay to be aware of how the fish are moving. The sight of rising fish will convince a good many anglers that the trout are taking the fly off the surface, and on observing such activity, they automatically reach for a dry fly outfit.

But early in the buzzer season, this may be a mistake, particularly if the trout are locked in to the pupae, as the majority of fish will totally ignore a surface imitation even though the trout appear to be rising inches below the surface.

Such a rise can leave the angler fishing dry fly frustrated, as he is caught between two methods, and left with that nagging feeling that most of the action is happening sub-surface but can't convince himself enough to make the switch. If a fish does take a dry,

Lough Mask brown trout – I doubt there is a more thrilling and beautiful fish in the world.

and there are always one or two trout willing to break the rules, then this can make the angler even less inclined to change to what might be a more productive method.

A good fall of adult fly will entice the trout to the surface, where they then move well to the dry fly. It is a question of being observant, and recognising the feeding pattern. Look for the head or the neb of the fish actually breaking through the film to take the surface fly, and do not confuse this with a surface movement of the water, where a trout has taken a food item just below the film.

Sub-surface Takes

If the trout are taking sub-surface, you see a boil in the water as the surface is disturbed by the movement of the fish, or the back and dorsal, or the tip of the tail lobe of a rolling fish. These may be surface movements but they are not always indicative of a trout actually taking fly off the top of the water. Early season trout haven't fully locked into taking fly right off the surface, and it can sometimes take a lot of fly to induce them to. Always study the rise forms while you are fishing, as wild browns can be very particular.

Dry fly is my favoured method, but a slight change in weather conditions will almost certainly put the fish down again, and you do not want to waste valuable time fishing the wrong method, when chasing the early season trout. If fish are moving near the surface, don't automatically assume that they will take a dry fly. Get it wrong and the bag count will be light. Experience has taught me that these little windows of opportunity do not last for long.

Effects of Weather

When you are out in a boat exposed to the elements from all points of the compass, subtle changes in the weather can occur at any time during the day, and if you are in tune, you instinctively know when a positive change in weather conditions has occurred. Late afternoon or early evening are likely times for these changes in conditions, if they are going to happen. A slight drop in the wind and we feel as if the temperature has risen, but in all probability, it is the chill factor which has dropped. A little cloud cover to prevent the evening temperature falling quickly, and conditions feel more comfortable. We sense this, and the insects sense this

also. Suddenly we become aware of adult fly on the wing all along the margins, and around the boat. The wave has fallen away to a light ripple, and the rise forms of trout taking midge pupae can now be clearly seen. If they are locked in to the pupae, you will catch very few on the dry fly. In such a situation I would continue fishing nymphs, until I had actually observed the trout taking off the surface. Only then would I switch from nymph to the dries.

For my dry fly leaders I use copolymer monofilament. The only time I would consider fluorocarbon is for fishing a single fly in a flat calm, and even then that would only be if the co-polymer failed, which rarely happens. Copolymer may be an absolute swine to fish with, as it twists and kinks very easily, but for fishing dry flies I find it infinitely superior to fluorocarbon.

As a second choice I prefer standard nylon to fluorocarbon for top water fishing. The big disadvantage with fluorocarbon is that, because of its greater density, it drags the flies down too quickly. This sinking problem is accelerated in a wind. It is also a stiff material which can cause rejection as the fish takes. Accept the twists and kinks, try to smooth them out as much as possible, and stick with the copolymer monofilament for top water fishing.

Accept the twists and kinks, try to smooth them out as much as possible, but stick with the copolymer monofilament for top-water fishing

Dry Fly Leaders

A typical leader would be about 20 feet long, made up from 0.205mm diameter monofilament, with two droppers for midges or small fly imitations such as olives or the smaller sedges. My top dropper would be 10 feet from the fly line, with 5 feet between the first and second dropper, and the same again between the second dropper and point fly. This would be the standard type of leader I use for all small fly top water fishing throughout the season.

The only time I change this configuration is when the fish are proving difficult, and I feel the need to go finer to deceive the trout. In such a situation I would drop to 0.185 mm, and fish either a single fly or two flies.

Flies for Buzzer-rising Trout

For the buzzer-rising trout, I have reduced my dry flies to two presentation types. One sits low in the film, and the other sits with the body penetrating the film. For the flies that sit low in the film, a simple pattern such as a Bob's Bits or a Shipman's in a variety of colours are all that are required.

Personally I prefer the Bits type pattern. It is simplicity personified, a fly dressed with a natural fur body, and just a few turns of hackle. The colours that I prefer are claret, fiery brown, black, ginger, orange, hare's ear, olive and grey. These colours will cover both the early midge rises, the olives and later the smaller sedges.

For the fly that sits with its body through the film, I prefer a Klinkhamer or Klinkhamer variant. Cul de Canard patterns undoubtedly catch trout but they are messy and time-consuming to fish in a rise. They require too much attention to make them float again after the capture of a fish, and lost time can prove costly. It is far quicker to tie on a new fly, when using Cul de Canard patterns, than to try and dry or impregnate a fly with floatant after catching a trout.

If the fly is well-sodden, floatant remedies rarely work anyway. Whereas with the post hackle flies or the Bits dressings, all I do is wash the fly, and give it a quick squeeze to remove the moisture following the capture of a trout. In most situations there is no need to add floatant to the fly, particularly the Bits, as the air trapped within the fur will keep the fly afloat. A few false casts, and I am straight into action again, following the capture of a fish. No time is wasted and, in a rise this can prove invaluable, and has caught me many extra trout.

I have two dry fly patterns in my box that I would not be without.

One is a post-hackle dry consisting of a black rib, dark grey herl body, peacock herl thorax with a white polyester or antron post, and a grizzle hackle. This fly is for fishing with the body penetrating the film, when the trout are taking emerging fly.

The second fly, I call the Duster; a Grey Duster variant with no tail whisks, just a body of grey seal's fur instead of mole skin body fur, and finished off with two turns of a well-marked badger hackle. From late March, this simple fly is deadly and has caught me more quality browns from Corrib and Mask than any other single pattern of fly in my box.

My Love of the Duster

I discovered just how effective the Duster can be, quite by accident about 15 years ago. We visited the Corrib for the olives, and possibly some mayfly fishing in early May. Our first day, following an overnight frost, was one of bright sunshine and flat calm, or very light wind, conditions which were far from promising. It wasn't until mid-day, that we motivated ourselves to venture out. We didn't know where to start, and just pointed the boats in a general direction and cruised. If nothing else, it was a good day for seeing the lake.

So it was much to my surprise therefore, that in a shallow bay just off the main boat channel, outside some markers, we noticed fish rising. Conditions may not have promised much in the way of fish but if these trout were rising, then we reasoned, they were catchable. It was just a question of finding the right formula. Easier said than done.

We threw everything at those trout for two hours or more, without the slightest interest from the fish. The trout were feeding on both emerging midges, as well as the adult egg-laying fly. As the day became warmer, the adult fly came out in droves. With all this fly littering the surface, the fish were totally locked into food suspended in the film. It was just a question of determining the colour, and presentation preference of the fish. But nothing that we tried would pull them off the natural fly.

Just before lunchtime, after countless fly changes, I was looking for yet another pattern which might induce a positive reaction from the trout. In the fly patch of my waistcoat were some flies that I had been fishing with on my last fishing trip, which had been to the River Windrush. I thought I may as well give one of the river patterns a go. A Grey Duster variant, tied with seal's fur instead of mole's fur for the body, took my fancy and so I tied one on. I had made no more than a few casts with the new change of fly when a trout took me, a fish which unfortunately shed the hook just as I was drawing my hard-won prize to the boat. We had arranged to go in for lunch with

friends, and it was time to go, but I now felt confident that, on our return, I would catch those trout.

In the afternoon session, I took eight good fish on the fly, before the trout went down. No other fly that I tried on that particular day would work, and no one else in our party took a fish. It was the day of the Duster, and the only pattern I had with me was a leftover from my last river fishing sortie. That fly became my key possession.

With no fly tying kit between us, we could not tie up some similar patterns, and although there were a few Grey Dusters in the fly boxes of other members of our party, they did not resemble the body colour of my fly. The flies were tied with the classic mole skin body fur, or rabbit skin under fur, and the fine hair, when wet, was just too dark.

The effectiveness of the Duster for wild brown trout rising to adult midges, had been established, and that particular fly, a scraggy leftover, spawned many others on my return to England. Body light grey seal's fur, hackle a well marked badger – simple but deadly. I would never be without it now.

THE ARRIVAL OF THE OLIVES

Eight wonderful weeks, during the months of April and May, provide the best day-time imitative fishing on the western limestone loughs. There may be days either side of these months in March and June when, blessed with the right conditions, we can expect to make good catches, but the best fishing, particularly to rising fish, will undoubtedly occur with the peak of the spring hatches of fly.

The three main insects of interest to both angler and trout are: the buzzer – the earliest of the spring flies to hatch; closely followed by the lake olive; and finally the mayfly which provides the grand finale. These three flies are the essential element of spring fishing, and for the imitative fisher they provide the champagne period of the season.

Above: Vaughan Lewis plays a good fish on the lower Corrib, keenly watched by his self-appointed gillie, Dee.

131

The appearance of the beautiful lake olives on the surface of the lough will often attract the attention of the bigger fish. Although not quite as large as the mayfly (which usually emerges a little later), it is nevertheless a worthwhile early-season meal for a trout, and will be taken as a freshly hatched dun (as here) or later as a spent fly.

LAKE OLIVES

Lake olives are members of the mayfly family (*Ephemeroptera*). They hatch in huge numbers during the early part of the season, a prelude to the largest mayfly (*E. danica*). Olive fishing can also be affected by the weather, but less so than buzzer fishing. For the angler who enjoys imitative fishing, but who does not want to join the mayfly jamboree, or run the risk of the buzzer season weather lottery, the olives are well worth consideration. Overlapping and sandwiched between both the buzzer, and the mayfly, the lake olives enjoy a lengthy season of at least six weeks. Through late April and May, they can provide excellent day-time fishing.

By late April, the daytime hatches of buzzers are waning and, as the season progresses, they tend to be either earlier, or later in the day. Olives on the other hand hatch from mid-day to early evening.

Best Times to Fish

The intensity of these olive hatches is such that it will pull the trout off the buzzers during the day. That is why, if I intend to fish the olives, I very rarely venture out early, for the best of the fishing will occur sometime between 11am and 6pm. On some days we may experience two hatches, one from 11am until 2pm, and another from 4pm to 6pm, but two hatches would be exceptional. The time, intensity and duration of an olive hatch depends on the prevailing weather conditions which vary from day to day. But the time of emergence does tend to follow a pattern. So if the main hatch for instance commences around 12-noon, it would not be unreasonable to assume that their emergence would occur at a similar time on the following day, or for several days following.

Life Cycle of the Olive

Olive fishing gives you a greater opportunity to fish dry fly to moving fish for it is predominantly a top-water pursuit. To understand why, we need to consider the life cycle of the olive. The trout have very little opportunity to take the nymphs before they leave the sanctuary of their burrows in the muds. Unlike the buzzer pupa which may, if the conditions are not suitable for emergence, hang in a zone somewhere between the bottom and the surface for several days or more, the olive nymph is an active swimmer and once it has decided to hatch it will rapidly ascend to the surface where it will hang, momentarily, before emergence.

Trout, therefore, lack the opportunity to take them in large numbers. The most vulnerable periods are those prior to emergence and the period immediately following emergence – before the duns take to the wing. As with buzzer fishing, a day of light wind is desirable, as the surface film then becomes more difficult for the nymph to puncture, thus slowing the period of emergence. Better still, a light wind on a cool day with fine precipitation can be ideal for surface sport. This not only slows the emergence of the fly, but also slows the drying out period following emergence, causing the duns to sit on the surface for longer. These conditions, which make the olive vulnerable to predation by trout, can produce some superb imitative fishing and a dry fly angler's dream day.

Leaders

For dry fly fishing I use copolymer 0.205mm or 0.185mm monofilament leaders; and for nymph or wet fly fishing in the upper layers, I favour a standard nylon 0.205mm or 0.225mm. This is a small fly period, and I rarely fish flies larger than a size 12, even in a big wind.

Poor Weather Tactics

During the early part of the season, strong winds make dry fly fishing with small flies next to impossible. If the presentation is suffering I would opt for the wet fly. Trout will sometimes show a marked preference for wet flies in wild conditions; whether this is because the fish are focused on taking the emerging or drowned flies I do not know. The exaggerated movement of the wet fly does appear at certain times to be attractive to the trout, when static dries may be ignored.

A good tactic on windy days is to fish a team of small wet flies on standard nylon, with the leader greased up to keep the flies high in the water. Even with a slower retrieve the flies will hold up, and the longer the flies are in the critical zone, the greater your chance of a take.

On dull days the trout tend to hold higher in the water, and this is why for this kind of fishing I prefer the standard nylon which holds the flies up better. I would not consider fluorocarbon, unless the trout had obviously gone deeper.

Today, anglers automatically reach for the fluorocarbon monofilament as a leader material for all feeding situations. This can be a mistake for spring fishing when, on many days, a fluorocarbon leader in conjunction with an intermediate line (a popular combination with wet-fly anglers) will drag the flies below the taking zone. Always consider, before tying

up a leader, the type of presentation you are trying to achieve, and use the leader material which is most applicable.

- For top-water dry-flies, use copolymer.
- Fishing nymphs or wet-flies high in the water, use standard nylon.
- For deep nymph or quickly fished flies, use fluorocarbon.

Stick to this basic formula and you won't go far wrong.

Best Flies

A tactic that has worked well for me is a combination of an olive bumble pattern on the top dropper, and two nymphs for the middle dropper and point. This has proved itself to be a useful combination in strong, squally winds, conditions which seem to have been such a feature of spring fishing in recent seasons. Nymphs such as Pheasant Tail, Diawl Bach, Hare's Ear and Olive Nymph, in sizes 12 and 14 work well. For the top dropper a size 12 Olive Bumble, or a palmered pattern (consisting of light olive, a bit of yellow and ginger in its make up) would be fine. If the fish show a preference for a top dropper which causes a bit of fuss on the surface, a good wake fly such as the Mini Muddler can prove effective. Deer-wing emerger patterns can also make good wake flies when fished on the top dropper with a bit of movement.

When the Fish Stay Down

If the conditions are such that the trout stay down, then deeper nymph tactics with nymph patterns, such as those already suggested, and of course buzzer patterns are a must. Trout take buzzers throughout the season, but there are times when they take buzzer imitations for other fly nymphs, and the olives are a classic for this mistake.

I have on occasion taken trout on buzzer imitations, that have been stuffed to the gills with olive nymphs, and not a midge pupa in sight. The trout may have taken the buzzer imitations for what they represented, but I feel that they took them for olive nymphs.

If this is the case, it just goes to prove that trout do not see our flies as we see them; they are deceived by certain triggers of shape and colour, irrespective of the imitation's resemblance to the real thing.

John Donlon and Mike Hartnet drifting the middle narrows on Lough Corrib.

Nymph fishing at this time of year is very productive, and it is possible to take good catches of quality trout in the right conditions. Once feeding fish have been located, make a note of which patterns and presentation the trout prefer, as it will no doubt be repeated for several days, maybe even longer.

EARLY SEASON DRY PATTERNS

The dry flies which I have found effective at this time of year are: Claret Bits, Ginger Bits, Hare's Ear (tied with a red game hackle), Grey Duster and a Klinkhamer variant (with a slim body of hare's ear and dark olive seal's fur mixed and a cree or red game hackle).

When the trout are hitting the duns, the Ginger Bits and the dry Hare's Ear take some beating. When the fish are focused on the emerging fly, the post-hackle Klinkhamer-type flies are excellent.

The Duster and the Claret Bits are good all-round patterns for the olive season, and if there are buzzers on the water the Duster can prove indispensable. In dull light, the Claret Bits can, for whatever reason, pull fish. Under a low cloud-base and damp conditions, it is amazing how effective the Claret can be for trout feeding on the emerging duns. My favourite flies however, for fish taking the duns, would be the Ginger Bits and the dry Hare's Ear.

The intensity of a good olive hatch can excite the trout to say the least. Trout sometimes move a lot of water in their eagerness to capture the escaping fly, and these frenzied rises can be seen a good distance from the boat. So the angler, if he is observant, has plenty of warning of an approaching fish.

Tactics During the Rise

I enjoy casting to rising trout. It is one of the finer moments of stillwater boat fishing. The tactic is simple, and one that has caught me a lot of trout. The secret is to be ever-watchful and to see the fish early. If a fish rises during the olive hatches you usually have plenty of time to make a smooth lift and to put the flies down where you anticipate the trout to move onto them. Never put the cast of flies or the fly-line over the fish (there is no excuse for poor casting here).

If you line the fish in any way they will invariably go down, just as they would on a river if you were to line them. If you are uncertain about the distance or the direction in which the trout is moving, keep the cast short; at least this way you will not end up spooking the fish. In an olive hatch there is every possibility that the trout will rise again, and offer you another chance.

To give some idea of just how effective a well-presented dry fly can be at this time of year, one day in early June I went out at around mid-day, and was off the water by 6pm. Fishing with a Duster on the point, Ginger Bits on the middle dropper and a dry Hare's Ear on the top dropper, I caught an exceptional brace of trout, by quietly stalking fish which I knew, in the prevailing weather conditions, would show in a small shallow bay.

Light rain was falling and cloud cover was good – ideal conditions for the duns to stick, and the fish were taking advantage of the situation, confidently taking the flies with slow leisurely rises. As the rises were slow and deliberate, the better fish stood out, and by targeting specific rises I was fortunate enough, in a golden twenty-minute period, to catch trout weighing 5lb 7ozs and 4lb 2ozs on size 12 dry flies. Those cracking fish were a testament to the quality of brown trout that the Corrib can produce when conditions are favourable.

Wind Conditions

Light winds and a bright day comprise very demanding fishing conditions, so a good turnover of your leader is essential. In situations like this, where casting a three-fly cast on a long leader is difficult, it is advisable to reduce the number of patterns to two or even one, on the longest leader that you can handle. On days with a fresh breeze, and cloud cover I would fish three flies on a twenty-foot leader, with a distance of at least six feet between the droppers.

In clear water at this time of year, trout may be cruising deeper than you think, and they will have no problem seeing the flies spaced six feet apart. There are days when for some reason, one fly will draw the trout in and you see a swirl under the fly, and moments later it will take one of the other patterns. I have seen this happen many times in the mayfly season but it also occurs with the smaller patterns.

Also, the effectiveness of one pattern can alter if you change another member of the team: just as in wet fly fishing when the top dropper can pull the fish and the fly following behind is then taken.

Splashy misses or abortive takes would suggest that either the presentation is at fault or the pattern

may need changing. The commonest fault for such a reaction from the fish would either be that the leader line is too distinct, or that the fly is riding too high in the water. If neither of these two faults is responsible, change the pattern or the size of the fly.

The Lift

When lifting off to recast, make the lift a decisive movement, and if you attempt to cover a trout and fail, allow the fish time to pass before lifting off for another attempt. With luck you will have at least another opportunity, if not several, to cover the fish. Far better to make one good presentation to a confidently feeding trout, than any number of poor deliveries. This is all common sense, but sometimes difficult to put into practice in the heat of the moment. Try not to disturb the water with clumsy casts, and make every presentation a delivery that will fool a trout.

Short Casts

Until your target has been located, it is advisable to keep the cast short. This avoids creating a large exclusion zone around the boat, through lining the fish. The secret of productive top-water fishing for wild browns, is always to approach with caution and thus avoid disturbing the trout before they see your fly. When there are no signs of rising trout, do not assume that there isn't a feeding fish close by. It is essential to maintain concentration at all times, which can be difficult, particularly on the slow days.

However, you will catch far more trout by spending your time scanning the water, observing and remaining focused. If you are searching and alert you are truly fishing; the fact that you are not continually casting your flies onto the water does not mean you are not fishing.

The spring olive fishing (from mid-April to early June) provides, I feel, the most consistent top-water fishing of the season. Hatches peak around the last week of April to mid-May, and no matter what the conditions, a rise of some sort is almost guaranteed. Even in the mayfly, heavy hatches of olives may keep the trout focused on the smaller flies, and anglers preferring to fish the bigger mayflies will miss the small-fly feeding fish.

The mayfly is a big fly, and it is the sight of these large flies sitting on the surface of the water (no matter

This 5lb Corrib brown shows a little pike damage between the adipose and the tail. The pike on this lake grow to immense proportions and a trout of this size is by no means too big for the predator.

how few hatch) that anglers notice. Most anglers appear to be blinded by the larger flies, ignoring the hordes of smaller flies that are coming off, and more importantly the trout which are feeding on them. I have had some good days during the mayfly with olive-feeding trout, in the bays neglected by anglers as a mass movement of boats seek out the open-water mayfly drifts.

Mid-summer

Again in June, there are some excellent days to be had. Cool, humid days with plenty of cloud cover are the days to look for. Following the gales of May 2003, when the mayfly hatch came abruptly to an end, the olives provided me with some wonderful dry fly fishing with trout from 3lbs to 5lbs during the first two weeks of June.

Why the size of trout taken on dries is larger (on average) than those taken on wet flies, I do not know, but I feel it must be down to presentation. When you think about it, a fly sitting in the surface film has to be one of the most natural-looking presentations, and it is a presentation that you can emulate time and again. It is that natural presentation and the consistency with

which we can achieve it, which fools the better fish. I can think of no other reason for the disparity of weight between the wet-fly and dry-fly caught wild trout on these clear western limestone loughs.

MAYFLY

As the season progresses from April into May, daytime feeding on the olives reaches its peak, and the stage is set for the next part of season, the Mayfly: a fitting crown to the spring imitative fishing. By this time the trout are tuned in to looking to the surface for food, so dry fly is the method and no matter what the conditions, it is a method which appears to produce trout of a higher average weight than wet fly.

There are periods throughout the fishing year on the Corrib, when certain methods seem to catch bigger trout. One is buzzer fishing with nymphs, and another is dry fly for both the olive and the mayfly fishing throughout May and into early June. Buzzer fishing can be excellent if the conditions are right, but it is very weather dependant, and therefore difficult to predict, whereas the olive and mayfly fishing is far more consistent.

If I had to pick a window for a good fish on the dry fly, it would be the second or third week of May, when fly hatches are at their optimum, and although more risky as an alternative, the second week of June, when the hatches are falling off but the fish are still looking for fly. Although the fishing is slower in June, if your luck is in, the size of the trout when they do come can more than compensate for the fall-off in fish activity.

Flyline for Mayfly

For the larger flies, such as the mayfly and the bigger sedges, I use a minimum of 8lb 0.235mm copolymer. The heavier line reduces leader twist but it does not eliminate it. Kinking is a perennial problem, especially with the larger flies, but it is a problem which is made worse if we use a finer monofilament. Normally I would make my leader up with about 12 to 14 feet between the fly line and the top dropper, and about 7 to 8 feet between the dropper and the point fly. In strong winds, for better control I would use a thicker monofilament, and reduce the distances to 10 feet from the fly line to dropper, and 6 feet from dropper to point.

Avoid a 3-fly Rig

A lot of anglers on the Irish loughs fish three big flies on a leader, and I feel this is a mistake. Actively feeding wild brown trout cover a lot water, especially in the mayfly season. Trout looking up in clear water would find it just as easy to spot two large flies spaced 7 to 8 feet apart, as they would three flies spaced 4 or 5 feet apart.

Presentation, accuracy and the speed of covering a rising fish are all better with two flies, rather than three. These flies are large, light, wind-resistant concoctions of fur and feather and with three of them it is next to impossible to lift them off the water and put them down accurately, with a swift movement. The delivery time is slower and the presentation is very often clumsy. If you don't believe me, try it. See how much quicker it is to cast when you reduce the number of flies to two or even one.

A single fly would appear to be an obvious choice where the mayfly is concerned but when lake fishing for browns from a drifting boat, we very often do not see enough rising fish to justify the single fly. It is therefore a question of balancing the team, to make the most of both fishing blind, and casting to rising trout. In the mayfly when the fish are going mad, when a trout rises within casting range, you have a very good chance of taking him if you cover the rise quickly. Time is key to success. If the delivery is slow, your trout will be well away from where you last saw him rise, and a good opportunity has been missed.

Choice of Artificial Fly

With the mayfly, as with the midge and the olives, I fish a narrow range of flies, tending to concentrate more on finding undisturbed feeding fish. The flies which I find successful are tied in four body colours with dyed yellow grey squirrel for the wing and the tail, except for the Grey Mayfly which sports an undyed wing and tail. In order of preference I would list them as follows: Grey, Ginger, Green and Yellow. The Grey and the Ginger probably account for at least 80% of my mayfly trout but that is because I fish them most. There are special conditions which suit certain colours of fly.

For a dark overcast day with a strong wind, a high floating Yellow or the Grey fly works well. It is important, in a strong wind, that the fly sits well up in the water. Very often in such conditions, I will fish with just my leader and the two flies on the water, holding my fly line just above the waves. This keeps the flies floating for longer: they are not drowned by the wave slap.

It is important, in a strong wind, that the fly sits well up in the water

If the wind falls off, I change to less buoyant flies, as short rising may become a problem. On a day of high broken cloud with periods of sun and good light, the Ginger can be very effective. For light cloud, or when there are a good number of spinners about, the Grey usually out-fishes any other fly.

Towards the end of the mayfly, I find the Green to be effective, particularly during the early evening. Green is also a good colour on Lough Mask. The two colours that I find to be most effective over the whole duration of the season are the Grey, and the Ginger, in that order. If one of these two flies isn't working, I normally find that I am in for a tough day.

Keep the casts short, and be watchful for rising fish. A sizeable percentage of trout will come blind, but any surface movement from a fish that is within casting range should be covered without hesitation. The fishing isn't difficult. Dry fly is one of the simplest techniques, and I see no reason to over-complicate it. Mayfly fishing is great fun, so enjoy what is without doubt the best time of the wild brown trout fishing year on the limestone loughs.

DAPPING

Dapping is a very traditional method of flyfishing and it has a long history. It is used on both rivers and lakes, but is particularly popular on the Irish limestone loughs, such as Corrib, in mayfly time.

It is a method in which a natural bait (often a mayfly) or a bushy artificial fly pattern is suspended on a nylon leader attached to floss or blow-line. The floss, used with a long rod, is allowed to trail out in the wind and the fly is danced on the surface of the water in front of the drifting boat.

In a stiff breeze (which is considered ideal for this method) the blow-line carries the fly out a good distance from the boat. There is nothing very complicated about dapping, but in the right conditions, and in the right hands, it can be deadly. I have seen large numbers of good fish caught by this method. The trout find the dapped fly where they expect to find it, in the surface film. The fly is suspended from a nylon tether, so there is no fish-scaring monofilament lying flat on the water. It is an uncomplicated presentation.

The long rod helps to elevate the blow-line, allowing it to carry the fly away from the boat. Dapping rods of up to 16 feet or more can be seen pointing to the heavens during mayfly time in Ireland. However, I much prefer a light rod of around 14 feet. Playing a fish is much more enjoyable and I feel I have more control over the fly with a shorter rod.

In a strong wind, the rod is lowered to an angle of around 45 degrees to hold the fly or bait on the surface of the water. In such conditions the blow-line streams out at a very shallow angle almost parallel with the surface of the water. The advantage of rod length in such conditions is somewhat negated, as you can achieve the same results just as easily with the shorter rod. Holding the rod lower prevents the fly from being lifted by the wind and, depending on the wind strength, the rod is raised or lowered to keep the fly a respectable distance from the boat.

The lighter the wind, the nearer to a vertical position the rod should be held. So it is only in a light wind where a longer rod will offer an advantage (and in light winds I would always opt for the dry-fly!)

Instead of a fly-line, we use a floss or blow-line for dapping, of about 6 to 10 feet in length. The floss is attached to a monofilament running-line (14 to 20lbs BS) held on a fly reel or a centre pin reel. A leader of 6 to 8lbs BS around 6ft in length is attached to the business end of the floss line, and a size 10 hook (for natural bait) or an artificial fly is attached to the leader tip. As the leader does not touch the surface of the water, line diameter isn't so important. For dapping I prefer a standard nylon to either copolymer or fluoro-carbon as it is softer.

Other Naturals

Depending on the season, mayflies, daddy-longlegs, grasshoppers or shop-bought crickets are used as natural baits, and these natural baits should be kept in a well-ventilated box. Whether you are using a natural or an artificial fly, the method is to hold the fly on the surface so that the trout will come to take it. Some anglers maintain that it is better to move the rod from side to side, sweeping the fly across the surface of the water. I have found with seatrout that the moving fly produces more rises.

But for brown trout I prefer to hold my fly on the surface of the water, and let the fly drift with the wind. This is a more natural presentation, and if I can drift the fly down the side of a wind-lane, so much the better. Never let the monofilament leader lie on the surface of the water, as this will spook the fish.

While employing dapping tactics, there is no rapid arm movement from the angler to cast the flies; the angler sits perfectly still. The trout sees no fish-scaring movement from the angler; he sees only the fly, which is exactly where he expects to find it, suspended in the surface film.

When using a natural bait one is advised to lower the rod as the fish goes down with the bait and delay the strike. However, I haven't found it necessary to delay too long, and with an artificial fly, the angler should strike immediately following the rise.

To me, dapping is a very sociable method of fishing, particularly suiting less-accomplished fishers. Every member of the boat will have the chance of catching a fish or two, and it is a great way to spend a breezy day out on the lough.

SUMMER FISHING

There is normally a fallow period following the mayfly but this, I feel, has more to do with the lack of fly activity, than with portly trout lying back allowing time for the food to digest after a period of over-indulgence. The next phase of insect activity following the mayfly of interest to the dry fly angler will be the summer hatches of fly over open water, the caenis in shallow bays or the sedge and midge hatches in sheltered areas behind islands, or in a few bays with easy access to open deep water.

Sedge or the midge fishing is largely a late evening pursuit but if you are keen enough to forsake your bed, the early mornings for caenis feeding trout can be very productive. For the bigger sedges, such as the Peter, Red Sedge or the Cinnamon, I fish the same leader set-up that I use for the mayfly, and for the smaller Silverhorn Sedges, I fish three flies on the finer 0.205mm nylon.

The midge fishing is a late evening affair, later than the sedges, and although always risky where the weather is concerned, if conditions are favourable then a good movement of fish can be expected.

Sometimes these rises can last well into the hours of darkness, as long as the fly continues hatching. If the light has gone, seeing the artificials or the rises can be difficult and it can pay to move the flies across the surface of the water, instead of leaving them static. You are maintaining contact with the flies all the time, so if a trout takes, you feel it, a bit like seatrout fishing in the dark. With either the sedge or the midge fishing, I would aim to cast to rising fish before the light completely goes, opting for the short evening or early morning sessions, especially if the conditions looked at all promising.

In the daytime, the majority of trout will come blind. It never ceases to amaze me how an area that appeared to be devoid of trout during the daytime, can become alive with moving fish in the half-light of a summer's evening. Early mornings, and late evenings are the key times to be on the water. They require some effort but the rewards are there, the fish are bigger.

An area that appears to be devoid of trout during the daytime, can become alive with moving fish in the half-light of a summer's evening

Lunch break on Illaundaullaur island on Lough Corrib looking towards Inchagoil.

FISHING THE BACK-END

Towards late summer and the back-end, many fly fishermen will be chasing open water daphnia-feeding trout with wet flies. Daphnia feeders definitely respond better to wet fly tactics but why they take a fly that bears no resemblance to the tiny crustacean they are feeding on, remains a mystery.

Trout, both rainbows and browns, which are locked in to daphnia-feeding, take coloured flies with some gusto. It must be a combination of movement and colour that triggers a response from the fish. Either way, this is certainly not imitative fishing. I have long given up trying to understand why some trout take a particular fly at a certain time in the season.

Daphnia feeding on the large Irish limestone loughs has been identified as a recent feeding phenomenon associated with enrichment of many of these great waters. But how recent? Brown trout which I caught on Lough Arrow in 1977 were stuffed with daphnia. Lough Arrow was a rich water but how far back do we have to go? I feel that daphnia feeding has always occurred, although probably on a more limited scale,

and at some time, a larger percentage of the stock have switched to feeding on this minute organism.

Fishing a remote hill loch in north-west Scotland, which had a bed of limestone, I once caught brown trout that had been partially feeding on daphnia. This was a remote loch, so enrichment was limited to a few upland grazing sheep, and yet it contained enough of those protein-rich minute organisms to interest the fish. Eric Taverner in his book, *Trout Fishing from All Angles*, stated that the main source of food supply in Lough Derg consisted of plankton crustacea. If we look hard enough through old angling literature, we will find there is very little new in angling.

The observations we make today are not so novel as we would like to think. Most rich limestone waters have always supported a population of daphnia but what has happened on many Irish limestone loughs, is that with nutrient enrichment, the daphnia population has proliferated.

Daphnia Feeding

Some of the largest animals on earth are plankton feeders, so fish do not have to pursue big meals if a small item is available in sufficient numbers, and is easy to crop. Because of the greater abundance of plankton crustacea, a greater percentage of the trout stock have switched to this readily-available source of protein, and anglers have now become aware of this. Daphnia-

Becalmed near the mouth of the Cong Canal on Lough Mask.

A good wave on Lough Sheelin with Derrysheridan in the background.

feeding has now been identified as part of the wild Irish brown trout seasonal fishing cycle, and although some of the stock may have been feeding on these crustacea for a good part of the season, it is in the late summer and back-end when fly fisherman concentrate on the open water plankton feeders.

I prefer shortlining with either a floating or an intermediate line, and a standard nylon leader for the late season wet fly. It is a no-nonsense approach but one which allows me to fish my flies quite high in the water, a presentation when combined with movement, and the right colour, which fish find quite attractive. The current trend is faster sinking lines, coupled with fluoro-carbon leaders, and longer distance casting, but my own approach lies in finding confidently-feeding trout.

First Find the Fish

Anglers can become too obsessed with technique, and overlook the obvious. Trying to tempt spooky wild fish that have been previously fished over, is always going to be difficult, no matter what method you employ.

Far better to seek out fresh stock. Then if you do find fish on a new drift or a line that has not previously been fished over, there is a good chance the trout will take. Also, unlike the early season fish zone feeding at depth, late season trout in warmer water temperatures tend to move higher in the water, and are prepared to chase.

Savage Autumn Takes

Autumn fish will at times swim a long distance to take the fly, and the hits can be quite savage, suggesting that the fish are moving at speed when they take. The aggressiveness of the takes may also suggest that the trout may quickly swim up to take the fly, and then equally as quickly return to the holding depth.

Because the late-season trout will travel to follow the fly at this time year, I do not believe it is essential to fish at a specific depth, provided your flies are not fishing below the trout. Fish a density of line that you have confidence in, and if you feel that casting a longer line gives you more confidence, then do so. But you do not need to cast a long line when searching out undisturbed feeding fish, because the boat is always drifting down onto them.

Wet Fly Patterns

We all have our favourite flies but for wild brown trout, if I had to choose colours for successful wet fly patterns, it would have to be claret, yellow, green, ginger, brown and, to a lesser extent black. I am trying to avoid the trap of naming an endless succession of wet fly patterns, and thus adding to the confusion of which fly to use on a specific day. I find some of the articles that are now being written about the different patterns we require for specific feeding situations, somewhat irritating. Particularly when a writer suggests a list of flies, and then recommends a totally different list of flies for the same feeding cycle, a year later. It would be understandable for a few new patterns to be added to a foundation of established favourites, but a completely new list of flies just leaves me reaching for the waste bin. For a newcomer to the sport, this must only add to the confusion. In terms of different fly patterns, or new methods of presentation, I feel that the trout are evolving defence mechanisms faster than we can invent solutions for breaking them down.

There is no doubt that, for certain periods of the season, such as the spring buzzer, and olive fishing, modern tactics and imitative fly patterns are often superior to some of the more traditional methods or forms of presentation.

But there are still days or certain times of the season, when the traditional approach will out-perform the contemporary methods.

Although I have had good days with dry fly, and much prefer to fish dries if conditions will allow, I have to concede that the late season fishing is really the domain of the wet fly angler. The fish are now feeding hard to improve condition for spawning, and this heavy feeding, particularly on daphnia, and the trout's more aggressive behaviour, make the moving wet fly a more productive method.

Traditional and Modern Combinations

When it comes to choice of fly pattern, it may be a question of combining something old with something new to attract the attentions of the fish but the method is the same. We search the upper layers of water in front of a drifting boat with a moving fly. There is nothing new when it comes to late-season tactics either: pulling is the method that works best, and for me, more than half a dozen pulls on a short line, combined with a smooth drawn out lift, works best of all.

Fishing with a twenty foot leader, I recommend five or six pulls finished with a long lift, over undisturbed water that hasn't been lined with the fly line. Fanning my casts left, middle, right, middle, left, I am covering new water all the time, and hopefully presenting my flies to trout that are totally unaware of my presence.

I want them to see the fly, and the fly only. An undisturbed fish is a confident fish, and is more likely to take my fly. The majority of takes will come either just after the fly has landed; within the first few pulls; or on the lift – so by fishing short casts, I fish out my retrieves much quicker, and therefore fish the most productive part of the retrieve more often.

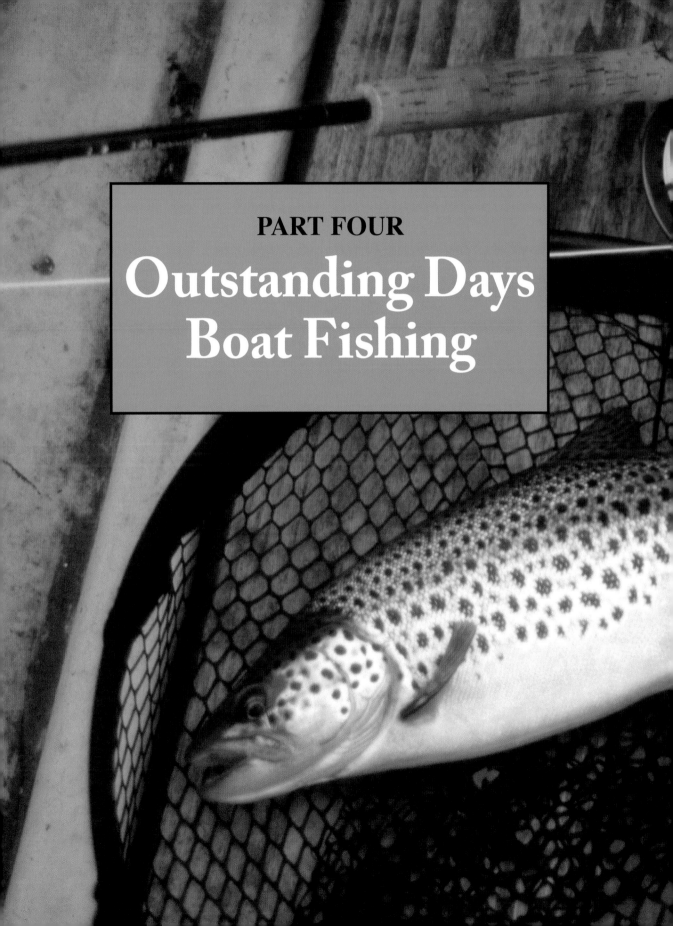

PART FOUR
Outstanding Days Boat Fishing

One to be returned: a fit Corrib brown trout.

CHAPTER 10

A Spring to Remember

It is a morning in late March or early April. The boat is lying idle in its mooring, protected from the main force of wind and wave. The wind is due north, a strong blow, at least a 6, possibly 7. The sound of the wind is all around as it hustles its way through the low trees and bushes, and the wave crests, broken by its force, produce an angry sea of white caps. The sky is a leaden, uniform grey, with no hint of colour.

The blasts of wind make you pull yourself deeper into the protection of your clothing. The lough is an inhospitable place to be. We scan the sheltered areas out of the wind for signs of fly life, small indicators to give some encouragement on such a cheerless day.

A lone chiffchaff calls from a thicket of scrub sallow and alder, one of the earliest summer migrants whose repetitive call is always a welcome sound. The

thicket of sallow shows hints of olive, yellow and green, its catkins providing an early flush of colour, before the leaves break bud.

It is the spring season, although the weather still has the bite of winter, and for fishing the buzzer conditions could not be worse. But at this time of year, the trout will be feeding hard to recover condition after spawning, and a few fish will surely come my way, even in these conditions, if I venture out. I'm tempted to go, but my spirit is fading with every breaking wave. This isn't my day. I turn my back to the boat and to the wind, and walk away. Time to wait.

Over the prime weeks of the buzzer and duck fly season, we will experience many such days, when the conditions are totally against us. It is possible to catch fish in adverse conditions but today there will be no surface movement, and unless we can find shelter, we will have to endure the bitter wind every time we start a new drift, which takes much of the pleasure of being out in a boat. For the imitative fisher, strong winds are a curse.

A good proportion of hardy early season anglers are visiting rods, wishing to experience maybe for the first time, the delights of the duck fly. The spring season is now a popular period of the Corrib year, almost as popular as the mayfly. A lot of duck fly anglers will go out in harsh conditions and sadly many of these eager fishermen will return disappointed. Fish can be caught, but they are taken sub-surface by those anglers who have found the feeding depth locating pods of buzzer-feeding trout in the many duck fly holes (localised areas that abound on the Corrib).

Whenever the conditions are such that surface activity is unlikely, fishing buzzer imitations sub-surface is the only way to take fish consistently but it could never be described as easy fishing, and it will test the best of anglers.

Trout give a clear answer to our offerings but sometimes we ignore it

When any hope of rising fish is non-existent, then we have to go down for them. Trout taken on nymphs at this time of the year are usually quality fish of a high average weight, and it is possible on the Corrib to catch wild brown trout averaging over 2lbs. This is what makes the duck fly so rewarding.

One Spring I waited eight consecutive days for conditions to improve, as we were hit by a run of strong northerly winds. I realised how lucky I had been in the past on my previous visits to the west of Ireland, to strike good fishing conditions as often as I did. Fishing for wild brown trout feeding on an organism whose life cycle is highly dependent on the weather, I had no way of cheating the prevailing conditions. If I wanted to catch wild brown on or near the surface, or indeed to enjoy the opportunity of casting a fly to a rising fish, the conditions would have to change.

Any improvement in the weather conditions from mid-March to mid-April will encourage the buzzer pupae to rise in the water, and to undergo their final metamorphosis. As the pupae rise to hatch, the trout quickly respond to this upward movement, and follow the ascending pupae towards the surface. If the surface tension delays the insect's emergence, so much the better for the angler. That is why, for fishing the emerging buzzer, we prefer a light ripple or calm conditions: it traps the emerging fly and the trout can feast before the winged adults leave the water.

Once the winged adults have broken through the surface film, they're off. In the shelter of marginal cover they wait until conditions are suitable for them to take to the wing, mate, and commence egg-laying. Early morning or late evening are the peak egg-laying times. When the conditions are right, clouds of dancing adult fly can be observed billowing like smoke in the wind over the sheltered edges of the islands, and marginal cover. Mating complete, the adults leave the shelter, and fly back onto the water to lay their eggs.

A big fall of egg-laying adult fly can produce some classic dry fly fishing. Anglers often mistake egg-laying adults, believing the fish are rising to the ascending pupae. This is understandable because the conditions which are suitable for a rise to the struggling, emerging fly, are also the very conditions preferred by the adult flies to lay their eggs. So in calm conditions in spring – which the duck fly fisher longs for – it would not be unreasonable for the angler to expect to cast to rising fish, but it is then down to him to decipher what is going on above, or below the surface. Use your eyes, and believe what you see.

But back to that awful run of eight days of hopeless weather conditions. Day nine did not look too promising either but the forecast was good. At last a good buzzer day was in the offing.

The account which follows is about waiting for the right conditions, and taking full advantage of them when they come. With wild brown trout, weather conditions are key to success. The weather will influence the hatches of fly, the way the trout respond to those hatches, and of course the way we fish.

We will not find good buzzer fishing over the vast open stretches of the lough. The right conditions are more likely to be found in sheltered areas of the bays, or in the lee of certain islands.

In the buzzer and olive season, the areas where I concentrate most of my fishing effort are those areas of the Corrib with a limestone bed and some adjacent cover and shelter. Shallow bays, areas between islands,

A wonderful sight in late March: smoke–like columns of duck fly rise over the island scrub on Lough Corrib.

and stretches of water between shallow reefs with a silt or marl bottom that has an overlying growth of chara, these are the areas I favour. The soft weed, chara, blanketing the bottom muds, is a good indicator that you are over the right type of water. Bays situated along the north end of the upper lough, the eastern shore of the upper lough down to the narrows, along both shores of the narrows, and localised areas within the lower lough basin are my favoured drifts.

If you seek better than average sized trout on the fly, avoid the popular areas, and wherever possible fish undisturbed water. It is no coincidence when you move in to a quiet bay, and discover a pod of fish confidently feeding, that the best trout are usually the first or early fish you catch. As the disturbance from catching fish, or just drifting over them has its effect, so the trout just slowly melt away, and it is the bigger fish that disappear first. There are of course exceptions, such as if the trout are mad on the mayfly, when they can come at any time.

When I heard the favourable weather forecast, I knew which area of the lough I was going to head for. Although it was still blowing due north, the wind had lost much of its venomous icy edge as I pushed the boat out from its mooring. With the wind at my back, I headed southwards to commence my first drift. After no more than 10 minutes motoring, I stopped off the point of a small island.

Here, with a north wind in the lee of the island, is a short drift that has produced many fish for me. I cut the engine well above the productive water, hoping to drift in undetected by the trout. Fishing with two buzzer pupa imitations on the droppers, and a Pheasant Tail nymph on the point tied to a 5lb .185mm fluorocarbon leader, and a #6 weight floating line, I made my first casts.

On wild fisheries I rarely fish depths greater than 6 to 10 feet, unless the day is bright and sunny with very little cloud, conditions which may drive the trout deeper. When the fish are feeding on buzzer pupae, they will only go down into deeper water when their food descends with the increasing light intensity.

In disturbed water, it is the bigger fish that disappear first

On this day, with conditions improving all the time, the wind was falling leaving a nice foam-flecked ripple, and the cloud was lifting. Midway through the drift, a reef of rock cuts out from the eastern edge of the island, fish work along this reef and into the water sheltered from the prevailing wind. A classic duck fly hole. As I approached the reef, a trout bulged just off the shallows. I instinctively covered the fish, but either the trout did not see my imitations or he refused them.

One of the old clinker-built boats on Corrib, as beautiful to look at as they are sturdy on the water.

Either way, no take was forthcoming.

Several casts later however, casting well forward and letting the flies sink to around six feet, I felt a nice steady draw on the line, one of increasing weight as a trout confidently moved off with the fly. My first fish of the day was a picture of a trout around 2¾lbs. It took the Pheasant Tail nymph on the point. Towards the end of the drift, I took another fish of around 1½lbs on the middle dropper. The fish took with another steady draw on the line as it confidently made off with the fly.

There were no other boats in the immediate vicinity, so I decided to try the drift again before moving on, and took another fish of around 2lbs again on the middle dropper. Three quality trout, and I had been out for no more than 40 minutes. This had the makings of a good day.

Only a short distance away the next drift covered a much larger area of productive water, and would take about an hour to cover, drifting off a shallow neck across a bay, and into a narrow throat between two reefs that opened up again into a small corner of the bay. This is a good drift during the olive season, as well as in the buzzer period, over water averaging 10 to 12 feet. The marl bottom, covered by a blanket of chara with scattered pockets of potamogeton, is perfect for nymph fishing.

It is normally an excellent bay which holds a good head of fish, but on this day no takes were forthcoming, and I finished the drift without an offer. There seemed no point in covering this drift again, so another short session on the engine took me around a rocky peninsula, and into another bay which cuts back in on itself, with a large island at the narrow point. The light wind by now was beginning to swing westerly, ideal conditions for buzzer fishing and perfect for presentation. During the next hour I took two more fish, on the dropper patterns, well-conditioned trout averaging 1¾ pounds and I also missed several takes. With the bay effectively covered, and being close to an area of shore that I particularly like, I went in for lunch.

What a difference a favourable change in the weather can make, so early in the year. After days of cold grey, heavy lead skies, rain, and high winds – the cloud base lifts, the wind drops, and the temperature rises. Suddenly I am in a different world: the drone of the insects on the wing, and bird song all around. Song thrush, blackbird, blackcap and willow warbler, some of our best songsters, are in full cry. Black caps and

148

willow warblers newly arrived from North Africa feast on the abundance of fly.

The limestone shoreline of Lough Corrib in spring is a wonderful area for wild flora, with early purple orchids, gentian and a profusion of primroses, all of which add interest to the day. Sitting back against a rock looking out over the water, a smoky haze hung over the marginal trees and bushes, as countless adult midges took to the wing.

They moved in clouds like a giant amoeba as they swarmed over the tops of the bushes, and as soon as the wind freshened a little, they immediately dropped back into the trees for shelter. As soon as the wind dropped, the flies were on the wing again. Prospects looked very promising, and I was confident of taking more fish before the day was out.

As I had only taken the one fish on the point fly, and this is a key position when nymph fishing, I decided to change the Pheasant Tail for a Diawl Bach. My next drift was behind the island, at the mouth of the bay. Beginning from a jungle of rocks on the southern tip of the island, a westerly wind would take me out over several shallows, followed by a large tract of open uniform water. The bed of the lough drops away to 15 feet of water just off the rocky point, and this has been a good area for some big fish in the past.

In the water between the island and the shallows, I took two more fish, one about 2 pounds on the point, and the other a trout of ¾ pounds. My smallest fish had taken the top dropper. The open water proved unprofitable, and I moved down to the next area, which in a westerly wind would give me a lovely parallel drift along the shore of a big island.

I had noticed that the last two fish took much higher in the water, and I felt that the trout were moving up towards the surface. This was confirmed on my next drift, as I saw my first rise but unfortunately could not cover it, as it was too far over to my left.

Not long after, another fish head and tailed down-wind of me, slightly to my left. I covered the area just in front of where the fish had last appeared, and the trout took my point fly on the second pull. This was a good solid take, and after a strong fight typical of Corrib brown trout, I boated a fine fish pushing 3 pounds.

I lost the next two trout, both takes coming higher in the water, no more than 4 to 5 feet down.

They were steady confident draws on the line, which normally result in well-hooked fish, but for some unaccountable reason these two trout came adrift in play. Sadly, one was a heavy fish which I estimated to be around 4 pounds.

With the odd fish now showing, I searched the water well ahead of me looking for a rise to cover. Just then, a lively trout of around 1¾lbs took my top dropper on the lift. The capture of this fish put the remaining trout down. As the evening was now well advanced, I moved back to the island at the mouth of the bay. Here in the lightest of ripples I found a concentration of fish that were moving well, the surface interrupted with the swirls and bulges of rising trout.

The sight of so many trout rising tempted me to try dry fly, but I found to my cost this change of method was a mistake, for I only had one half-hearted rise in possibly 40 minutes fishing. I was annoyed with myself for wasting so much time on a method which obviously wasn't working. It is not necessary to show your flies to countless fish to realise this. They are not blind. The trout give a clear answer to our offerings but sometimes we ignore it. Eager to fish dries, I had made the mistake of not studying the rise form, and had fished the method I preferred, which did not suit the trout.

Realising the mistake, I quickly changed back to nymphs, and with the trout so high in the water, fished two hackled pupa imitations on the droppers and the Diawl Bach on the point, tied to a standard nylon leader. During the next hour, casting to moving fish, and maintaining contact with the flies immediately after they alighted on the surface, I caught five more trout: four on the hackled flies; and the last fish of the evening on the point fly.

My largest trout weighed 5¼lb and 4lb 6ozs respectively, with another fish of around 2¾lb and two around 1¼-1½lb. This made up a tremendous catch of wild brown trout. In the fading light, several of the fish that took me could be seen rolling over the dropper flies, their golden flanks reflecting back what little light remained, a memorable sight before the line drew away and I tightened.

The wind overnight changed to the south east, and the following day out with a friend I took ten fish, the biggest 3½lbs on dry fly before lunch time. Although the morning was cold, the wind remained light with good cloud cover, and there was a huge fall of adult fly. The surface of the lough was covered with fly, and this time I could clearly see the trout were taking off the top of the water, so dry fly was an obvious choice. For 2½ hours the trout moved well, with no shortage of target fish to cover. This is my kind of fishing, and like a dog with two tails fishing a Duster on the point, Ginger Bits on the middle dropper, and a Klinkhamer variant on top dropper, I took full advantage of the rise.

It makes no difference which species of fish an angler may be pursuing, stalking a visible target has a greater interest than taking a fish deep or randomly, covering the water blind. Once you are targeting an individual fish, or group of feeding trout, you are totally absorbed by the scene which is being played out before you.

It has to be one of the finest moments in fishing. You are totally focused, and then follows the agonising moments as the fish approaches the offering. You are willing the fish to take; but will it? There are so many imponderables that could go wrong: the cast, imitation selection, presentation. Only the fish can now determine the outcome, and you watch that fish all the way – inch by agonising inch. Will it take? This is my sport. Give me a day of light wind, a hatch of fly and rising trout: the ultimate day's flyfishing.

I believe that many experienced lough fishers fail to exploit these rises, because they cannot come to terms with presenting a small surface fly to a moving particular fish. And yet these anglers recognise if they see trout rising, that it is a good sign. They move to the general area, but do not present their flies to individual rising fish. Even worse, they continue flogging away with wet flies, just covering the water in front of the boat with a long line. Casting a long line, and pulling a team of wet flies through an area of rising fish, is not the right method. It will not consistently take trout in such conditions. The fly pattern is wrong, and the presentation is wrong, and worst of all, the angler is lining the fish.

When trout are moving close to the surface, they are easily put down, especially if you put the fly

With wild fish, when the weather conditions fall right, exploit them: do not wait for tomorrow.

line over them. Covering wild browns from a drifting boat with small surface flies, is much more demanding than searching the water with a team of wet flies, but it is also far more rewarding. Judging which direction a trout is moving, placing a fly ahead of the fish to ambush it, and then pulling the hook home when the trout takes, requires a proficient level of skill. You cannot just rely on luck, to do it consistently.

Certainly there are far more unknowns, when presenting a fly to a stillwater fish, than in casting to a fish in a river. In the lake, we are not casting to a trout, which is holding station in a known lie, facing head upstream to the current, where, if you do not spook him with clumsy casting, you will have more than one opportunity to pass a fly over his head. In a river, not only do we know where the fish is, but if he does take the fly we know which way he will go when he returns to the lie with the fly. This makes hooking the trout easier, as we know in which direction to pull, to set the hook (ie. downstream, away from the direction the fish is heading).

The boat fisher's situation is totally different. From a drifting boat, he will have only one opportunity, or at best if a trout is rising regularly and moving across the front of the boat, two or three casts, to take the fish. They will not tolerate a sloppy presentation.

When the opportunities come your way, you have to take them. Good judgement, and a good eye, are key. You need to see the fish, to determine the direction in which it is heading, and where the trout is going to be when you place your fly. If you feel that you cannot cover a moving fish comfortably, because he is on the limits of your casting range: wait. The fish may move into a more favourable position. If the trout does move within range, then by holding your hand, you have made a positive move; and if he doesn't you haven't put the fish down with a clumsy cast. With luck you may have another crack at him later as they cover a lot of water.

The morning session fishing dry fly was sublime, but after lunch the wind rapidly freshened, and became gusty, dispersing all the adult fly. With a lack of surface fly, and no signs of a hatch, the fish went down. As we had enjoyed such a good morning, we felt the best of the day was over, and as conditions were clearly deteriorating, decided to come off the lough early.

The next four days were absolute howlers, but

This Irish lake trout has relatively few, widely-spaced black spots on the flanks. It is a stunningly beautiful fish.

the fifth day was perfect: mild, with a light southerly wind, and just the occasional hint of sun. Fishing either nymph or dry fly, depending on the mood of the fish, I boated 17 trout, the biggest weighing 4¼lbs. From a total of fifteen days, at a key time of the year, I fished on three days boating 41 quality trout. Only two of the smaller trout around 1½lbs were retained, all the other fish were returned. Superlative wild brown trout fishing, on one of the best top water loughs it has been my privilege to fish.

These were exceptional days, but I took advantage of the conditions. With wild fish we have to fish through some tough days, but when the weather conditions fall right, exploit them: do not wait for tomorrow. In good fishing conditions, I would expect to enjoy some exceptional top water fishing on the Corrib during the buzzer, olive and mayfly season, and this pattern repeats itself every year.

Some years are better than others, depending on the duration of the hatches of fly, and the frequency of favourable fishing conditions. The dry fly fishing is

superb, and if it were not for the popularity of dapping on the Corrib, the dry fly fishing would be even better than it is. This is why I prefer the mayfly to come late as it delays the dappers, and extends the best of the small imitative fly fishing.

Although I would expect to make some good catches during the spring season, I am not saying that every day would be a good day: far from it, because if you guess wrong about location, you are going to struggle. So a good knowledge of where there are healthy concentrations of trout, that have not been over-exploited, is a huge advantage. This is why, for the visiting angler, the services of a knowledgeable local boatman can prove invaluable. Weather will play a key role, and of course luck will also play a part. There will also be days when fish, for no reason, come adrift; or you get takes but cannot convert them into results. Over the course of a season, you have to be prepared to take the rough with the smooth, but make sure you seize the opportunity to make a good catch when it presents itself.

151

CHAPTER 11

Mayfly time on the Corrib

Lough Corrib in May is a wonderful place to be, as the area becomes infected with piscatorial madness. Villages and small towns along the loughs shores fill up with anglers from all over the world. The largest of the spring flies, the mayfly (*E. danica*) excite the trout into a feeding frenzy, so even in the wildest of conditions, a good catch can be expected.

Mayfly fishing is the social high point of the fishing year on the limestone loughs and when the word is out that the fly is up, even anglers who fish at no other time will take their week. All are intent on making the most of the two short weeks that have become known as 'duffer's fortnight'. Traditionally, most anglers concentrate on the upper lough, and it was at Oughterard on the western side where Bruce Vaughan and I went for a week's mayfly fishing that eventually brought us an unexpected bonus.

It was lunchtime before we motored out of Portacarron Bay towards Inishcash Island. As this was going to be a short fishing day, we decided to fish an area of the Corrib known as the Long Shallow, an area of offshore shallows just east of Inishcash. With a fresh south-westerly wind and good cloud cover we drifted from Ard point to the Black Rock, a drift that took us over the offshore shallows, and we got off to a flier. The browns were taking emerging duns, and we were fishing dry mayflies: a grey on the dropper and a ginger on the point to 0.235mm nylon.

We enjoyed a wonderful afternoon's sport with trout up to 2lb 12ozs. It was evident that the trout were on the surface fly, and were ignoring all wet flies even those that were fished only inches below the surface. As we were fishing on a heavy wave, Bruce was struggling to see his dry flies, and several times he tried the

152

wet fly to ease the strain but the response from the fish was poor. When we came off the water at around six, we had accounted for and returned around 25 brown trout. We couldn't have wished for a better start.

So we were in good humour that evening when we met Danny Goldrick, then of the Western Regional Fisheries Board. A good friend had suggested that we meet Danny, as he had some interesting information about the lough. Danny recounted tales of his experiences on Mask, the River Erriff and Ballynahinch, as well as the Corrib, into the early hours. Talking to someone who has fished Irish waters for as long as Danny is always going to be an experience.

It was late before we started talking about the Corrib. He suggested various drifts we should try, and he mentioned the fabulous fishing to be had on the lower part of the lough which came as a real surprise. Both Bruce and I were led to believe from talking to various anglers around the Corrib, that the lower section was full of pike and bream, and that there were few brown trout present. Yet it was obvious from Danny's experiences that this was a misconception based on the views of anglers fishing the upper reaches only, who had had no real experience of fishing the lower Corrib. If Danny's predictions were to prove correct, here was an excellent area of the Corrib totally ignored by the vast majority of anglers who fished the lough.

Danny did warn us that this area of the lower reaches of the lough did not hold the same density of trout stock as the upper Corrib, but he said it could be well worth a visit if we wanted to try something different. Wild browns of such a high average weight as he had caught, on one of the prolific great western

Back you go: Lawrence McCarthy returns a handsome brown trout to Lough Mask.

loughs, had whetted our appetites, and we just had to give the lower Corrib a try. Danny suggested we hire a boat from Annaghdown on the eastern shore, and motor down through the narrows to Shankill Bay, Rabbit and Muckrush point, where he'd join us after lunch.

Conditions were certainly not favourable the following morning with bright sun, cloudless sky and a flat calm. As we approached Shankill Bay, I cut the engine and let the boat drift in with an occasional stroke of the oars. It all looked very uninviting after the high of the previous day, and I really didn't feel like flogging away on what looked like a hopeless case.

Instead of taking up the fly rod, and becoming too involved in the fishing, I took time out to have a good look around. We were over eight to ten feet of water, and the clarity was such that I could clearly see the bottom over a wide area. It looked hopeless

for trout, but there was a good variety of fly coming off. The surface was spattered with lake olives, dark sedges, adult midges that were busy egg laying and the occasional mayfly.

What I do know is that, even if the weather conditions are far from favourable ie. bright sun and flat calm, trout will still rise if there is food on the surface for them to rise to. Compared to the previous day, the mayfly hatch was sparse, but there were certainly sufficient flies to tempt a trout the surface.

Once trout switch to the mayfly, they'll take it in preference to anything else, even when there is a good hatch of other species. At that moment, I witnessed a classic example of this preferential feeding, when a mayfly emerged within a group of seven or eight lake olives, and was promptly taken by a trout. Things were looking up! I broke off my leader and attached finer 3lb nylon. As I had seen a variety of fly life on the water,

particularly sedges, I decided to present the fish with a mixed offering, and tied a dark sedge on the point, and a grey mayfly on the dropper, both dries. I would normally have switched the position of the flies around, with my preferred fly on the point, but as the trout the previous day had shown a distinct preference for the dropper, I decided to start with my mayfly pattern on the dropper.

Scanning the surface of the lough for a rise, we did not have long to wait for the first opportunity. A cruising fish came within range, rising intermittently, and I covered the trout with the mayfly which it took with a leisurely head and tail rise soon after the fly had alighted on the surface. A gentle lift, and the fish was off like a torpedo. Unlike most brown trout I have caught, Corrib fish make dashing runs and pull hard. Some of the bigger browns can occasionally take you down to the backing, with reel-screaming runs. They are among the hardest fighting brown trout I have caught, and this fish in shallow water and on a light line, was no exception. At 2lb 8oz it was an encouraging start. Soon after this fish, I took another trout of 2lbs followed by a bigger fish of 3lbs around mid-day. Both these trout fell to the grey mayfly, in conditions most would have considered hopeless for wild browns on a dry fly.

Once trout switch to the mayfly, they'll take it in preference to anything else

The trout were taking the fly confidently, but by early afternoon, locating a rising fish was proving difficult. A good trout rose close inshore over some submerged rocks. The faintest of breezes came across the lough from the west, assisting my cast and making it easier to cover the fish. The trout appeared disinterested in my flies, but I felt that it was still in the area, probably feeding on ascending nymphs and taking the occasional emerging dun.

I left the flies sitting, just in case. After what seemed an eternity the fish came up without warning and sucked in the fly. As I tightened, feeling his great weight, the trout rolled on the surface and went straight down, smashing the light leader on the submerged rocks below. There is always the chance of coming across a big brownie on the large Irish loughs, so I rarely fish fine, particularly at mayfly time. Because of the conditions, bright sun and flat calm, I was not expecting a fish of this class to be feeding, and had been caught out with a totally inadequate leader.

With such a fine leader, there was nothing I could have done to prevent the fish from swimming through the jungle of rocks below and I had had no choice but to let the trout run. It was not going to happen again. I vowed to fish stronger nylon for the rest of the day.

We went in for a late lunch following the loss of the big trout, to meet up with Danny. He was surprised

A female mayfly takes shelter under the leaf of an alder. If you are wanting to dap the live mayfly this is a good place to collect the naturals.

A brief moment for admiration, before his Lordship returns to his rightful kingdom.

to hear of the sport we had enjoyed, considering the conditions. His beaming smile on hearing the news said it all. As usual, lunch was a relaxed meal with much talk of fishing, and favourite drifts. It also gave us time to take a good look at the diversity of fly life, and how the flora on the lower lough differed from our usual haunts on the upper Corrib.

The margins were rocky with a very shallow gradient, and the bottom appeared to be made up of fine marl and silt deposits. Vast tracts of common rush and phragmites backed the bays with a flat landscape of scrub, pasture and bog as a backdrop. It looked not unlike a lowland lake, only many times bigger. The bed of the lower Corrib is limestone, and the flora and fauna are typical of a limestone lake, as are the marginal plants.

The mixed marginal growth is wonderful habitat for a myriad of different insects, and the appearance of brimstone butterflies probably searching for buckthorn amongst the scrub, the vivid sulphur yellow of the males illuminated by the spring sunshine, were a striking sight on that particular day. A flock of whimbrel took

off from a rocky point. Known locally as the maybirds, large numbers of these waders similar to but smaller than a curlew, pass through from late-April until mid-June. The peregrines follow these waders, and if you are lucky you may see this dramatic falcon stooping on the whimbrel as they congregate off the rocky headlands.

And looking out across the lough, everywhere as far as the eye could see, the bottom was in view. It looked empty. It looked fishless, but we knew better. Danny said that the midge and sedge fishing can also be superb, and I believe it. The lower lough extends for over 6,000 acres, and in good light you will not lose sight of the bottom over most of it – ideal habitat for fly life.

The wind picked up over lunch, and when we pushed the boat out there was a fair breeze blowing from the west, but the light was still bright with an odd patch of cloud. I put a Ginger Mayfly on the point position and left the Grey on the dropper, both tied to a stronger 8lb 0.225mm leader. By the time we started our first drift a good wave had built up, making it difficult to see my flies. Even though there were still no obvious sign of rising fish, I elected to stick with the dries. We had wind, but conditions were still far from favourable. Danny had positioned the boat to drift across Muckrush Point down to Billybeg, and my luck was in: I took a beautiful 4lb wild brown on the first drift. Its flanks were heavily spotted, with a good rudder for a tail, a cracking fish as only a Corrib brown can be.

As Danny was keen for us to see more of the lower lough, we tried drifts along Rabbit Island, Adam's Rock, Fly Island and from Annagh Bay down to Little Sca, either catching or moving fish off every mark. I added two more trout to my bag, fish of 2lb 4oz and another cracker of 4lbs making my total catch for the day, six wild browns for 17lb 12ozs, all on dry fly. As Danny said, it was an average weight that would run the best Midland loughs close.

With such ideal habitat it is not difficult to understand why the average size of the trout is so good, but the stock has not always been as healthy as it is now. There was a time when the stock used to be so low, that anglers would not consider it worthwhile fishing for them. This all changed when the Western Region Fisheries Board embarked on an intensive develop-ment programme. They removed pike, replenished fry stocks in the feeder streams (previously damaged by arterial drainage schemes) and patrolled the loughs and streams for poachers, illegal nets and traps. This work, carried out by Danny and his staff, led to an increase in trout stocks from 1976 onwards.

The work still continues, not only by the fishery board but also by local clubs, and individuals with an interest in the lough.

Will all this work, I wonder, be sufficient to maintain stock levels given the intense rod pressure the lake is now being subjected to?

A lot of hard work, time and money have been invested in the future of Lough Corrib

I was particularly pleased to take this fish, in early morning when nothing but the odd caenis was showing.

CHAPTER 12

A Night to Remember on Sheelin

In mid-May one year came the news I had long been waiting for. Stuart McTeare telephoned to tell me that the mayfly on Lough Sheelin had been up for six days and that the first fall of spent gnat was expected at any moment. My fishing partner Bruce Vaughan and I immediately booked a morning flight to Dublin.

Hopes were running high as we boarded the plane, and we had visions of mighty Sheelin brown trout rolling on the surface and sucking down mayflies. After 50 minutes flying time and an hour and a half of manic driving, we reached the lodge. Baggage and tackle were hauled from the car as Stuart and Fiona came out to greet us. Time was precious, and Stuart fed us with snippets of information as we munched our way, with embarrassing haste, through lunch.

Apparently, Sheelin was enjoying the heaviest mayfly hatch for at least 20 years, and a 7½lb brownie had been taken the evening before off the Crover shore.

Things were looking good!

By 2.30pm we were walking through lush pasture to the boats. The hawthorn bushes were festooned with mayflies which, in a few hours, would take to the wing to begin their nuptial flight. We stepped into the traditional Sheelin-style wooden boat and laid down our rods ready to go. I eased the boat out of the bay: it was 2.45pm and hard to believe that we had left England only a few hours earlier. With thoughts of the big brownie taken the night before uppermost in my mind, I made for the Crover shore to begin our first drift.

Once out of the shelter of the bay and into open water, a wonderful sight lay before us. Countless mayflies were hatching: wherever we looked, the erect wings of the emerging duns could be seen stretching away into the distance. I have seen good hatches of mayfly before, but never in such numbers as we saw coming off Sheelin that day.

Flies may have been hatching in profusion, but conditions were less than favourable, with a cloudless sky and a hard wind from the east raking the surface of the lough. The misty haze, so often experienced with poor air quality during an anti-cyclone (and with an east wind) produced a milky, diffused light. Even though the day did not look too promising, surely, with all those mayflies, sooner or later we would find some rising fish.

Had we been on an English reservoir, the rainbows would have been gorging themselves silly on the glut of fly. But Sheelin is no English reservoir and we were fishing for well-fed wild browns – and wild brown trout, as we know to our cost, are influenced more by the vagaries of the weather than the more freely-rising rainbow trout.

As we motored across to the Crover shore there was no sign of surface-feeding fish, and no trout came to our wet mayflies during the drift. Our plan was to move around and cover as much water as possible until we found moving fish. But drifts off Stony Island and Gaffney's Bay were unproductive also, so we moved on to the sandy bay where the boats from the Sheelin Shamrock Hotel come down the Upper Inney River to fish Sheelin. Still the mayflies continued to pour off, and, although the bay was covered with fly, we struggled to find that elusive rising fish. With nothing showing on the surface, I changed to a team of nymphs, while Bruce put on a dry mayfly, both of which the trout continued to ignore.

So that we could take advantage of the spent-gnat fishing, dinner had been arranged for 7 o'clock and time was pressing. The milky light persisted as we rounded Inchicup Island to begin to begin our last drift before dinner. Behind the island the wind was blowing onshore, but the boat kept a good line close to the margin.

Here our luck changed as a good fish took Bruce's mayfly. That fish fought well, giving a few anxious moments before Bruce could sink the net and hoist aboard a superb 3lb brownie. It was a fine way to open the score card. With several hundred yards of unfished water remaining, we continued fishing until the drift was almost exhausted, and, as the boat drifted into a bay just before Curry Point, a trout rose 20 yards downwind of Bruce. Covered with a Grey Wulff, the fish took on the third throw – a fine two-pounder.

Facing page: The great dance of the mayfly, over the tree-tops of Sheelin.
Below: Sunset at Stony Island on Lough Sheelin: time to put on a spent gnat.

We were back on the water by 8.30pm, when the mating mayfly spinners were on the wing in force. Adult flies were massing over the marginal bushes. Soon they would be making for open water to lay their eggs and, we hoped, we would be in position to take advantage of the evening fall of spent gnat. The wind had eased and shifted a little, as it so often does during the late evening and as we settled in the lee of Inchicup Island it was blowing slightly offshore.

I looked to the trees to see if the flies were still on the wing. We were in time and obviously had made the right decision in our choice of location as the dancing imagos were thicker than ever – like a seething mass of mosquitoes moving in clouds along the margins. They had collected here in huge numbers, presumably because of the wind, which had blown onshore for most of the day.

Now, in the light air of the evening, the wind had shifted to our advantage and would blow the egg-laying spinners onto the water. We talked softly, staring into the setting sun for signs of a moving fish.

As the sun sank over the western shoreline, the wind felt cold on the back of my neck. Would the drop in temperature keep the fish down? We sat and waited, but nothing moved. A few flies began drifting onto the water and a cuckoo called from the trees, the sound accentuated by the evening silence.

We were drifting out of the bay towards a sunken reef when a fish moved on my side of the boat. I immediately lengthened line and covered him. The trout took with a slow head-and-tail rise as the fly settled almost on his nose. A slight pause before tightening resulted in a heavy swirl as the fish rolled on the surface and then sounded. Hanging beneath the rod, pulling and boring in typical brownie fashion, he felt a good trout.

Minutes later I was admiring a cracking fish of 4½lb. Tiny-headed and thick in the shoulder, she was a typical Sheelin fish. Recovering from the excitement, we realised that the air was full of mayflies.

Like snowflakes in the wind, great swathes of egg-layers came flying by in an endless stream intent on performing their final egg-laying act.

I was captivated by the scene before me: the surface of the lough was littered with struggling spent gnat. Surely the trout would rise now. Bats were on the wing and the light was fading quickly before we spotted another fish well downwind of us. Two pairs of eyes were transfixed on the disturbance as we inched closer. The trout remained on the top, head and shoulders breaking the surface as he gorged himself on the dying flies. Several more trout materialised from the depths, and suddenly we had four or five trout feeding in front of us.

We selected a target apiece and began casting. My first cast gave just a little too much lead and the fish moved inches wide. I lifted off and covered him again, but the fish ignored the fly. My third cast was short and, judging by the murmurings from the other end of the boat, Bruce was having similar problems.

My fourth cast was spot on, and the fly disappeared. When I tightened, the trout boiled on the surface and then went down. Bruce was still casting feverishly at the fish moving in front of us and some of those browns looked big.

The sight of them was too much for me, and I really bent into my fish, trying to bully him to the boat. With rod bent double and the line taut as a bowstring, I cursed the fish, which had not looked very big when he rose to me.

At last, however, the pressure told and my fish came to the surface, wallowed and was netted. Feeling his weight, I now knew why he had put up such a strong fight. Probably not much over 21 inches in length, another Sheelin beauty of just over 5lb lay in the net, giving me a wonderful brace of wild brownies.

Lost in the drama of my triumph, I looked up from my fish. Bruce had stopped casting, the fish had all gone down, and the waves rolled silently by. It was over. A night to remember.

Facing page: Lawrence McCarthy returns an early morning riser to the Corrib.

CHAPTER 13

Corrib Caenis at Dawn

On the Corrib by mid-June, the best of the spring and early summer imitative fishing may be over, but we still have one fly, which the majority of stillwater fly anglers may not be aware of, that will produce a consistent rise. From June and throughout July, many consider the best chance of a rise will be late in the evening.

Late evening fishing however tends to be an unpredictable time, as the conditions have to absolutely perfect, and even then there is no guarantee that a movement of fish will materialise.

Throughout the summer months, sedges and midges will entice the trout to the surface if sufficient fly come off. If your luck is in, and you time your visit to coincide with a hatch, there is a good chance of a big trout, especially to a dry buzzer imitation. Buzzer or sedges are not however, the flies that I am looking for

to produce a consistent rise at this time of year.

I may loathe rising early, but the morning rise is, I have found, a more consistent one, and in my experience a hatch of some sorts will occur most mornings throughout June and July. But I did not realise just how consistent these rises were, until a few years ago when I agreed to go out with a friend Larry McCarthy on Lough Corrib, to try the dawn for a fish.

We were motoring out across a shallow bay to try a known buzzer area, when it came to our attention that the odd fish was moving out over open water. Not anglers to pass up an opportunity, we cut the engine and scanned the immediate area. The odd trout was showing, but nothing to get too excited about. However in a very short time the fish came on in great numbers and a prolific rise took place. What the trout were

161

Drifting a sheltered bay on Lough Corrib. It is always worth fishing carefully into the shallow rocky shoals.

taking wasn't immediately obvious, but as the quantity of spent fly built up, the penny dropped. The fish were taking caenis. That rise went on in flat calm conditions for at least three hours, and was our introduction to many early morning stints on the lough.

Caenis hatch at any time of the day if the conditions are right, but on Lough Corrib, early mornings in particular are the key periods for a hatch. The fly largely ignored by the majority of boat fisherman hatches in huge quantities and can induce a frenzied rise. From June and throughout July, caenis consistently hatch around or just after sunrise.

In the west of Ireland in high summer, particularly on a large lough like the Corrib where there is a lot of reflected light, dawn can break early, possibly two hours before sunrise. Providing you are in position just before sunrise, that is early enough, and you should get two or three hours' good fishing. I rarely find that a rise occurs first thing, unless there has been a good overnight hatch of buzzer or a big fall of adult egg-laying sedge, until the caenis start coming off.

There are six species of caenis, but the two species of greatest interest to hatch on the Corrib are *Caenis moesta* and *Caenis macrura*. One is a sooty grey, the other a creamy white. Slightly larger than other species of caenis, they prefer to come off in the morning rather than the late afternoon or evening. It is difficult to differentiate between the species, but the colour is

easy to define. The adult female naturals are beautiful, mayflies in miniature with a black thorax and black leading edge to the wings, pale creamy abdomens with a few bands of brown. For such a small fly it certainly stands out, particularly if the morning is overcast and the reflection off the water's surface looks a dark basalt grey.

Sunrise appears to be the trigger for them to hatch, and once they commence hatching, the fish soon start moving. The duns following emergence will moult, casting their skins within minutes of hatching. That is why if you are out on the water in a caenis hatch, your clothing can quickly become covered with the shucks of moulting caenis.

From the time the duns emerge, this is a fly in a hurry. Once they have moulted, the spinners immediately begin mating, and the females will then lay their eggs and fall spent on the water within a very short time of hatching. The main hatch may be a short frenzied affair, but in that time an unbelievable quantity of spent fly can build up. On cooler mornings, the fly may come off in short bursts with intervals in between.

This does not mean that the rise will be curtailed prematurely. This is because the main rise does not come to the emerging fly, but to the vast quantity of spent flies that litter the surface. How long the rise will last is highly dependant on the strength of the wind, and how long the fall of spent fly remains accessible to

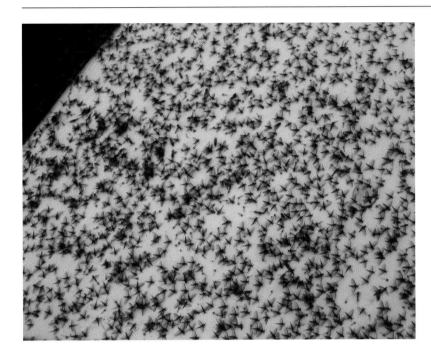

Caenis mass on the cuddy cover at the bow of the boat. The 2-cent coin gives an indication of scale.

the fish before it is dispersed. At times the surface of the lough can be covered with spent fly, and the trout will feed greedily on them. In a light wind, this carpet of spent fly can last for several hours or more, possibly until 9 or 10 am and the fish will continue feeding on them long after the main hatch has finished, providing there is sufficient spent fly to hold the trout's interest.

In a strong wind the spent fly is dispersed much quicker, and even though the trout may follow the floating carpet of spent caenis for a while, the concentration of fly becomes scattered and consequently the trout go down. To avoid disappointment, a windy morning is the time to stay in bed, as the rise will be of much shorter duration and if it is too windy or raining it may not happen at all.

Of all the elements, rain is the one condition that will prevent them from hatching, and if the hatch has already begun it will cease if precipitation occurs whilst the hatch is on. Heavy rain will not only stop the hatch, it will also drown the adult flies if they do not find shelter, spoiling any chance of a good movement of fish.

If the wind falls light overnight, and it does not build too much in strength before 9 or 10am, I would be optimistic of a movement of some sorts. A light wind is good, but combined with a little cloud cover to keep the temperature up or a humid morning following a night of light precipitation is ideal, these are the conditions to look for. Anglers on holiday with family attached, would do well to bear this in mind, as it allows them to put in possibly three or more productive hours without disrupting family plans for the more sociable part of the day.

The best hatches of caenis, occur over shallow water with a marl or silty bottom. Unlike the adult fly, the active crawling nymphs do not appear to interest the trout as much as the adult fly. We have never found this phase of the life cycle productive. Perhaps foraging for nymphs requires too much effort in relation to the size of the return.

Irrespective of where the flies hatch in a bay, we look for the nearest sheltered areas to the area of emergence such as weed beds, in the lee of islands or peninsulas. Sheltered areas where the duns can make the final moult, and the adult fly can take to the wing to mate without being buffeted by the wind.

A lot of flies will quickly collect in such areas, and as the adult cycle is a brief one, it doesn't take long for a mat of spent fly to build up on the surface of the water. This mat of flies, will be taken by the wind in a steady progression towards the windward shore. The stronger the wind, the quicker the fly is dispersed, so ideally, we want a light wind to slow the dispersal rate down. In light winds dense mats of fly form, and these dense mats are very attractive to the trout, particularly the bigger fish.

For eight weeks or more, caenis will come off most mornings throughout June and July, and the fish are looking for it, not only this they also look for greater concentrations of fly even if they have to cover considerable distances to find it. These dense mats of fly are made up of a multitude of spent flies, and when the flies come close together two or three or more individuals will clump together, forming a cluster.

So, within a mat of fly, we have these clumps or clusters as well as a large number of individual flies, all lying inert on the surface of the water, being carried by the wind. Manna from heaven to a hungry trout, and the big fish know this. Not only do they look for the denser mats of fly, they also target the clumps of fly.

Over several seasons I have noticed that the smaller trout hunt in packs sometimes forming huge shoals, when looking for a fall of caenis. They look like a shoal of mackerel sporting in the sea, cruising up and down the edges of wind lanes, searching for fly. Why the smaller fish should form such tightly packed shoals is a mystery, but as single fish they perhaps feel vulnerable, and open to predation. In a pack they have protection from numbers, and the extra pairs of eyes and senses. The bigger fish, however, hunt alone or in pairs, feeding in a more leisurely manner. They may be joined at times by other larger fish, or a pod of smaller trout.

There was a time when to catch a trophy fish on the fly from the limestone loughs, I would have chosen the spring period, mid-March to the end of May, as the best time for a big trout, and the next best period would have been the back-end. High summer can produce good fish, but I have in the past always found summer fishing to be less predictable. Now I have to review

Caenis fishing would not suit every angler, as it is very challenging. It is not called the angler's curse for nothing

my thoughts. In 2004 and 2005 I missed much of the spring fishing, in fact I basically missed the olives and the mayfly for both seasons. Fishing between the hours of 10 to 6pm was impossible, so I either went out for the late evening or early morning rises whenever the opportunity arose. As it turned out, this didn't prove to be a handicap. In the summer of 2004 whenever time would allow, I fished for buzzer-feeding trout during the late evening, and for caenis-feeding fish in the early morning. Late evenings or early mornings in 2005 provided some exceptional fishing, and left me unprepared for the sheer quality of fishing that I experienced.

Caenis fishing would not suit every angler, as it is very challenging. It is not called the angler's curse for nothing. The difficulties placed on the angler hoping to ambush a trout feeding on spent mayfly are not to be under-estimated, but it is considered by some advocates to be the crème de la crème of stillwater flyfishing. But the spent caenis is even more difficult to fish than a mayfly rise, because we are competing with a much smaller insect and a greater abundance of fly.

Once the trout are up and taking spent caenis, the fish remain high in the water, therefore considerably narrowing the fish's cone of vision. Your casting has to be accurate, and judgement in tune with the fish, as your fly has to be placed where the trout is going to rise next. With so many flies on the water, a trout isn't going to deviate one pectoral fin to take a fly which is not already on its cruise line.

Forget the wet flies and the nymphs. Keep the approach simple for early morning caenis fishing and fish one method only: dry fly. There is no need for vast quantities of tackle. It's definitely a one rod affair matched with a floating fly line, and a few dry fly patterns.

If it is possible to have the boat set up and ready to go for an early start, so much the better. I'm very fortunate to now live close to Lough Corrib, and my boat is moored a short walk from my house in an area where there is an abundance of good caenis fishing, all within 20 minutes motoring of the mooring. With my rod already made up, I can be away in minutes. I try to avoid long drives using the boat and the outboard, particularly during the early hours when most people are still asleep.

My boat has proved to be a very good indicator

A big fish makes an energetic run as the dawn light gathers strength on the Corrib.

of when the caenis is up. From June onwards, I check my boat regularly in the mornings for the first signs of a hatch. Once the mayfly falls off, the flyfishing on the Corrib slows and it isn't until the caenis start hatching, that surface sport improves again.

I'm looking for the shucks and spent bodies of the adult flies lying on the boards, and in particular on the cover of the outboard motor. If there has been an early morning hatch, the shiny surface of the outboard cover will be littered with the bodies of spent fly, and once I make this discovery, I know that for a good few weeks a hatch of some sort will occur on most mornings. It is now down to me to leave the comfort of my bed and rise early.

Just before sunrise, I like to study the weather, so that I can determine the areas that might produce the best opportunities. Once in the chosen fishing area, position the boat well up-wind, if there is any, and wait. Avoid any unnecessary disturbance to the fishing ground until the fish have begun rising, and if conditions are suitable, rise they will. As the sky lightens to the east, the first indicator that the hatch has begun will be the arrival of hordes of swallows and martins searching for insects. They time their arrival to perfection. Once the hatch has finished, they then depart, ignoring the vast quantities of spent fly.

Although martins and swallows are aerial feeders, they do take vast quantities of emerging fly of other insects, particularly the olives, whose upright wings make an easy target. The spent fly of the caenis, however, lying flat on the surface of the water, appears to be difficult to take, so once the hatch is over, they leave.

Caenis hatches are rarely prolonged affairs, and once they start to hatch they come in a rush. You will quickly become aware of the

As the sky lightens to the east, the first indicator that the hatch has begun will be the arrival of hordes of swallows and martins searching for insects

emerging flies as they settle on your clothing and then quickly moult. It does not take long for the empty skins of the moulting flies to litter your clothing, and if you wear glasses as I do, you will be continually taking them off to remove the empty shucks, for as long as the hatch lasts.

As the sun rises over the horizon your clothing may be bedecked with them, and this proliferation of flies will not have gone unnoticed by the trout either. By this time the fish will be moving. If you are lucky and have chosen the morning well, you may now have three hours of fishing which is as good and as taxing as any top water fishing you are likely to experience.

The choice of fly pattern is always a testy subject and every angler has their favourites. I have seen anglers arrive at a venue carrying an ensemble of flies that would do any retail shop justice, but is it really necessary to carry so many flies? For wild fish, I do not think so. These fish are honed in to feeding on certain seasonal prey items, and this cycle of feeding will be repeated each year. So a pattern of fly that worked at a certain time of year to a particular hatch of fly, will work again during the same season the following year.

A fly larger than the natural works better with the mayfly, olives or the buzzer, and this applies even more so with caenis

We are not talking about stock fish which are pellet-fed, then released into an environment where they undergo a feeding learning curve, and then instinctively feed on natural food items but are conditioned to refuse certain patterns of fly through over-use. We are talking about wild fish, and a natural feeding response to an artificial in a particular hatch of fly.

So a good fly that worked in say a buzzer or an olive rise, doesn't suddenly become redundant. All the flies in the world will not catch you more fish if you cannot get the basics right. Location is key, and presenting a fly to the fish without them detecting your presence, is also vital. We are dry fly fishing, the simplest and perhaps easiest method to fish. You know where the fish are, and you can see what they are taking, so you should know which patterns of fly will work.

We have found fish, good numbers of trout are moving, but how do we catch them? Just because the flies are small, do not fall in to the trap of going ultra-light and fishing small imitations. I have been down this route, and I haven't found it successful.

Just as in the mayfly when a large dry imitation is very often taken in preference to the natural fly, so the same appears to apply to the caenis. You want your fly to stand out, so a size 12 or 14 is fine although there are times when even a ten will work; but it has to be in the right place, sitting in the surface film directly in front of the fish, on its cruise line. The trout will not change direction to take your fly. There is so much fly on the water, it doesn't have to. So accurate casting is a must.

For trout feeding on the spent fly, flies such as the Duster, Ginger Bits or a Bits tied with natural cream-coloured seal's fur for the body, a pinch of black for the thorax and a badger hackle, work well.

Another pattern that works well in the spent rise, is the Cluster in sizes 10 or 12. This is a good fly for the larger trout that are taking clumps of spent fly. A small Hare's Ear or pale coloured Klinkhamer are excellent patterns that sit low in the surface film, although I have found these flies more effective for trout that are taking the emerging fly. You are not going to rise every single trout covered, but this does not mean that the imitation isn't working: in all probability the fish hasn't seen the fly.

Do not continually change your flies, just because the trout are refusing. Keep your leader set-ups simple, and in the light breeze of the morning, if you find turnover difficult with a team of flies, reduce the number of flies you are fishing. One fly presented correctly is better than three flies lying in a heap. In caenis fishing, speed, precise casting and good presentation are essential.

In the low light of early morning, I always fish a pattern that is easily visible on the top dropper of both the two-fly and three-fly leaders. This fly, usually a size 10 or 12, acts as a sighter for the patterns behind it.

It helps you focus on where your flies are, but knowing the general whereabouts of your flies isn't enough. You have to know where the fly behind it is. In a buzzer rise, the density of fly isn't so great, so the probability of a fish taking if it rises behind the sighter is much improved.

Worth the early start: Larry with a Corrib caenis-feeder.

Thus you can strike with a high level of confidence of a successful outcome. With caenis, there is such an abundance of natural fly on the water, that a fish may rise two or three times within inches of your fly without taking, and if you strike when it is taking a natural, you have blown your chance. The same applies to freezing when you are unsure if the trout has taken because you cannot see the fly clearly. Delay and your chance has gone. Remember these are big trout, you are not going to get many opportunities. When they come you have to take them.

Some may think that the sizes of fly listed are too big, but size doesn't seem to be a problem: quite the opposite in fact. Close imitation doesn't seem to work, and my nearest copy to the real thing is a caenis imitation tied on 14 or 16 hooks. But with so much fly around, these smaller flies do not stand out, and it then becomes a lottery whether the fish will take or not. I have found a fly larger than the naturals works better with the mayfly, olives or the buzzer, and this applies even more so with caenis.

Often the flies clump together, forming a larger mouthful. These clumps or clusters of fly are very attractive to the larger trout and they definitely home

in on these clumps when the conditions are right. This discovery was an eye-opener for me and fishing companion Larry McCarthy, when we were out on a tricky morning, of little wind and poor light. We needed a sighter we could pick out easily. I wasn't too worried about the size, as I thought the point fly would do the business.

In my fly patch was a fly that Larry had given me, one on which he had caught well from the previous evening buzzer session. A size 10, this was a big fly, one which I would be able to see clearly. Within minutes of making the change, we came onto a group of three large trout feeding together. One of the fish came my way and when he went down, I made my cast. The point fly was in a good position for when the trout came up and began feeding, inches from the fly, but the trout passed it and carried on feeding.

While the trout was up I left the flies before making another cast, the fish continued feeding right into the sighter and then the fly was taken with a confident rise. As I tightened, 5lbs of very wild brown trout lifted from the water, and powered off. I boated three fish that morning for around 14lbs, two on the Cluster. Following this I experimented with fishing the fly on the point, and for big trout it proved a winner. These big trout have been around, so they know all about clumping caenis. So in a caenis rise, do not always think small.

If there is a light wind, I fish a team of three flies but invariably in the early morning as the breezes come and go, making turnover difficult, I opt for precision. We are not fishing the water blind in the hope that a trout will come on to our fly, we are targeting specific trout, and the fly must alight without alarming the fish, inches in front of the trout's nose. So when the wind is erratic I often fish two flies and in extreme cases, a single fly.

No matter what pattern we try, the one that wins hands down for caenis feeders, is the fly on the point. The fly arrives uncluttered, so the fish see no nylon and there is no risk of lining or alarming them. Light winds or flat calms are the conditions preferred for caenis fishing. So take the opportunity to take trout off the surface and fish as long a leader as you can comfortably handle, but do not meddle with turnover.

For this type of fishing I prefer copolymer monofilament 5lb (0.165mm) for calm conditions and a single fly, or 6lb (0.185mm) for two flies in light breezes. There was a time when I would have gone finer, believing the fish to be line shy. But now I realise

that in many situations it wasn't the diameter of the line or the point of attachment to the fly that was at fault, it was either the presentation that was found wanting – or the fish just simply hadn't seen the fly. In a caenis rise, the trout are so high in the water, locked onto the spent fly, that they hardly notice the line attached to the fly. In fact, I have had fish rise to a natural fly that was adjacent to my leader on more than one occasion.

The biggest risk is in lining the trout with the leader when you cast, or the movement and distortion of the surface film as the leader alights on it. If the fly pitches into the trout's window without alarming it, the fish will take it. But why not every time? Even with a fly pattern that is working and with good presentation, refusals in a caenis rise are common, but this does not mean that you haven't found the answer. When trout are rising to an abundance of small fly, it is always going to be difficult to get them to accept your offering. If you have found something that is working, albeit with moderate success, stick with it. When the density of fly falls off, you may then find that your catch rate improves.

The fly will come off irrespective of wind direction, but the fish are harder to stalk in an east wind. This is because the eastern sky is much brighter, and with this illumination behind you, the trout see your

5½lbs of fine Corrib trout, showing a beautiful patterning of large dark spots and yellow under-fins.

silhouette more clearly. It is always important to keep movement to a minimum, but never more so than in an east wind. Keep low, and make your casts slow and deliberate. No excessive false casting. Leave your line out on the water, lift off and put the fly down in the direction you think the fish is moving. If you start waving the rod around, or make any sort of movement, the fish will detect your presence and just melt away.

If you observe the fish, particularly in a heavy hatch, you will notice that they are continually sipping in fly, one after another. On occasions the neb of the trout appears to be glued to the surface film; so close are the rises that it is sometimes difficult to differentiate between individual rises. They may rise twenty or thirty times covering no more than a metre of water before dropping down, and then re-emerging a bit further on. Why they drop down in the water is anyone's guess. In *An Angler's Entomology*, Harris thought it was perhaps in order to swallow a mouthful of fly. He may be right, but I feel they drop down to look for another cluster or denser concentration of fly.

By dropping down in the water, they automatically increase the size of their window, and this allows the fish to scan a wider area for the next dense mat of fly. I do not think they are looking for individual flies. You can use this pattern of feeding to your advantage, and try to cover the fish when they are down. This way there is less risk of spooking them by the casting movement. When the trout are down, try to guess where they will re-emerge, and cast your fly into the zone.

If the fish passes the fly, it is highly probable that the trout hasn't seen it, so do not assume it is a refusal and change the fly. Do the same again, lift off when the fish is down and try to guess where it will re-emerge. Do not hesitate. Remember, quick precise presentation without alarming the fish is the key. You may cover a trout a number of times without a response, until the fly falls right and it is taken.

This is totally different to the dry fly fishing earlier in the year when the trout were feeding on midges or olives, cruising deeper in the water. Then you could give the trout plenty of lead and they still came on to the fly. With caenis you have to put the fly right in the fish's window: I cannot emphasise this point enough.

When a trout passes the fly, do not rip the leader off the water. Lift with a deliberate but controlled movement, and put the fly back down where you expect the fish to rise again. Do not waste time with unnecessary back casts before putting the fly back down; controlled speed is essential. These fish will be high in the water, and if they are facing you they will certainly notice the rod movement.

The secret is to leave the line out on the water until a fish rises within range, wait until the trout drops down, lift off and put the fly back down in front of the trout with no more than one false cast. Minimise any movement, particularly the rod movement. If the cast is a poor one, leave it until the trout has turned away from you or gone down, for even if you do not obviously scare the fish with a recast, it is highly probable that the trout will see the rod movement, and consequently change direction.

When the density of fly falls off, you may then find that your catch rate improves.

My last piece of advice is to remain seated. This will keep your profile low and allow the fish to come in closer to the boat. Do not be tempted to stand to cover a fish which is rising at the limits of your casting range. More often than not these trout will work their way in towards the boat. In a caenis rise there is no shortage of rising trout, believe me. Have patience and wait for the fish to work its way to you.

They are totally focused on the fly, and if you do not make any silly moves, the trout will not notice you, they will only see food. The carpet of fly may lead them right into the boat. Even in a flat calm you will be amazed how close the fish will come before they veer away.

Step out in the early morning mist to witness the dawn, that period of half light, sandwiched between night and sunrise, which in high summer the majority of the population miss. In the evening, the last hour of natural light is a time when our senses become alert to the changes that are taking place. As day gives way to night, a fisherman's instinct will tell you if it looks a good evening for a fish.

I have witnessed many sunsets, and never tire of them. They are all different, but all carry that mystical atmosphere, full of expectation. But the dawn has a different quality, and in high summer, in my opinion is the best period of the day. Making our way to the boat, inhaling the fresh morning air, cool, fragrant and sweet, a heady mixture of grasses, honeysuckle, meadowsweet and bog myrtle awakens the senses. Along the shore we can observe spearwort, marsh orchid, purple loosestrife and in the limestone, just above the high water mark, the burnet rose, and bloody cranesbill will now be in bloom, adding a striking splash of colour against the grey of the rock. Bird song builds all around, and hare's run through the dewy grasses leaving a drunkard trail. If only it could always be like this.

But in the west of Ireland, development has raced on at an unprecedented level in recent years. It is progress, but progress is now encroaching on those areas we selfishly thought could never change. For years that timelessness, so quintessentially Irish, particularly in the west, had always been the same but the Celtic Tiger has arrived, and what once was, is now rapidly changing. People now enjoy a better standard of living, they have more disposable income and unemployment is low, all positive changes but I can't help feeling that there is a cost.

Yet in the early morning stillness, much remains the same. As we approach the mooring, the lough is calm. Not a ripple disturbs the boat, the unbroken mirrored surface looking like liquid mercury, reflecting the shoreline in monochrome. Placing the rod, net and flask in the boat, we untie the mooring ropes and are ready to go. A redshank rises from the shore, startled by our intrusion, and the air rings to the distinctive sound of its warning call. Then peace descends on the scene again.

Conditions look promising as we pull out of the bay. The lightest of dawn breezes catches the surface, but the main body of water remains calm. To the east the sky is growing brighter, and the first rises appear on the surface. Just odd ones at first, but soon the surface of the bay is alive with moving fish.

My line is out; I keep perfectly still, waiting for the trout to move in. In the faint breeze, I have positioned the boat well upwind of the main area of feeding trout. Like a school of feeding mackerel, they collectively follow a haphazard route and I watch them intently, following them in. It seems to take an age, but in truth it is no more than a few minutes before they

are in range. Then things happen at a pace. Fish, one after another, come into casting range.

Now is the moment to make your play. Do not become over-excited, and make sudden movements or stand up to get an early cast in. Remain calm, watch the fish and pick a target. Even if there are a number trout moving together, pick a single fish. Lift off the line that is already out and lying to the side of the boat, and make your cast just ahead of your target fish, but not so close that you spook it.

Your fly is sitting in the surface film, so low in the water it is just a mere speck. The cast is good, and the heart rate jumps as the fish rises only inches from the imitation. He is taking natural fly, one after another. There is no mistaking where the fish is, and then a rise occurs just beyond your fly, and you know he has passed it.

Let him go: don't rush, there is plenty of time to cover this fish a number of times. He has passed on and gone down, then just as suddenly he reappears about a metre further on. Now make the cast slow and easy. He refuses again: you begin to have doubts about the pattern. But you must remain focused: do not waste time changing flies, just cover that fish again.

Another refusal, and you feel sure you should have changed the fly. He moves on and is joined by three or four fish, all nibbling away at the surface, sucking in fly. The trout now has competition around him. The fly alights again in his path and the nibbling continues just as before, but this time the fly disappears. In disbelief you tighten and the morning silence is broken by the sound of a screaming reel. You are in heaven.

My best brace of wild brown trout from the morning rise weighed 5lb 12ozs and 4lb 8ozs. It was a period of quality fishing for trophy trout the like of which I may never experience again, but one I will never forget. The biggest fish, a stunning-looking trout with broad shoulders and deep silvery flanks, exploded from the water when I set the hook.

The fish roared off into the distance just below the surface with the line trailing in its wake. I was over water no more than four or five feet deep, so the fish couldn't go down – it had to run, and I only managed to stop it just short of a dense weed bed with twenty to thirty yards of backing out, and the rod hooped over. There were heart-stopping, anxious moments as we reached a stalemate, but eventually the fish grudgingly turned and I won the day.

When I hear anglers say that they have never had the backing line out to a running fish caught within our shores, I dearly wish they could share that experience. We hear much today about hard fighting fish from distant waters abroad.

It is perfectly understandable that UK and Irish anglers want to hook up into something big that pulls hard without putting in too much rod effort. But we still have fish that swim in the waters within our island's shores, that can run a good angler ragged if they are prepared to look for them, and to put in the time and effort to catch them. A big wild brown trout is a superb fish, and to catch a native specimen is, for me, so much more rewarding than any number of big fish from exotic overseas waters.

Although rising early does require a certain amount of effort on my part, I find the period just before sunrise relaxing. Soaking in the timeless atmosphere of the early dawn period is always a pleasure, enjoying the subtle changes in light, the incessant sound of rambling sedge warblers among the reeds, the mist rising from water and hanging in the hollows.

But once the rise commences, I am all concentration. Once the rise has begun, I know that the next two or three hours are going to fly. This is challenging fishing, make no mistake about it, but it is the best top water fishing on the Corrib that summer provides.

Get it right, and you may well bring four to six hard-won fish to the boat, all targeted prizes.

But get it wrong, and most surely you will come off the water empty-handed.

Caenis feeders are like that.

One of the fish that ran me to the backing.

171

CHAPTER 14

Sheelin Bloodworm

Success with wild trout, seatrout or salmon, is largely about taking advantage of opportunities, when they arise. If you are fortunate enough to visit a wild brown trout fishery in good weather, with a hatch of fly, then a memorable day's sport could be in the offing. The same applies to migratory fish.

Several times now I have travelled to the Western Isles to fish for seatrout and salmon on loch systems, which after prolonged drought conditions have come into spate just as I arrived, and experienced superb fishing. If a golden opportunity does present itself, seize it, for it will not come your way that often.

Thoughts of wild fishing were buried deep in my subconscious when the phone rang late one July night. I was surprised to hear the voice of Stuart McTeare who then ran a guest house at Finea, adjacent to Lough Sheelin in Ireland, murmuring in hushed tones, "They are on it." "On what?" I exclaimed. "The wormmmm," came the drooled, hushed reply. "You have been drinking," I retorted. Stuart's voice rose a pitch or two above normal, as he quickly assured me that he had

not been drinking but had in fact been out on Sheelin fishing the bloodworm, and had just returned from a successful evening's fishing.

He then reminded me about a conversation we had much earlier in the year, in which I had shown a great interest on hearing of the superb bloodworm fishing on Sheelin the previous summer. Having never experienced trout feeding on bloodworm trapped in the surface film before, I had asked Stuart to call the moment he thought conditions were right. Apparently they had been taking them for two days. He was unsure the previous day that the worm was really up, and had waited for the second consecutive day for confirmation.

He now felt confident that they would be up for a few days. If I was interested, he recommended I should try to fly over to Ireland that week, as the feeding spell would not last for long. The thought of wild trout rising on an un-crowded lough appealed. Here was a golden opportunity to fish for Sheelin's legendary brown trout, and it was an offer I just couldn't refuse.

Stuart was a little anxious when I met him at Dublin airport, on the following Thursday evening, concerned that the bloodworm may have stopped rising. Feeling in a mischievous mood, I reminded him that it would be bad form to invite a friend over from England to fish Sheelin, if the trout were not indeed rising! Stuart pointed out that the fish had risen to the worm every day for the last six days, and he was hoping that the bloodworm would remain up for at least a few more days, to give me an insight into the superb, surface fishing available during high summer.

The largest trout taken during this spell was a fine fish of 6lbs caught by Stuart earlier in the week, but a number of trout up to 4lbs had fallen to rods staying at Stuart's guest house.

I was intrigued by the concept of the bloodworm lifting to the surface, and the trout rising to them even in hot sunny conditions, which would normally spell disaster with wild trout.

Although the English reservoirs abound with chironomid larvae, and I have caught many trout which have been feeding on bloodworm larvae at depth, I have never seen the larvae rise to the surface where they then hang in the surface film, and the fish feed on them.

I once had the good fortune to catch trout that were rising to asellus, a bottom-dwelling crustacean that had risen to the surface and become trapped in the surface film.

This was definitely a unique event, which lasted several days but was never repeated. My theory is that, for some reason, large numbers of asellus were dying, and then floating to the surface whereupon the trout found them an easy meal. Whatever the reason, it was a situation that provided some great surface fishing in warm bright conditions, and I was grateful that I was around to experience it.

It would appear from Stuart's observations of the Sheelin bloodworm that they ascend to the surface, hang in the surface film for a period of time without pupating, and then descend back to the bottom again. The conversation continued into the wee hours, as we sampled the delights of the dark Liffey water in the local bar that evening.

We were joined by a couple of local anglers, and the talk was of the lough, the great trout and the

It is hard to believe that the meagre morsel of a bloodworm will tempt such huge fish as this plump Sheelin specimen. But when they are on the bloodworm little else will appeal to them.

fishing. I was looking forward to the following day with eager anticipation.

We made a leisurely start the following day, as nothing happens at pace in Ireland, all part of the charm of an Irish holiday. The wind from the south was already warm on the back of my neck as we motored up the River Inny from Finea, and through the great beds of phragmites that extend around the outflowing river from the lough. These great tracts of reeds act as a screen, and we were unable to see the lough until we broke through the reed beds, and then the vastness of Sheelin opened up before us.

At 4,500 acres, Sheelin is a big water, a rich limestone lough, approximately 5 miles long by about 2 miles wide, with extensive shallow bays and offshore shallow marks. Much of the water over the southern half of the lough is no more than 12 feet deep, and most of the best drifts are over water between 5 and 10 feet deep. Stuart and Denis O'Keefe (the boatman who works for Stuart) with many hours of experience between them, know Sheelin well and the best drifts to put you onto fish, under the prevailing conditions.

That day, as we cleared the reeds, Stuart hesitated momentarily, studying the wind direction, and the way it was striking the surface of the lough. There was a pause, and then he announced it would be perfect for a drift from Sailor's Garden down to Derrahorn.

Easing gently into position, Stuart aligned the boat for the first drift over an area where bloodworm had been seen previously. As the boat slowed, we scanned the surface of the water, and just as Stuart had predicted, the chironomid larvae were present in the surface film. There were several species of larvae on the surface, some up to an inch long and differing in colour from a dark blood red to almost translucent grey.

It was a truly amazing sight, one which I had never witnessed before. Many of the larvae could be seen twisting and squirming below the surface film, but some had actually pushed through the film and were writhing on the surface of the water.

We were intrigued as to why the larvae should come to the surface if they were not pupating. Several theories were proffered. The two we considered most plausible were that the larvae were surfacing under warm summer conditions to collect oxygen; or were surfacing to use the wind and wave action to migrate to another area. We observed the bloodworm for several

minutes before our attention was drawn to the sound of a rising fish. Dinner was on the table, and the trout had come to dine!

Having tackled up earlier with a 10ft rod, floating WF6# line and copolymer leader to which three size 10 Dry Bits patterns were attached, with Red on the point, Dark Fiery Brown on the middle dropper and a Claret on the top dropper, I was ready to make a start. Having been told previously that many of the bloodworm were a good inch long – no exaggeration – my size 10 dries were not too big.

Conditions were ideal, with good cloud cover and a light southerly wind, perfect for dry fly fishing. Stuart positioned the boat to drift over several offshore shallows, before pulling the boat inshore to drift down onto Derrahorn. The wave made a gentle rhythmic slap on the side of the clinker-built boat, as we drifted slowly down onto the first shallow. We could see the submerged boulders ahead of us as I searched the water in front of the boat with the dry flies.

Upon nearing the shallow, a fish took the Red Bits on the point with a confident rise, which was easy to time. Lifting the rod to set the hook, my strike met with satisfying resistance as a fish of about 2lbs boiled on the surface, and went down pulling and boring, typical of a brown trout, before coming to the side of the boat where I could release the fish without netting.

We then continued on down beyond the shallow where the bottom dropped away. Strands of potamogeton stretched to the surface, above the soft silty bottom beloved of bloodworm. Beyond the weed beds, there were increasing numbers of midge larvae on the surface that were being swept along by the wave action.

Drifting beyond the weed beds, a good trout of at least 4lbs rose about 20 yards below us and slightly to my right. I lifted off and covered him with my flies. Within moments of my flies alighting on the surface, the head and shoulders of the trout appeared through the wave, as the fish took the Red Bits on the point.

We had only been out for a short while, and the sight of the big brown so early in the day, was all too much and forced an error. There was a huge boil on the surface, and the great tail of the fish disappeared below the waves, as I broke the line with an over-exuberant strike. It was the class of fish I had come to Sheelin

Stuart McTeare coaxes in a fish in front of the Sailor's Garden on Lough Sheelin.

for, and knowing how difficult the lough can be, I was more than a little annoyed with myself for committing what could be a costly mistake. Remonstrating with myself and determined it would not happen again, I replaced the point fly.

As I tied on a new fly, Stuart pulled the boat a little closer inshore so that we would cover a new mark on the next drift. Looking around, there were only two other boats in the bay. It was wonderful to think that we had acres of undisturbed water to fish for confidently-feeding trout, without the risk of another boat moving in and spoiling the drift. The trout were obviously moving well, as I rose another fish to my top dropper soon after starting the next drift.

This had all the hallmarks of a good day, as I drew my second fish, a shade smaller than the first, to the side of the boat for releasing, but I knew from previous trips to the lough that feeding spells can be short-lived.

Little did I know at that time that it would be the best day I have ever experienced on Sheelin. Stuart had to be in early as he was expecting another guest, whom he would have to take out for the evening, but

he had made arrangements for me to go out with Denis O' Keefe after an early dinner. By the time we motored back down the River Inny for tea, my tally had reached six browns, the best fish pushing 3lbs, and I still had the evening to come!

We were out on the water by eight, and there were still a few fish moving to the bloodworm. It wasn't long before I took another trout on the Dark Fiery Brown. But then the mood of the trout appeared to change, and the Dry Bits patterns failed to work. There were increasing numbers of cinnamon and peter sedges resting on the gunwales of the boat, and I became aware that the rise pattern had altered.

The trout had switched to the sedge, and were no longer feeding on the bloodworm. I broke down my leader and tied on a new leader of 8lb (0.205mm) copolymer with one dropper to which I attached a Dark Fiery Brown Sedge, and on the point an Hare's Ear Emerger Sedge. On a water like Sheelin which produces big browns to dry sedges, the 8lb leader would not be too coarse, particularly if there are weed beds nearby.

The soft evening light illuminated the surface of the water, as the wind fell away and the ripple

A slow drift at Goreport, Sheelin, with Bill Seward.

died. Just the occasional breeze would come wafting down, creating small crazed patches on the flat calm surface. We scanned the area around us for a moving fish. Sedges were breaking through the surface film, hesitating for a moment to get their bearings, before scurrying shore-wards, producing that tell-tale wake that proves so irresistible to trout.

Deep in concentration, searching for a sign of a rising trout, I found what I was looking for. Downwind in the ripple, the neb and then the dorsal of a good fish broke the surface and simultaneously I received a gentle nudge on my right shoulder.

Denis had marked down the moving fish also. Game on. He pulled on the oars with quiet, smooth deliberate strokes, and positioned the boat in the area where we last saw the trout move. There wasn't a word spoken. We just looked and waited. The quietness that comes as day gives way to night descended upon us, arousing all our hunting instincts.

Our expectations were running high, as we had seen the fish move and fully expected him to rise again. The trout bulged on the surface about 35 yards away, moving our way quite fast. My heartbeat moved up a gear, as I cast into the anticipated path of the trout.

Silhouetted against the light of the western sky,

the artificial dry flies were easy to see. A natural sedge emerged close to my point fly, dithering momentarily, trying to get its bearings before making its charge for the shore.

The fly was taken within moments of emerging. Like a cat stalking a mouse, just waiting for the right moment to pounce, I instinctively knew that the fish was going to take and my hand tightened its grip on the handle of the rod as the nose of the trout broke the surface again, and my point fly disappeared.

A firm strike, and the rod hooped over as the fish boiled on the surface, before powering away. The loose line slipped quickly through my fingers, and he was onto the reel, running fast straight out from the boat before kiting round to my right, and coming in under the rod, pulling with short powerful surges. The fish played on a short line until at last he came up, and I led him into the net. Weighing around 4½lbs, this fish was a picture, typical of Sheelin brown trout with a small neat head, broad and deep with heavy shoulders and a narrow wrist that ended with a wide broad tail.

Following the capture of this fish, we quietly pulled closer inshore where we could see several trout moving, and I took two more fish of 2¾ and 3lbs. We then moved out again to try a shallow, where several fish had moved earlier in the day, and in the fast failing light I took a final trout of 3½lbs that put up a tremendous fight, taking the whole line and several yards of backing on two very strong runs. It was a fitting end to a memorable day of exceptional wild brown trout fishing.

The conditions changed the following day, and the bloodworm failed to show on days two and three but they were up again the week after, and anglers enjoyed good bloodworm fishing into September. For my short stay the changing weather conditions may have slowed the daytime bloodworm fishing, but it did not the affect the evening sedge fishing which was superb, and my final fish on day two was a cracking brown of 5½lbs.

The final evening of my short holiday provided an excellent example of a boatman's skills with the oars when I went out with Denis after dinner. After a still, warm, humid day the wind started to build into a big blow, and conditions were rapidly deteriorating. As we motored out onto the lough, a fine rain began to fall. It was looking like the evening could develop into a dirty night, and the odds of finding a rising fish were far from favourable.

We motored slowly down the lough, past Sailor's Garden on down around Derrahorn, and into the Bog. Around the Bog we chugged on, and still Denis could not find what he thought would be suitable water. We continued on down past Lynches Point, and into Goreport, and here he looked up at the trees, their swaying tops lost in the swirling mists above us.

He didn't like it, and suggested that we continue on down into Corru. Here on a point at the top end of Corru, he brought the boat slowly in. It felt right. If ever there was going to be a trout rising on the lake that evening it would be here, we both agreed, so Denis tucked the nose of the boat in under the shore.

Denis held the boat in position with quiet strokes on the oars, and within a few minutes of our arrival, a fish rose on the ripple edge where the wind cut the point. I felt the familiar nudge on my shoulder, but Denis knew that I had seen the rise. The two flies went out to search the ripple edge, and the trout took the top dropper within moments of the fly landing on the surface. Weighing 5lb 10oz, it was the best fish of my trip. I had fished that evening no more than 15 to 20 minutes.

Denis rubbed his hands and said, "There is another one in Sheelin yet," and I knew what he meant. I wondered how many boatman would stay out on a filthy evening like that until eleven or later. All around us was a low oppressive sky, and the rain was getting heavier. There was a plane to catch the following morning. I had had an exceptional run of good luck, and even I could sense that my good fortune was up. Why push it further?

"Time to cash in," I said to Denis. "We have had an exceptional run, but we can't go on throwing sixes." On the way back to Finea, Denis was deep in thought, he was going over successful days in the past. Then with a wink and a nod that meant he was satisfied with the answer, he exclaimed, "Do you know Dennis, that is the first trout I have ever seen taken from that spot." Denis had boated for countless anglers on Sheelin, and yet we had taken a fish from an area that he had never seen a trout taken from before.

However, that hadn't stopped him from going in to look. On the night in question, it had felt right, and was probably one of the few places on the lake capable of producing a fish. When your luck is in, as mine was on that exceptional trip, you should just take it, for luck, as we all know is a very fickle spirit. A memorable period of wild brown trout fishing had come to an end.

Sheelin is a rich water that can produce the best average size wild brown trout in Ireland. The average weight of trout, caught during the mayfly season by rods staying with Stuart at that time, was 3.47lbs. This is an incredible average weight for wild fish. However, on Sheelin, timing is of great importance as there are periods when the fishing can be slow, particularly during the first six weeks of the season or if the trout become preoccupied on daphnia. But if conditions are right, and this coincides with a hatch of fly, who knows what opportunities could be in the offing? I know of no lake in Britain where I could go and reasonably expect to catch a wild brown of 4lbs on the fly, and yet this was a distinct possibility on Sheelin. There is still wonderful fishing in Ireland, and it is on the big loughs such as Sheelin on its day, that fishermen can rediscover the excitement of fishing wild waters that retain the mystery of the unknown. Sheelin has since been in decline, but there are indications that this vast lough is returning towards its full potential once more.

CHAPTER 15

A Very Late Night on Lough Arrow

In high summer, on the limestone loughs, the prospects of covering rising fish during the day are slim. If we wish to cast a fly to moving trout at this time of year, we need to fish at the most productive times of day. From June to late August, this will be either early morning or late evening. I find early mornings are more productive for rising trout, particularly for caenis feeders which, once the hatch begins, produce a more consistent rise. Buzzer and sedges in the late evenings, however, do produce the bigger fish.

Although less predictable, as the light levels fall, the larger chironomids and sedges will emerge, and the adults will also return to lay their eggs. This increase in insect activity as the twilight deepens can excite the fish into a feeding orgy. The bigger brown trout become more confident, and trout that have been lying dormant for most of the day in deeper water are attracted to areas where the hatches of fly and insect activity are greatest.

Areas for an evening rise are more localised, dependent on a density of fly and the weather conditions. On the large loughs, with their localised weather

patterns, these factors aren't so easy to judge. Once you know of the areas that produce good hatches of fly during the summer months, you then need to determine how wind direction will affect the area you have chosen to fish.

This knowledge is vital for success. Your chosen area requires shelter. If it is exposed to the wind, it will rarely produce a good rise. Just like the early season buzzer fishing, the wind is a great spoiler. So choose your drifts with care, taking into account wind direction and the weather. Avoid cold clear evenings, especially those with a strong or gusty wind.

If we select the right evening, and the temperature does not drop too quickly as the wind falls off, there is a good chance that in certain areas, the margins and the shallow bays which earlier appeared lifeless will come alive with rising fish. And some of these fish could be big trout. They know the right time and where to find an easy meal, and as well as the large chironomids, sedges will also be high on the menu.

Certain species of sedge provide a big mouthful for a hungry trout, and a good dry imitation may produce the best fish of the season to a surface fly.

There are nearly 200 different species of trichoptera, and they inhabit a diverse range of habitat. On the loughs, the sedges that interest us most are the: cinnamon, brown, longhorn, medium brown, silverhorns, grousewing, welshman's button; and of the larger species: mottled, large cinnamon; and the largest of the all caddis flies: the great red or murrough.

The size range of most of the caddis flies would be between 10 and 15mm but the larger species, of which the Peter sedge *Phryganea Varia* or *Phryganea Obsoleta* are members, range from 20 to 27mm and it is the bigger flies which hatch during the evening that will attract the heavier trout. The bigger sedges are unable to take to the wing following emergence, as their wings have not fully dried, and as they cannot take off they are, at this stage, very vulnerable.

To overcome the danger, they hatch in falling light levels, and in the dark. Following emergence, the insect senses where the shore is, and wastes no time in trying to make for it. They achieve this by using their wings as a propulsive force, even though they cannot use them for flight, and scutter along the surface as quickly as possible to the sanctuary of the marginal cover along the shore. This spluttering run for the shore is the next best thing to flight, which it cannot yet do, but this haphazard run for cover is fraught with danger, as it is a great attractor to trout.

The active cased larvae of the sedge is a bottom-feeding organism which, once it has finished growing, is then ready to pupate, and will attach itself to a stone or piece of wood etc, on the bottom and seal itself within its case.

The period of pupation varies according to species, but once the insect is ready to hatch, the pupa ascends to the surface, either by free swimming or crawling up the stems of water weed or reeds to get as close to the surface as possible, or best of all for the larger caddis flies emergent vegetation.

From the uppermost end of the weed beds, the pupae have to run the gauntlet of open water to reach the surface. Here is where the trout take them. I have rarely caught a trout with a cased caddis larvae in its stomach, after the first few weeks of April.

Early season bottom-feeding fish certainly feast on them, along with shrimp, hoglouse and snail. This is why the Hare's Ear and the March Brown are such good flies in the early part of the year because they imitate this type of fauna. But I have found the pupae and the winged adult fly in a good many summer fish which I or my friends have taken. Even though the fish may not be feeding on the caddis nymphs during the summer, they will take representations of this part of the fly's cycle, but it is questionable whether the trout take them for what they are supposedly representing.

On the limestone loughs, the big sedges, called murroughs or peters, bring up some hefty trout. During high summer on loughs such as Owel, the peter fishing is regarded as highly as the mayfly, and there are those who maintain that the sedge brings up even bigger fish. Certainly, if I were looking for a big trout on an imitative fly, I would choose either the buzzer, spent gnat or the sedge. I have taken some very good trout on dry sedges, but my biggest fish of all have either fallen to the mayfly or the buzzer.

Shallow, weedy bays with plenty of marginal cover close to deeper water, are the areas that provide good sedge fishing, especially bays surrounded by mature trees. The trees not only provide cover for the adult fly, they also shelter the area from the wind.

During high summer the trout tend to lie up during the day in deeper water. They seem to sense that there are going to be easier pickings later in the day, and move into the shallows to feed as the evening progresses. As the trout move in from deeper water, they may commence feeding on the sedge pupa as they ascend to the surface, but the bigger fish may not start moving until the pupae begin emerging.

Once the fly starts emerging, the hatch may not last too long. I have rarely fished to a hatch of the larger sedges late in the evening that has lasted any length of time. When the fish move, they move in earnest and they cover a lot of water very quickly, taking in fly as fast as they can. It does not take a trout long to fill up on fly as large as a sedge.

The rise may only last for twenty to thirty minutes. It isn't only the sedges that feel vulnerable, the trout also feel exposed even in the low light levels of late evening, and they feed as hard and as fast as they can to minimise their exposure. They move swiftly through the water taking as many flies as possible in a short feeding frenzy, before leaving the area for the sanctuary of deeper water. So be prepared and take advantage of the movement of these better fish, as and

It was almost too dark to see the rise, let alone the small sedge which attracted this late night reveller. All we have to do now is find our way home!

when it happens, for they may not rise for long.

Trout feeding on the pupae ascending from deeper water rarely betray their presence by disturbing the surface. It is only as the pupae near the surface, or when the adult flies return to lay their eggs, that we see fish rising to sedges. Therefore knowledge of the water we are going to fish, and the areas where the sedges are going to hatch is essential, particularly if you want to fish before the rise commences.

For the trout feeding sub-surface on the pupae, a team of nymphs on a long leader is the best approach. For this type of fishing, it can pay to anchor off the edge of weed beds, and fish into the deeper water beyond it. A good team is a Hare's Ear on the point, Sedge Pupa on the middle dropper and a Sedge Pupa or Amber

Nymph on the top dropper. Fish the flies slowly, and if you are fishing over submerged weed beds, try to keep the point fly just over the top of the weeds without fouling them.

When fishing over weed beds from a drifting boat, it is difficult to prevent the flies from fouling up. In situations such as these, it is better to fish the flies higher in the water well above the weeds, thus avoiding the risk of continually snagging up.

The takes should come as slow confident draws on the line, which should be felt by hand if you miss sight of the line sliding away. I would not advocate fishing nymphs in an area you intend to fish later in the evening, if it is going to disturb the water. You are far better advised to wait, for there is a greater chance of a bigger trout later, when the fishing will be visual and more exciting.

For rising trout, the dry fly is the best tactic to employ, and when I set out in the evening with the sole intention of fishing a sedge rise, I will only take a dry fly outfit with me. When fishing the larger sedge imitations, I fish two flies just as I would mayflies, spaced six to eight feet apart.

Where big trout are concerned, I fish a minimum copolymer leader strength of 8lb (0.235mm) and if necessary in exceptional circumstances of thick weed and heavy fish, go up to 10lb (0.260mm) and a single fly.

In low light levels and plenty of cover, confidently feeding fish are not going to worry about leader diameter, providing the line is well degreased and is sub-surface up to the fly.

Dry flies I favour for sedge fishing are: a pattern I call the Flopsy Bunny, tied with a hare's ear body and the guard hairs well picked out, a wing of deer

Chocolate Drop

hair and a red game hackle; this pattern and a ginger, a brown and a dark brown sedge called the Chocolate Drop tied up the same way, but with a seal's fur body and hackle of the relevant colour. These are the flies I fish most.

The seal's fur for the Chocolate Drop is first dyed in hot orange dye and then immersed again into a dye mixture of fiery brown and a little black. This produces a dark shade of brown when you look at it against a solid background, but when you hold the dyed fur up to the light the hot orange comes through. Tied with the dyed fur for the body, a dark deer hair wing and a dark furnace or coch y bondhu hackle, this fly is a great taker of quality trout.

The smaller caddis flies such as the medium sedge, grouse wing, silverhorn and the longhorn sedges are found on most waters, and in a good year hatch in profuse numbers. They usually hatch in the late after-

noon and early evening, and the adults return to the water to lay their eggs as the light fades or early in the morning if conditions are suitable.

On warm afternoons and early evenings, the adults can be seen dancing over marginal vegetation, occasionally drifting out over the open water to sense whether conditions are favourable to commence egg laying during the day, but the main fall will occur later in the evening as the wind drops. Find a good area where there are plenty of adult fly on the wing, and a slight offshore breeze, and there is a good chance that a rise will occur as the light fades. I have had some excellent evening fishing on certain waters, when there has been a good fall of silverhorn or grousewing sedges.

The most exciting sedge fishing is with the bigger fish if they move late, on June or July evenings, to the larger sedge flies. July is the month for the peter fishing, and when the trout are on it, this large caddis fly provides some wonderful fishing.

One of my earliest recollections of fishing to a hatch of the larger sedges, was a July evening on Lough Arrow many years ago. Arrow used to enjoy a tremendous peter hatch, and produced some superb fishing to those who fished the lough at this time. I enjoyed a classic introduction to the peter fishing through a local farmer, when I enquired about fishing the lough.

He was returning from the fields leading a horse and cart, when I had the good fortune to meet him. He could sense that I was keen to fish the lough. He showed me hospitality as only the Irish can, and suggested that I should call on him around 9pm that evening.

This seemed awfully late to be going out, and although I felt a little unsure, I dutifully called at the appointed time. The door to the farm house was open when I arrived, and I was called in to the kitchen where I found Mr Ballantine drinking tea. I was advised that it was still a little early. There was no rushing the tea. Eventually the rod was taken from its rack, and he checked his made-up cast of two flies which appeared to be fine. He then asked, "Do you have any Murroughs?"

At that time I had not yet heard of the Murrough or Peter. Although I understood the principles of sedge fishing, this was terminology that I had not heard before. Although I had sedge flies with me, they were totally unsuitable, so he kindly gave me two of the same patterns he had already mounted to his cast.

They were flies he had tied himself, and they were both large dry flies tied on size eight hooks. One had an olive green body, and the other a fiery brown body and they were finished with a good stiff red game hackle, plenty of it. With my two flies tied to an 8lb leader, we set off for Laundry Bay, an area where he knew the sedges would hatch. The bay was surrounded by an heavy growth of emergent vegetation, and inside the bay were thick beds of potamogeton (broad-leaf pond weed) giving way to deeper open water - a classic area for sedges to hatch.

Hare's Ear Sedge

There was barely 45 minutes of daylight left when we arrived at the chosen area. I thought we were too late: the sun had already sunk behind the horizon. As we quietly rowed into position, there were no trout rising so we moved the boat into the wind, and positioned it so that it came to rest on the upwind edge of the broad-leaved weed beds and waited.

For ten to fifteen minutes we waited and scanned the surface of the lough for signs of a rise. I was growing impatient to fish. This wasn't quite what I had in mind when I came out that evening, and nothing I had experienced previously had prepared me for this. But I followed the advice, particularly as it came from a man who had caught a 6lb fish the previous evening!

The wind had fallen and now only light breezes caught the tops of the reeds behind us making them rustle. Nothing disturbed the surface of the lough.

Then the first flies emerged well downwind at the head of the ripple, and began scuttering towards the weed beds and safety. These early flies made it to the weed beds, avoiding any molestation from the trout.

An odd fly at first but soon there were good numbers of these large sedges coming off, and the surface of the lough was punctuated by the flies making for the sanctuary of the weed beds. As the activity built up, so the first trout moved in and began feeding with wild frenzied rises. There was no mistaking these rises, as the water was thrown up by the explosive takes.

At the first sign of a moving fish, we moved the boat out from the resting position against the weeds and began fishing. The method that evening was to cover a moving fish with the flies, and then move the fly with a series of short quick pulls to make the fly skate. When the trout took, they hit the fly with a wallop, with hand-wrenching takes that snatched the rod down. There was no missing these fish when they took.

We fished on into the darkness, but the aggressive behaviour went with the last of the light, and though the fish continued moving, the rises were less explosive. As the frenzied behaviour stopped, so the fishing slowed, although we fished on well into dark. We took no big fish that evening, but they were all good quality trout, well over two pounds with the best pushing three.

It was a great introduction to fishing the large sedge rises on a wild limestone lough, and I had experienced nothing like it before on the reservoirs. In fact there were no reservoirs in England that could have prepared me for such an event, although Draycote at that time was enjoying some tremendous caddis fly fishing to the smaller grousewing and silverhorn sedges. The rises on Draycote however were different, being of a longer duration and occurring much earlier in the evening over open water.

That evening on Lough Arrow provided a wonderful insight into the world of sedge fishing on limestone lough fisheries, and what I learnt has served me well over the years. Although I now use different patterns of fly, and would in most rises fish them static, the principles of location and the way the trout feed remain very much the same.

Sadly, waters that once provided superb sedge fishing such as Arrow and Sheelin, are now in decline, but whenever the occasion should arise for the chance of an evening of sedge fishing, I jump at it.

On the western limestone loughs, the areas to fish a rise to the larger sedges are limited, possibly because of habitat, but more than likely because of the very changeable local weather. If you know of such an area where a late rise to murroughs occurs, guard that information with your life.

Carra provides the best opportunities of the four western loughs to fish a sedge rise, but these loughs are now popular fisheries and boat disturbance and a good rise do not go together. The best fishing, like all wild trout fishing, comes from an area that is lightly fished. Find such a bay that receives little pressure, and one that has a good hatch of fly and you have found a gem.

In the right conditions during the summer months you could go out for a couple of hours' fishing, and come in with the brown trout of a lifetime, taken off the top with a dry fly.

I have caught four wild Irish brown trout over 7lbs and this one fell just short by 2oz.

CHAPTER 16

The Back-End

Bleached by summer sun, straw-coloured grasses laden with ripening seed bow their heads to the wind. The pale creamy cups of grass of parnassus look to the heavens, whilst the magenta of knapweed, and the wedgewood blue of scabious provide a late flash of floral colour. Robins have become more vocal, establishing territories before the onset of winter. The drying leaves of spent bracken cloak the hillside in shades of brown, trees are turning gold and copper, closing down with the receding sun. Cool nights produce misty mornings and heavy dews, the legacy of the moisture-laden air left on every spider's web. For the lake fisherman it is late season, the final run in to the end of the fishing year, the back-end.

Tactical changes are required of our fishing approach at the back-end. But do we think positively about what we are trying to achieve from our fishing day, I wonder? On the western lough systems, open water drift fishing for shoals of daphnia-feeding trout now dominates the scene as the majority of boats forsake the inshore shallows and bays.

Many lough fishermen now consider open water drifting for daphnia feeders to be the best method for the final six weeks of the season. They believe the trout only feed on daphnia at this time of year, and it is out over deep, open water where the daphnia concentrations are greatest.

Thus it is out over open water where all the fish are – so goes the thinking. But are they? What happened to the traditional approach, fishing inshore? Have the trout all forsaken their old haunts and, like the anglers, migrated to deep water.

Towards the end of the season, following the fallow period of high summer, there is an increase in daytime fly activity, but there are no really heavy or consistent hatches of fly, such as we witnessed earlier in the year.

So trout looking to the surface for fly feed at random. That it to say, they are not preoccupied on any one item: they couldn't afford to be, as there is not sufficient fly of any one species around to sustain them. These trout will take any number of fly patterns wet or dry, and if you were to kill one of these fish and spoon it, the stomach content would be made up of a jumble of different flies and crustacea.

Trout that are feeding thus tell you very little. They tend to be in small fragmented groups and although similar in size to the shoal fish, they are not with the main concentrations. You may come on these small nomadic groups at any time, whether fishing open water or inshore.

I do not believe that these fish are going to spawn, therefore they have not joined the pods of trout waiting inshore to run the rivers, but for some reason they also haven't joined up with the main groups of shoal fish feeding on daphnia. To me, these small nomadic groups of trout are bonus fish.

For the back-end of the season, I would adopt one of two approaches. The first option is to try for the shoal fish, which entails open water drifting for daphnia-feeding trout with wet flies. This is a reliable approach at this time of year, one that will produce on the right day good numbers of fish. Many anglers favour the open water drifting, but it is a tactic that produces very few big trout.

The second option, totally against the trend, is inshore drifting close to marginal drop-offs, or features such as shallow reefs, islands, or off river mouths, fishing either dry fly or wet fly to these more localised pods of trout which are waiting to run the rivers to spawn. These localised pods of trout will contain some heavy fish, and although the fishing is slower than the open water drifting, it is these larger trout that I tend to target towards the back-end of the season. I find the capture of a larger trout, if it is caught by design, more satisfying than putting a bag of smaller fish together. However, I do enjoy both approaches: flyfishing always provides a lot of pleasure and it just depends on the weather conditions and the company I am in as to which approach I choose to fish on a given day.

Daphnia-feeding trout tend to move around in shoals cropping the concentrations of this small insect. At the back-end it is not uncommon to witness two anglers fishing from the same boat playing trout at the same time – that shows how tightly-packed these fish can be. If you spoon one these trout, you will find a predominance of daphnia in the stomach.

This is good information if we are fishing for daphnia feeders, as it confirms that our approach has been correct and that we have probably located a shoal of trout. If we wish to take advantage of the information, the area should now be marked which is not always easy to do over open water, and fished over again if the position has been noted correctly. Very often it is possible to take several more trout from the shoal, before they move off.

Trout feed on daphnia all year round, but in the colder water temperatures of spring and early summer the wild fish of the western loughs, unlike those of the English reservoirs, are harder to locate.

However towards the back-end, with higher water temperatures and decreasing light levels as the sun

Evening light at Inishaird on Lough Mask, a magical time for fishing the skerries, and rocky inlets along this rugged shore.

approaches the autumn equinox, the daphnia blanket consistently moves higher in the water and hence so do the trout. This makes locating the fish on these large western loughs much easier. Possibly because they feel vulnerable swimming around in open water, daphnia-feeding trout tend to move about in shoals, and range in size from ¾lb to about 2½lbs.

This does not mean that you will not catch fish over this weight, but I have taken very few open water shoal trout over 3lbs. When the shoal trout are moving to the fly on an overcast late season day with a nice unbroken wave, it is hard to leave them, as they provide excellent wild sport.

The fishing can at times be frenetic, keeping two rods busy. However, as good as the sport is, I find that after several days' fishing for daphnia-feeders, a certain amount of repetition begins to creep in, which can take the edge off the fishing. I find myself doing the same things, with little if anything of interest happening either on the surface or in close proximity to the boat.

It is a bit like open water dry fly fishing on the blind, when there are no visible signs of trout moving, only now I am wet fly fishing, drifting down vast tracts of featureless open water until I locate a pod. There are no bankside distractions, no shallows or features. A sameness pervades the scene. The fish themselves also tend to be uniform in size, with little prospect of something bigger.

Although bigger-than-average trout are taken over deep water by anglers fishing for daphnia feeders, these larger trout are rare. Certainly I never feel confident that something bigger is going to come my way to spice things up a little, and if I don't have confidence then I am trusting too much to luck, and that is bad fishing.

If you want to target the bigger fish then you have to adopt a different approach and fish over areas which hold them. Some of these fish may be very big specimens, and pursuing such trout with a fly requires a more dedicated approach: it isn't everyone's cup of tea.

Towards the back-end the brown trout which are going to spawn during the coming winter months, undergo physical and chemical changes as the ova and sperm develop. As well as these changes, the trout also feel the need to migrate inshore. Not all the trout in the same year classes will spawn, but even some of the non-spawning fish will undertake this inshore migration.

This inshore migration doesn't appear to involve a mass movement of fish, but over a period of several weeks, trout will move into certain locations and hold in these areas prior to making the spawning run. It is similar to swallows or martins which gather in certain areas before making the mass migrational movement southwards. It is easy to observe the birds as they collect in the same areas year after year.

As late summer gives way to autumn, the sky can come alive with the twittering masses of these social migrants. Then comes the day when the air falls silent: we look up and they are no longer there. Much the same happens under the water with brown trout, only in a lake you can't see the changes occurring.

The trout gather near certain features year on year, prior to making the spawning run. Knowing where the trout amass is advantageous to the angler, as these movements are repeated anually. Now not only does the angler have access to some key areas to fish at a certain time of the season, but more importantly, a number of these locations will hold some pretty hefty trout. Search and find is the key.

Like the early season fishing, where the trout hold inshore, feeding over the food-rich shallows to gain condition and put on weight after spawning, we are now searching for groups of fish which are holding over or near to features prior to spawning. The only difference is the locations will be much tighter, and the fish are not gathering for food.

These groups or pockets of trout may hold over certain shallows near the mouth of bays into which a spawning river enters; around certain islands; along stony shallow shorelines; and off rocky points or promontaries. Shallow water over a clean gravel or stony bottom is also attractive to the fish at this time of year, as is the drop-off from a sandy delta where a river enters the lough. Remember: it isn't the need for food that has driven the fish into these areas.

On a big lough the wind direction and the strength of the wind will always play a big part on the area you choose to fish, but providing it isn't too rough, I would always favour a windward shore or a shore which is exposed to a lively wave.

At this time of year, trout will collect and move around certain areas irrespective of wind direction or conditions, but the action of the waves do tend to excite the trout. Salmon are also invigorated by the action of the waves in stillwater fisheries in much the same way. In a good blow, there is always a possibility that they may feel in the mood to take a fly, and the same applies to brown trout which are holding over shallow water prior to spawning. If the fish are in an excited mood, there is a good chance they will move to a well-presented fly, even if they are not feeding. These trout may be stimulated by reflex to an easy meal, or they may take out of sheer aggression but either way if they take the fly, the result is a positive one.

As the fish are not looking for food, the need to stimulate a feeding response from them becomes more important, and wet fly definitely has the edge over dry fly at this time of year. I have taken some good fish on large dries, but during the back-end fishing, especially over the last few weeks of the season, I have found that the trout respond better to movement than to a static dry. Unlike the imitative fishing earlier in the year, the trout are not so selective about fly pattern, because they are not looking for specific food items.

Movement and colour are more important. Also, I have found that larger flies are more likely to induce a response from the bigger fish. Because of this, I favour

dabbler flies, in claret, olive, ginger, black or with tinsel bodies such as Silver Invicta. Tried and trusted patterns, but with longer hackles or wings to produce extra movement, and a more streamlined shape.

Fishing with these larger flies is very much like the method for spring salmon or fishing lures on the reservoirs, using a floating or intermediate line. Unlike the reservoir fishing however, on a wild lough you do not need to cast a long line. A great many wetfly anglers when fishing for wild trout make the mistake of casting too long a line from a drifting boat. It is not necessary.

It is far more important to cover the water in front of you with a presentation that will fool the fish. I employ a longer line than I would for short lining, but nothing like the distances I see some anglers throwing, certainly no more than 20 yards which is the maximum you need to cast. What is important, other than size and colour of fly, is the movement of our artificials through the water.

To assist the presentation, try and throw a slight curve into the line. It is essential to get in to a rhythm, just as we would for short lining, and to keep the flies moving. Towards the end of the retrieve, accelerate slightly and then hold in the skin of the water before

A Corrib brown trout is returned.

David Reinger fishes upper Lough Mask while Tim the boatman looks on.

lifting off. Any following trout that hasn't already taken, will more than likely have a go at this point, resulting in a swirl at the fly or a firm take. Remember we are fishing for bigger-than-average trout, and we are fishing to much smaller groups of fish than the shoal trout, therefore competition isn't so great.

With shoal trout, if you are getting follows but no firm offers, I have found that on some days you can induce a take with a stop-start retrieve. They will accelerate forward following the fly, and then take as you apply the brakes by stopping the hand haul.

But this tactic doesn't work so well with the bigger chaps: they just melt away if you try this. These big fish are cute: they have probably seen most flies and every conceivable presentation, which is why it is so important to keep the fly moving without any form of hesitation. Fishing the fly through a slight curve in your fly line will assist this movement, and keep the artificial fishing all the time, right up to the moment you accelerate prior to lifting off.

Concentration is a must, and be prepared for that take at the end of the retrieve, every retrieve.

Another presentation which is now often overlooked are flies that cause a bit of a fuss in the surface film: wake flies such as the Muddler Minnow or a stimulator with a larger head than normal. These are patterns that can induce an aggressive take from back-end trout.

Why wake flies should prove so attractive to trout I do not know, but when the fish are in the mood, wake flies will certainly bring them up. When the Muddler causes a disturbance in the skin of the water, the fish follow, some slashing at the fly, missing more often than they strike, it is all very visual and exciting.

The biggest problem is inducing the trout to take a firm hold of the fly. I know of no other method where the hook-up ratio to offers-received is so poor. A minor tactic which I have found to work on days of strong wind is a wake fly fished on the top dropper and point, with a wet fly on the middle dropper.

This is a combination that has worked well in the past, fished with a fast retrieve for aggressive back-end brownies. It is advisable to grease the end of the flyline to prevent the tip of the flyline from sinking. If the flyline tip sinks, a fast retrieve will drag the top fly down, thus nullifying the effect of the wake fly.

The methods are basically straight-forward, not as subtle as the imitative tactics we fished earlier in the year, and far less demanding but still they require a thoughtful approach to their application. As with all types of fishing, if we apply a little thought it can make the difference between a poor result and a good day.

We will be fishing over relatively shallow water, preferably no more than 12 feet deep for a large part of the day, so good presentation even with the bigger flies is important. You do not want to put an interested trout down or fail to make it commit itself to take, because of disturbance to the immediate area through poor entry of the flies or line splash.

A lot of the fish will come to the flies over water where you can make out the bottom, and most certainly in close proximity to shallow features. These trout will not be lying deep, and will notice any unnatural break of the surface and react accordingly.

Over shallow water, fast sinking lines are not advisable, so a floater, sink-tip or an intermediate fly line will suffice. Conditions, and the depth I want to fish my flies, will obviously dictate which of the lines I fish, but any of the three fly lines mentioned will cover my needs. Where possible, I would always opt for the floater. If I want a little more depth, then either the sink-tip or the intermediate come into play, and for days of strong wind, the intermediate comes to the fore, as it allows better control of the flies.

For leaders I fish either standard nylon, or fluorocarbon from 6 to 8lbs breaking strain. Fine monofilaments do not balance the size of flies we are using, nor do I feel that going fine is necessary. If the fish are in the mood, and the presentation is good, they will have a go. Finding them is the hardest part. And if you do hook a sizeable brownie over rocky shallow water, it is nice to know that you have a leader with a bit of substance – it works wonders for the confidence.

Claret Bumble

Takes will be hard won. Some of these takes may come from good fish, possibly the trout of the season, so do not lose them through an inadequate leader!

On the Corrib, the back-end fishing has been very indifferent over the last few seasons, whereas on the Mask the open water has fished extremely well for daphnia feeders. The Corrib's fall off-in form is, I feel, due to fishing pressure, particularly during the spring months when we witness unprecedented numbers of anglers fishing the lough. For a wild lough fishery, this amount of rod pressure just isn't sustainable without some sort of reform to the fishery law, or a change of angler's attitudes to releasing fish, but that is another issue. What has happened because of the Corrib's lack of form is that increasing numbers of anglers have switched from the Corrib to the Mask once the Spring fishing is over.

As a result the Corrib trout get a welcome break over the last few months of the season, and personally I prefer it with less boats around. The risk of disturbance by another boat is greatly diminished, which suits my style of flyfishing when I'm after the bigger trout.

The back-end fishing for the bigger specimens which are lying close in to marginal drop-offs and shoreline features, is never going to result in large numbers of catches, but the quality of the fish I feel more than compensate for this. Over the last six weeks of the 2003 season from both Corrib and Mask for example, I took a number of trout weighing 5lbs or more.

On a day in mid-September, I elected to fish the Corrib. It was a day of south wind blowing 3 to 4, with good cloud cover and a nice wave running. Narrow foamy slicks were carving lines down the lough's surface before being broken up amongst a jumble of rock on the windward shore.

If ever a day was made for boat fishing, I thought to myself as I ran the boat upwind, this was it. Ten minutes on the engine, and I cut the motor to begin the first drift off a river mouth.

The trout I am after behave very much like salmon, and with a little luck are, hopefully, almost as big. These are fish that are waiting to run the spawning streams. They may not be necessarily feeding, but they can be tempted to take a fly. Large wet flies with plenty of movement can at times prove attractive to these fish, and knowing this I put up a team of wets attached to 8lb fluorocarbon, and a 7 weight floating line with five feet of fast sinker added to the tip of the line.

We drifted in water between 6 to 10 feet deep over and through beds of soft aquatic weed that was, due to the lateness of the year, only just dying back. The bay was protected from a south wind, so it wasn't until we were well across the bay that the wave picked up. A once-noted area for pike, it can throw up the odd big trout but not on this day. We completed the drift without stirring a fin. I then motored with the wind across a broad bay, until I came to the tip of a long peninsula with a rocky point. Outcrops of rock stretched out north-westwards from the tip of the peninsula.

Silver Invicta

A good area in the mayfly, particularly in a north-west wind, this is also a collecting area for trout that wish to run the river, the mouth of which we covered on our last drift. With the south wind there is a bonny wave running across the point, and the foamy slicks, the colour of the creamy top of a pint of Guinness, carve tramlines through the outlying outcrops of rock.

We began the drift just short of the point, and allowed the boat to drift down onto the rocky shallows, keeping to the western edge of the shallow reef as much as possible with the use of an oar.

Passing several large exposed rocks, their tops awash in the slap of the wave, I have a solid take well down in the water. There is no surface disturbance as the trout hits the fly, just a strong confident pull, and I know the fish is well-hooked.

My rod hoops over with the weight of the trout, and a strong-pulling specimen showing the first flushes of autumn colour is soon drawn in alongside the boat for release. A cock brown trout of around 2lbs, it had taken a Silver Invicta fished on the tail of the cast. Always nice to start the ball rolling, and on a day such as this a good sign perhaps, but no further fish are forthcoming from the remainder of the drift.

We push on northwards across the mouth of a long narrow bay, negotiate a way through a causeway and up to a triangular reef, which in the low water has a number of rocks protruding above the surface on the southern point of the reef.

This is a good area in the spring when the trout are in amongst the shallows hunting for shrimp and hoglouse, but today's fish will not be searching for such fodder. The trout will be holding just off the edge of the shallow, where the bottom drops away. We drift the eastern side of the reef and carry on down with the wind for several hundred yards over a number of shallows, before striking deep water.

At the beginning of the drift a fish comes with a rush to one of my flies, a Silver Dabbler fished on the top dropper, just as I am about to lift off. Following the fly up, suddenly the shape of the fish materialises from the rocky shallows below, and takes with a wild slash at the fly. An aggressive take, I feel the weight of the trout as it plunges down in the water. It is a similar trout to my first fish, but unfortunately it comes adrift after a few moment's play. Midway down the drift I receive a savage pull, but amazingly for such a strong take do not hook the fish, and with no further offers to show for our efforts, come away fishless from what looked on the day a promising piece of water.

I now move closer inshore to fish off another shallow which lies off the mouth of a small enclosed bay, a bay into which another spawning river flows. The bay is guarded by string of islands that are scattered across its mouth, and the shallow across which we intend to fish lies just outside these islands. It's normally a good area for a fish, but on this day the trout are not at home. I try a line closer in to the mouth of the bay, but again draw a blank.

Autumn colouring on a 7 lb Irish lough trout.

There is no point pursuing a lost cause, so I move on with the wind to an island surrounded by a number of shallows. We drift the western side of the island into a labyrinth of shallows, some of which cut across our line of drift and necessitate dexterous use of the oars to keep the boat moving. I take a small fish off these shallows, a trout of less than a pound on the Silver Dabbler: he came with a splashy rise to the top dropper, a rise typical of a small fish.

Having fished out the drift we pulled in for a welcome break. Only two fish in perfect conditions provided much food for thought, as I looked out across the lough towards the west, and the mountains beyond. With the south wind running there was a good wave pushing over a number of shallows.

To the south, the lake bed drops away to the main body of the upper lough. Flanked by islands to south-west and north-east, this is an area from which, between mid-August and the end of the season, I have taken a number of good trout. Indeed my biggest brownie from the Corrib came from this area. A white marker beacon, the waves breaking all around it, stood between us and those shallows.

The fishing ground lay to the west of this beacon, a marker to the entrance of a bay famous for its salmon. A river which enters this bay attracts both salmon and brown trout, trout that can make double figures have been known to run this river. Here were the right conditions for a good fish, a river which attracts big trout during the winter months, an area of offshore shallow features close to which the trout could hold and feel comfortable, and a nice wave running down the drift lines under dark overcast conditions.

Following our break, we motored out across the wave to fish the area to the west of the beacon. The first drift down produced nothing of note, so I tried another line about 100 metres west of the previous drift. Foamy white slicks snaked their way down the waves, passing over two shallows. A jumble of rock lies clearly visible beneath the surface of the water.

Drifting the left hand side of the shallow along the edge of the drop-off, I expected a take with every cast. I was throwing a slight curve and retrieving, pulling the flies back through that attractive curve, an action repeated again and again. Midway down the side of the shallow my moment came, and I received a solid pull.

No movement broke the surface: just the pull and a feeling of weight as the trout took the fly. This fish hung deep and felt heavy. Then it made a run downwind from the boat which is the way I wanted the fish to go, then changed direction and came round in a wide circle to my left, running in behind the boat and hanging beneath the rod.

This is where I wanted my fish, and I played the trout on a short line, letting the spring of the rod take the fire from the trout. The line was tight, all the stretch taken up by the pull. Against the strength-sapping bend of the rod, the trout quickly tired and came to surface: a good fish.

I wanted to weigh it, so I netted the trout instead of making a quick hand release at the side of the boat. Once in the net, I drew the trout to the side of the boat, and unhooked the fly, a Ginger Dabbler on the middle dropper, from the side of its jaw. I left the net and the fish in the water, whilst I quickly removed the spring balance from my bag.

Holding the spring balance I then lifted the net and fish from the water, and weighed the trout in the bag of the net. Maybe not quite 100% in accuracy, but close enough for my need. Allowing for the weight of the net, the fish weighed 5lbs 6ozs, a cracking wild brown trout. After a quick admiring glance at my prize, I returned her from the net and the trout momentarily paused before swimming off strongly. I wished her luck.

Further down the same drift, I hooked another fish on the middle dropper, a trout of around 1¾lbs, which I released by hand at the side of the boat. It was a cock fish this time, the colour of a good malt whisky on its flanks.

On my next drift I took another autumn cracker of 3¾lbs, close to a channel marker that shows one of the boat routes out of the bay, but then the fishing slowed with no further offers forthcoming.

With the light fading and about 25 minutes motoring against a headwind to the home mooring, we elected to call it a day. Five trout for a day for me was a good result.

With a little luck on my side (and we all need it) the afternoon had turned good and I had taken two big limestone trout on the fly.

Above: A quick photo of the beauty before I returned her to the water and she swam away strongly.

Facing page: Lawrence McCarthy holds his largest brown trout to date – 6lb 7oz – caught on the east shore of Lough Mask.

CHAPTER 17

The Longest Day

On a beautiful mid-summer's day 2004, I fished the dawn on Lough Corrib and arrived home just after six, too late to go back to bed I thought, so I took my dogs out for an early walk before having breakfast.

At nine I drove into the hospital to visit my wife. When I arrived she was sleeping but as I sat down beside her, Cathy opened one eye and smiled. She spoke softly in a sleepy tone: "Well and what have you been up to?"

I told Cathy about my morning and then we talked, in-between the blood tests, the ward rounds and the everyday life of a hospital patient. In our relationship, Cathy had been the main conversation maker, but

now the rolls were reversed. And that is how we spent a good part of the day. Sometimes Cathy would slip into a short sleep, but most of the time she would listen, quietly fighting the cancer that was eating away her life. It was a personal battle.

Cathy had already beaten doctors' predictions by three years. She had endured numerous chemotherapy and radiotherapy treatments, stem cell treatment, a bone marrow transplant and a new promising treatment from the US. We had placed a lot of faith in the new drug and I think it was the defining blow when the treatment failed. The body was now giving way before the mind. Well into the afternoon, Cathy fell into a deeper sleep. Time to go: I left her sleeping. My in-laws were visiting later that day, so I returned home and caught up with a few jobs around the house.

Shortly before nine in the evening, I was just settling into the chair with a glass of wine and a book, contemplating an early night as I was very tired, when the phone rang. It was my good friend Lawrence McCarthy, and I knew what was coming: "Well what do you think? Looks like a nice evening for a fish." He was right: it was a lovely evening, but did I want to go fishing? Lawrence was not letting me off that easily. "Look," he said, "I know just the thing for you: get your fishing gear ready and I will be around in 10 minutes." With that the phone went silent. I knew there was no way out of this.

It was a short car journey to Lough Mask where we had chosen to fish and en route Larry dived into a local petrol station and came out with several cans of a drink, a high caffeine drink that is supposed to give you wings. "Try this," Larry quipped, "it should wake you up." Always the optimist, he is a great foil when I am in a negative mood. Ten minutes later when we arrived at the bay, I was struggling to keep my eyes open. Larry's magic formula wasn't working.

Bleary-eyed, I tackled up. Larry had the boat ready and loaded before I had even finished tying my flies to the leader. My man was on a mission. "You can finish tying your flies on in the boat." Larry was in a hurry to go.

As we motored up the bay I tied two dry flies, both size ten to my .235mm copolymer leader: a Grey Duster on the point and a Klinkhamer variant on the dropper. The bay held good fish, we knew this from previous experience so I felt comfortable with the eight pound leader. It was 9.30pm and the sun was low in the western sky as Larry cut the engine.

We started our first drift close to an indented shoreline. The shoreline was a mix of limestone outcrops, burnet rose, juniper and, further back, dwarf birch, hazel, alder and scots pine. Bulldozer and modern farming practices had not yet left their mark on this area of the lough and our bay had a timeless atmosphere. This is how much of Mask's shoreline would have looked were it not for the interventions of

One of the 5lb fish caught from the bay on the night of the longest day.

Denis O'Keefe landing a good fish from the bay a few days later.

man. The reflections of the shrubs could be seen right across the calm surface of the bay.

We drifted the edge of a light ripple, over water about eight feet deep. The bottom was made up of gravel and marl, with a good blanket of the soft weed, chara – ideal ground for the aquatic fauna on which brown trout feed. We had been drifting for no more than a few minutes when a trout rose my side of the boat, a short distance down but off to the right.

Just the tonic for a tired fisherman: I was now wide awake. I lifted my leader from the water and covered the fish. Moments later, my point fly disappeared as the trout made a slow head-and-tail rise, a confident take, and on raising the rod I felt solid weight. My first fish was on! The rod hooped over and the line began to slip through my fingers – a good fish by the feel of him.

He made several strong runs before kiting round and cruising in under the rod tip. Under the rod he bored away, typical of brown trout, refusing to yield on a short line but not making any long runs. Eventually my fish came to the top and on the lightly rippled surface looked a cracker in the late evening light. At just over twenty inches it weighed around 4¼lbs! "Who's tired now?" asked Larry.

I slipped the fish back and continued fishing, now fully revived. We had drifted no more than fifty yards when another fish came on the blind, to my dropper this time. The rise was slow and confident, just a lazy roll and the fly disappeared.

Again I felt a solid weight on tightening, and again we repeated the sequence of play that I had just performed minutes earlier. It was not quite as big as the first trout, but still a very good fish, just over 3lbs. I had not long returned my second fish when Larry's rod went up, followed by the familiar chuckle as the rod took on its fighting curve. Another weighty trout slipped over the rim of the net, about 3½lbs. Three fish totalling about eleven pounds – it doesn't get any better than this, I thought.

This was a good start, but better was to follow. I looked across to the western horizon, the sun was low in the sky, a sinking ball of fire, so bright that it left a cascade of light on the surface of the water.

The illumination was such that it left the western shoreline deep in shadow. The light out on the water, however, would hold up for several hours which boded well for the late fishing.

Sedges were now out in force, fluttering all around us. The surface of the water was etched with the skating ripples of emerging sedges, and the boat was quickly covered with egg-laying adult flies. My first two fish had fallen to midge imitations but now I was thinking of changing the team. Larry's fish had taken a small sedge pattern and sedges were emerging in good numbers.

The sight of all the flies left me with no doubt. Time to change. I quickly broke off my two successful flies and replaced them with a Brown Sedge on the top dropper and a Chocolate Drop on the point. We moved the boat further into the bay, to an area we call the Inner Sanctum.

This is an area of shallow water four to five feet deep, with an overlying bed of chara. Clumps of potamogeton grow to the surface in places, providing cover for the fly. This was ideal ground for both sedge and midge and the big fish would know this. With the falling light, they would come in to gorge themselves on the rich banquet.

We started the next drift just as the last of the sun dropped over the ridge of the Partry Mountains. That mid-summer's day I had seen the sun rise and now I was watching the sun set. It sank very quickly behind the mountain ridge. On this day, just like the artic tern, which possibly sees more sun-time than any other creature alive as it follows the sun around our globe on its annual migration, I had seen maximum sunlight. This had been a long day, I thought, the longest day of the year. And yet in time it was no longer than any other day.

What happened over the next two hours was almost surreal. We came off the water taking a further ten cracking brown trout. Three of the fish were over five pounds, the biggest just under six and not one of the ten fish was less than three pounds. There had been a manic spell of hooking and playing big trout, with no time for other thought. It was a piece of pure theatre, a play of two acts.

Act One was the sedge. As the wind fell, so the adult flies came on to the water in droves and this lasted for well over an hour. The Chocolate Drop accounted for five of the six fish in the first Act.

But this was to all change in Act Two. As night deepened, the fish went down. We began to think we should call it a night. But just at that moment, we heard a distinct suck quickly followed by another. Soon there were several fish moving, all producing that same

audible sound. Except for the illumination from the western sky, the light was all but gone. If the trout were not moving in the illuminated area, the rises were difficult to see, but there was no mistaking that sound. They were feeding on buzzers. We began chasing fish, more by pinpointing the position of the sound than spotting individual rises, but they were ignoring our imitations. We couldn't induce an offer. Then Larry changed to a Balling Buzzer pattern and began twitching the fly

196

across the surface of the water. In a frenzied twenty minute spell, Larry took four beauties, whereas I couldn't attract so much as a sniff to my flies. Every time he set the hook, Larry would burst into laughter. The last fish, a trout of around four pounds, stormed off across the shallows, even though Larry tried to hustle it and keep the disturbance to a minimum. It was too powerful, and resisted gamely. The commotion finally put the other fish down. Thirteen trout was more than

we could have hoped for from the bay: it was beyond our wildest dreams. No more trout stirred. All was silent, the rise had finished. It had been a wonderfully long twilight, typical of a fine June evening here in the west of Ireland. And although there was still light in the western sky, we knew it was over.

I've had my share of good luck in fishing, and I've had disappointments too. But my luck on that midsummer evening could not have run better. It was as if every conceivable element of fishing law was on my side, willing me to succeed. The weather, the mood of the fish and the hatches of fly were all conducive to the perfect evening.

In three hours, from eight rises, I had hooked seven fish and landed them all. The average weight was well over four pounds. It was an exceptional session of wild brown trout fishing, perhaps the finest of my fishing life.

All this came, however, at a time in my life of great sadness. But it meant that, for a few hours, I could escape and lose my thoughts to those wonderful wild Irish brown trout. We all need a bolt hole at some time in our lives and for a few sublime hours I had found mine. Such moments, however, can only last for so long.

My life was being torn apart. As we slowly motored back to the mooring, basking in our success, I looked up to the night sky. The stars were shining brightly and I thought of Cathy lying in a hospital bed. Reality returned to my life and the ache from deep within came as strong as ever, and I was overcome by a feeling of guilt.

The following morning I was back at the hospital. When I walked into her room, Cathy was drowsing. I sat down quietly beside her, thinking how good and how cruel life can be. Cathy never complained about her situation, never questioned why, she just tried to beat the disease. Now her defences were slowly breaking down.

I didn't want her to leave, I couldn't imagine a life without her, but fate had already mapped out the ending and we knew what was coming. When she woke, the smile came immediately as it always had done. We hugged, not wishing to let go, and then talked about the events of the previous day and about my memorable evening.

My account of the previous evening finished, Cathy took my hand, looked at me with eyes that were full of affection, and said that she was delighted that I could find something to help me through what was happening in our lives. The words came spontaneously, straight and true; they came with love. Her eyes told me that. Emotion flooded through my body, I could feel it welling up inside me. I was almost choking on a floodtide, but I didn't want to show the tears. My evening had been memorable, and yet at the same time I had felt uneasy about it. A poor evening's fishing could not have changed what was happening, but that logic escaped me. Now after hearing those words, words which I will always cherish, I could come to terms with that uneasy feeling of guilt.

Fishing for me has been a way of life: it has been my career, it has helped me through periods of stress, and it has filled voids in time with a pursuit full of wonderful memories. I hope it will continue to do so, for as long as I walk and breathe.

My wife was a psychiatrist, she knew how to use words for effect, and even in her darkest hour could find the right words to help me. The woman I had chosen to share my life with was special, someone who brought sense and reason into my life: she was my lover, my partner, my best friend. Cathy understood what fishing meant to me.

Also published by Merlin Unwin Books
Tel: 0044 (0) 1584 877456
www.merlinunwin.co.uk

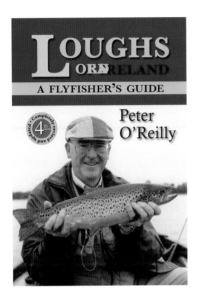

LOUGHS OF IRELAND

Completely revised and updated, this is the 4th edition of Peter O'Reilly's *Loughs of Ireland*.

This book has established itself over 20 years as the definitive angler's guide to the trout, seatrout and salmon stillwater fisheries throughout Ireland, both Northern Ireland and Eire.

It is essential reading for anyone fishing the loughs in Ireland, whether local or those wishing to plan a visit there.

Information includes:
* average size of fish caught
* the most productive bays
* numbers of fish caught recently
* telephone numbers for permissions
* which flies work best on each particular lough
* useful relevant websites and email addresses
* boat availability
* contact details of local fishing guides
* best times to fish each particular lough
* special angling tips for individual loughs

£20

TYING FLIES WITH CDC

Tying Flies with CDC is the definitive guide to using this extraordinary duck feather. It draws on the international ideas of celebrated flytyers: Dutch experts Piet Weeda, Hans van Klinken and Theo Bakelaar; Marc Petitjean of Switzerland and Marjan Fratnik of Slovenia; Elie Beerten of Belgium, Nicolas Ragonneau of France, Paolo Jaia of Italy, Rene Harrop of America, Tetsumi Himeno of Japan, and many others.

This is an inspirational book for the modern flytyer.

£20

Further reading from Merlin Unwin Books:

Once a Flyfisher
Laurence Catlow

Catlow's fishing diary follows the events of a season on the beautiful rivers of Yorkshire, Cumbria, Shropshire, Scotland.

As he fishes through the summer, the author's views unfold: forthright, at times extremely funny, unexpectedly moving and always challenging.

'Witty, illuminating and moving' – **Daily Telegraph**

£17.99

The Fisherman's Bedside Book
Compiled by 'BB'

A classic anthology in which 'BB' chooses extracts from his favourite fishing writers: Skues, Farson, Ransome, Chapman, Haldane, Chalmers, Waller Hills, Plunkett Greene, etc. As compelling now as it was when 'BB' first assembled it.

'The best fishing anthology I have ever read'

– **Arthur Ransome**

£18.95

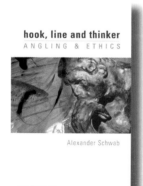

Hook, Line and Thinker
Alexander Schwab

Anglers feel instinctively that their sport is not cruel. This lively book explains why their instincts are right - and exposes the confused philosophy of their accusers. An easy-to-read guide to the thinking behind the arguments.

'I cannot recommend this book enough: it will, at the very least, give us anglers the philosophical ammunition to answer those who want to see the sport banned' – Charles Clover, **Daily Telegraph**

£17.99